100 THINGS
IOWA STATE FANS
SHOULD KNOW & DO
BEFORE THEY DIE

Alex Halsted and Dylan Montz

D1316560

TRIUMPH
BOOKS

Publisher's Note: A special thank you to Don Gulbrandsen for championing this book. We hope you enjoy it.

This book is available in quantity at special discounts for your group or organization. For further information, contact:

Triumph Books LLC
814 North Franklin Street
Chicago, Illinois 60610
(312) 337-0747
www.triumphbooks.com

Printed in U.S.A.
ISBN: 978-1-62937-107-8
Design by Patricia Frey
Photos courtesy of Getty Images unless otherwise indicated

Alex:

For the people who pushed me to reach for things like this, especially Mom, Dad, Katelyn, and Paige.

Dylan:

To Mom, Dad, Drew, and Carly. I'm lucky to have you in my corner.

Contents

Foreword

There was a reason I chose to attend Iowa State University on a basketball scholarship in 1991. I love this place. I love the history of Iowa State athletics. I grew up a stone's throw from Hilton Coliseum and Jack Trice Stadium and immersed myself in the popular athletes, coaches, and administrators who have made this place so special to me.

My father accepted a job as a professor at Iowa State in 1974, when I was just two years old, and I guess you could say the rest is history. I was there as a ball boy to witness the birth of "Hilton Magic" when Johnny Orr electrified the crowds with his powerful entrance to the *Tonight Show* theme.

Ames was such a special community to be raised in. To be able to spend time on the sideline at both Hilton Coliseum and Jack Trice Stadium was a thrill for me. My life has kind of come full circle now—I started playing basketball here, spent 10 years in the NBA, and then came back home to coach for five seasons. I feel very lucky, especially knowing how supportive the Iowa State community is of their athletic programs.

I am always intrigued to learn more about the former stars on the hardwood and gridiron at Iowa State, and that's why all Iowa State fans will appreciate this book. I thoroughly enjoyed telling my stories to Alex and Dylan and am looking forward to reading what the other Cyclones legends had to say about this special place.

Once a Cyclone, Always a Cyclone!
—Fred Hoiberg

Foreword

Growing up in the small eastern Iowa town of Maquoketa, Iowa State wasn't really a part of the conversation in my household. My dad was from Chicago, which made us fans of the Bears, Cubs, and Bulls, while my mother's side of the family was Iowa fans, just like most of eastern Iowa at that time. When Dan McCarney took the job as Iowa State's football coach during my junior year in high school, it was the first time that Ames and the Cyclones entered my radar.

After being recruited by Coach Mike Woodley and McCarney, it was an easy decision to accept their scholarship offer. Their sales pitch was simple: we would turn the program around by recruiting hardworking in-state kids and win with work ethic and commitment. At the same time, I would get a great education on the most beautiful campus in the Midwest.

Looking back, their pitch couldn't have been more true. Other players from Iowa started to choose Iowa State, and we built a bond to create our own legacy as the first team in school history to win a bowl game. Other than graduating, that was our only goal. Though there were some dark days in our first four years, the dream that McCarney and Woodley were selling came to fruition.

The 2000 season and the Insight.com Bowl game will always be special for me and every player and coach on that team. Though we had a lot of talented players, including J.J. Moses, Reggie Hayward, Ennis Haywood, James Reed, Ryan Harklau, and the best offensive line in school history led by Ben Bruns, our team won because of its unquestioned commitment to each other. We won because our team goal was much greater than the quest for individual accolades. We won because we worked harder than everyone else. We won because we believed in each other. We won because of the people: a mix of Iowans and kids from all over the country believing in doing something special that hadn't been done before.

We were rewarded with an epic experience in Phoenix with 25,000 Iowa State fans having our back. The stories that I get to hear of how people drove down to that game and the good times they shared with other Cyclones make me smile every time. It was special for everyone involved with Iowa State, and I feel lucky that I got to play a role in making it happen.

The landscape of college athletics has changed a lot since 2000. Big TV contracts, state-of-the-art facilities, recruiting, and social media have all reshaped the way business is handled in athletic departments. But one aspect that hasn't changed and never will is the unwavering support of Cyclones fans across the country. When Iowa State wins, we cherish and relish those victories and seasons. When we struggle, we continue to support and cheer on our team in hopes of better days ahead. Work ethic, commitment, and school pride will never falter at Iowa State, and it is because of the people. Cyclones fans are the best, and I'm happy to be one of them.

—Sage Rosenfels

Introduction

The yellow rally towels were stuffed inside the pockets of our jackets for safekeeping—who knew, they just might be a souvenir—and the hand warmers had long since gone from hot to warm to completely useless as we crept from Row 33 in Section 2 into the aisle at Jack Trice Stadium.

The evening had started with an unassuming walk to the stadium, where Iowa State would host No. 2 Oklahoma State. It was a cold Friday night on November 18, 2011, and Oklahoma State was supposed to win in convincing fashion. If for nothing else, the game was certainly worth checking out for the purpose of seeing a potential national title contender, and who knew what might happen, anyway? As we hurriedly moved down the concrete steps while Jeff Woody inched closer to the end zone with each step, the crowd roared. We reached the barrier just as the Iowa State offense set up four yards from the goal line. Woody took the handoff and charged into the end zone as we hopped over the concrete barrier. Pandemonium.

It was just more than one year earlier, off in the distance of that same north end zone on the seventh floor of an eight-story dormitory, that the two of us had met. Down a hall in room 7353, overlooking Hilton Coliseum and Jack Trice Stadium, the journey began in August 2010. It was happenstance—plus a lucky click of a mouse on a roommate board—that two journalism majors ended up in this same room. For the next four years we attended athletic events first as spectators and then as journalists at the *Iowa State Daily*, where we worked for three years, starting as reporters and eventually becoming editors. It was in the confines of that small dorm room where our journalism careers truly started; in the newsroom at Hamilton Hall and on press row at Hilton Coliseum and

Jack Trice Stadium where they were crafted; and now it is here, with these pages, where the journey continues.

In a lot of ways, *100 Things Iowa State Fans Should Know & Do Before They Die* is its own little journey through Iowa State history. During the course of many months, we conducted 39 interviews totaling more than 17½ hours. We sat and listened as Johnny Majors stood before us like a football coach and gave a speech just like he had some 46 years earlier, and as Jim Hallihan demonstrated a defensive scheme the Cyclones had used in the 1980s. We dug through newspapers from 1895 to present and everywhere in between.

The result is a collection of 100 vignettes encompassing the greatest players and coaches, moments and games, and things to do from throughout Iowa State history. Different sections will elicit different memories and emotions from each reader, and that's the great thing about this book. The journey through the book is up to you to control. You can start on the pages that follow and move through sequentially or hop around to the personalities and moments that mean the most to you. There are sections on players ranging from Jack Trice to Troy Davis; important moments, from the 1944 Final Four to the monumental upset of No. 2 Oklahoma State in 2011; and things to do from singing "ISU Fights" to experiencing Hilton South.

Remember, each journey is different. The 100 things in this book, and their associated rankings, might be different from what you would include. That's the beauty of it. This really is only just the beginning. There's so much more to explore.

So let's get going.

1 Jack Trice

The night before the biggest game of his life, Jack Trice sat alone in his hotel room at the Curtis Hotel in Minneapolis. The next day he would start his first varsity game, but for the moment he sat isolated and consumed by his thoughts. The hotel stationery and pen lay in front of him.

John G. Trice was born to Green and Anna Trice in 1902, in Hiram, Ohio, a small town some 40 miles southeast of Cleveland. Green was a farmhand and Anna washed clothes; his four grandparents had been slaves. John went by Jack. He was a jokester and a member of the Boy Scouts. When Jack was seven years old, his father died. After he finished eighth grade at 14 years old, his mother, feeling Jack was too sheltered, sent him to Cleveland to live with his aunt and uncle and attend East Technical High School.

Upon his arrival in Cleveland, Jack excelled. East Tech was considered a powerhouse in football, losing just once in both his sophomore and junior seasons before going undefeated during his senior year. Jack was a big lineman and was named All-State. "No better tackle ever played high school ball in Cleveland," teammate Johnny Behm told the *Cleveland Plain Dealer* in 1979. "He had speed, strength and smartness." The East Tech yearbook called him "undoubtedly the best tackle that ever played on a Brown and Gold football team."

After Jack graduated from East Tech in 1922, he began working for a construction road crew. That summer he met Cora Mae Starland, and the two were secretly married. Around the same time, East Tech coach Sam Willaman had been offered the head coaching position at Iowa State. Willaman invited six former players—including Jack—to come play in Ames. Jack obliged, leaving Cora Mae in Ohio, and became the first black athlete at Iowa State College.

Jack arrived on campus in the fall of 1922, and of the nearly 4,500 students at Iowa State, he was one of 20 or so African Americans. At that time, athletes didn't get scholarships, so Jack worked two jobs—as a custodian for a downtown business and at State Gym—to pay for tuition, meals, and lodging. Campus housing was segregated, so Jack found a room downtown, a few miles from campus. He enrolled as an animal husbandry major and did well in his classes. Although freshmen couldn't play, Jack made a name for himself in practice. He was six feet tall and weighed 200 pounds, and coaches saw a bright future for him. When Jack's freshman year was complete, he went home to Ohio and lived with his mother. In the fall of 1923, Jack returned to Ames with Cora Mae, who enrolled in home economics.

The 1923 season began on September 29, when Iowa State hosted Simpson College, a small in-state school that would provide a tune-up game. The Cyclones won 14-6, and while Jack didn't start, he blocked a kick, forced a fumble, and recovered another. Next up was Minnesota on October 6, and Willaman named Jack a starter.

The Cyclones traveled by train to Minneapolis the day before the game and stayed in the Curtis Hotel. The next day Iowa State arrived at Northrop Field on a sunny autumn afternoon. Back home in Ames, Cora Mae went to State Gym to follow the game on a GridGraph.

On the second play of the game, Jack injured his left shoulder, which would later be determined to be a broken collarbone. He refused to exit. Jack was bandaged and continued on. In the third quarter, as Iowa State passed to Norton Behm, Jack performed a rolling block, throwing himself in front of the defender. After the play, he lay on his back; he didn't get up.

When Jack Trice arrived in Ames in 1922 from Hiram, Ohio, he became the first African American athlete in Iowa State history. Following his death from injuries sustained in a game on October 6, 1923, Trice left an enduring legacy. (Photo courtesy of Iowa State Athletics)

3

As Minnesota fans chanted, "We're sorry, Ames, we're sorry," Trice was helped from the field. At the nearby University Hospital, it was determined Jack could take the overnight train back to Ames with his teammates. Jack lay on a straw bed on the ride home and, upon arrival, was taken immediately to the college hospital. Late Sunday afternoon, Jack began experiencing irregular breathing, and a Des Moines specialist, Dr. Oliver Fay, was summoned to Ames. The next day, Cora Mae was told to go to the campus hospital. When she arrived in Jack's room, she greeted him. "Hello, darling," she said. Jack looked at her but never spoke. At 3:00 PM the Campanile bells chimed. Jack was dead.

"If there is anything in the life of John Trice and his career that will be an inspiration to the colored students who come to Ames, he has not lived and died in vain," Jack's mother wrote in a letter to college president Raymond Pearson.

Classes were suspended the next day, and several thousand people gathered on Central Campus for Trice's memorial.

Player Profile: John Crawford

When John Crawford arrived at Iowa State in 1954, he became the first African American basketball player in school history, some 32 years after Jack Trice first arrived at Iowa State College and broke the color barrier in the university's football program.

Crawford, a 6'5" forward, became a three-year starter for the Cyclones from 1955 to 1958 after arriving from New York City. During Crawford's sophomore season, he averaged 12.6 points and 9.7 rebounds per game as Iowa State won its first conference tournament title in school history with a 1955 Big 7 Holiday Tournament crown. Crawford averaged a double-double the next season, one in which the Cyclones upset No. 1 Kansas in Ames. He was named first-team All–Big 12 as a senior.

When his career came to an end, Crawford was Iowa State's all-time leading rebounder (with 658) and second all-time in scoring (914 points).

Teammates carried a gray casket with a Cardinal and Gold blanket laid over the top. Pearson pulled out a letter. The night before the biggest game of his life, segregated from his teammates, Jack had begun to write with that hotel pen and paper laying in front of him. Following his death, the letter, written on Curtis Hotel stationery, had been found in Jack's coat pocket. It read:

Oct. 5, 1923

To whom it may concern:

 My thoughts just before the first real college game of my life. The honor of my race, family, & self are at stake. Everyone is expecting me to do big things. I <u>will</u>! My whole body & soul are to be thrown recklessly about on the field tomorrow. Every time the ball is snapped I will be trying to do more than my part. On all defensive plays I must break thru the opponents' line and stop the play in their territory. Beware of mass interference, <u>fight</u> low with your eyes open and toward the play. <u>Roll block the interference</u>. Watch out for crossbucks and reverse end runs. Be on your toes every minute if you expect to make good.

Jack.

When Jack sat in his quiet room consumed by his thoughts and began to write, he could never have known the big things he would do. The legacy of Jack Trice does not rest with a game or moment, or even a letter, it is one of courage and commitment that endures forever.

Heeeere's Johnny!

He had a funny way of talking. His colorful, raspy voice fit the bill of an entertainer more than it did a basketball coach. His charisma and larger-than-life personality set him apart, and whooee, did people love him. He was, after all, the father of Hilton Magic.

Every night as fans packed into Hilton Coliseum, Johnny Orr stood in the tunnel by the locker room. Pregame warm-ups were about over, and he was getting ready to take the court. "Coach, this is Oklahoma, now, this is a big game," his assistants would say. "You've got to really get the crowd going."

"That's hard to do as a coach," longtime assistant Jim Hallihan said. "You'd have a big game, you're real serious and you've got butterflies, and you've got to go out there and act like [he did]. Only he could do that."

What Johnny did was captivating. As he ran out of the tunnel and stepped onto the Hilton floor, the pep band began blaring its rendition of the *Tonight Show* theme. Johnny ran along the bench as players finished warm-ups, wildly thrusting his fist into the air, high-fiving anybody he could. No matter the game, Johnny always brought life into the building. It was that entrance to the *Tonight Show* theme that became his trademark.

"Heeeere's Johnny!" the crowd would yell.

John Orr grew up in Taylorville, Illinois, and played college basketball at Beloit College—where he was a two-time All-American—before graduating in 1949. After college, Johnny coached high school basketball, including at Dubuque Senior High School, before landing a job as an assistant at Wisconsin. A head coaching stop at UMass then led him to an assistant position at Michigan, before he took over as head coach of the Wolverines in 1968. Orr won 209 games at Michigan and led his team to the 1976 NCAA Championship Game against Indiana.

In 1980 ISU athletics director Lou McCullough was searching for a new basketball coach. Iowa State had just wrapped up its eighth straight losing season, with four different coaches in

Johnny Orr took the reins of a dormant Iowa State basketball program in 1980, and with a larger-than-life persona, including his trademark fist pump, Orr took the Cyclones to new heights and became the program's winningest coach.
(Photo courtesy of Iowa State Athletics)

that span, and he wanted somebody to reenergize the program. McCullough called Orr at Michigan, hoping he could speak with Orr's assistant, Bill Frieder, about the Cyclones job. During the course of the conversation, Orr learned that the ISU coach would be making more money than even *he* was making in Ann Arbor, and so he lobbied for the job himself. Just like that, Johnny Orr was bound for Ames.

As he was introduced as the new man in Ames, with a banner behind the podium that read *Iowa State Is Orr Right,* Johnny didn't quite know just what he was getting himself into. After many difficult practices at the start of his first season, Johnny went home and told his wife, Romie, exactly what was on his mind. That's how he always was.

"Son, You're Not Doing Your Job"

Even though he was always animated and spoke his mind, nothing caused Johnny Orr to do so more than his relationship with officials.

Iowa State played at Oklahoma in 1982 and held a small lead, attempting to run out the clock. OU players attempted to draw fouls, hoping to get more possessions to extend the game. "They're dropping like flies," broadcaster Pete Taylor said. Bogus fouls were called, and the Sooners eked out a one-point win.

Later that season when the two teams met in Ames, the same three officials were assigned to the game, much to the dismay of Orr. Bernie Saggau, the director of Big 8 officials, was at the game as the Sooners won again after a questionable technical foul was handed to Orr.

"I told the Big 8 I didn't want those three officials again," Orr said postgame. "We don't have them all year, and then Oklahoma comes back and we've got the same three guys. Bernie, if you're out there listening: Son, you're not doing your job."

Bernie, who lived in Boone, Iowa, was listening. The next season, a gag order was issued to coaches in regard to commenting on officiating.

"Romie," Johnny said. "It's going to be a long year, because we're no fucking good."

It took the program a few seasons to get off the ground, and it was Orr's infectious personality and ability to connect with recruits that helped turn the corner. A Michigan pipeline to players such as Barry Stevens and Jeff Grayer opened the doors for success, and that came to fruition through Orr's ability to relate to anybody. Part of Orr's personality came across in his colorful language, with some profanity sprinkled in.

"We went to somebody's house up in Detroit or wherever we were, and we said, 'Now, Coach, this family, the father's a pastor. So you've got to really watch your language,'" Hallihan remembered. "Somewhere along the line, he'd let out a little cuss word like a 'damn,' and if [the people he was talking to] laughed, the door was open."

Johnny's ability to hold the attention of a large group of people was part of his allure. He once went into a recruit's home, and when the boy's father asked if a scholarship offer was on the table, Orr told stories for 15 minutes and left without answering the question. Nobody seemed to remember the man's question being asked.

For as many people as Johnny loved, there was just one group he didn't care for: officials. In a game at No. 12 Iowa in 1983, Iowa State lost by 17, and Orr had remained relatively quiet throughout the whole game. "I mean, how do you get on the refs when you're losing by 30?" Hallihan said. The next day, everybody saw a photograph of Johnny giving the middle finger to a referee in the *Des Moines Register*. His unapologetic persona and up-tempo brand of basketball were the perfect fit at the perfect time for Iowa State.

"You had so many coaches who really pulled the reins on players, they didn't allow them to truly express themselves out on the floor," Grayer said. "Johnny Orr was just the opposite."

Johnny Orr won 76.7 percent of his games in Hilton Coliseum from 1980 to 1994 and is the winningest coach in Iowa State history with 218 victories. He guided Iowa State to six NCAA tournaments and a Sweet 16 in 1986 after a memorable upset of his old school, Michigan.

On November 17, 2013, Johnny Orr made his final appearance in front of the crowd at Hilton Coliseum to witness Iowa State take on No. 7 Michigan. Orr walked out of the very same tunnel he had all those years before, this time with his pupil Fred Hoiberg leading the team. He was the same old Johnny, just like he was when he first burst onto the scene.

"He showed so much life that day," Hoiberg said. "The guy just lit it up when he walked out there. I just tried to sit back and enjoy it."

Orr passed away on December 31, 2013, but what he built at Iowa State will never die. The sports bar in Hilton Coliseum named Johnny's, Orr's towering bronze statue on the concourse, and the banner overlooking the arena floor are all reminders that the father of Hilton Magic is here to stay.

"You can't tell me one person that meant more to Cyclones sports than Johnny Orr," Hoiberg said.

3 The Mayor

Before Fred Hoiberg ever became the All-American hometown hero, the competitive fourth-grader stood at the Pinewood Derby ramp in disbelief. He looked around and saw the souped-up cars his friends had made with their fathers, who were engineering professors. They had spoilers on the back and perfect aerodynamics.

Then he looked at his, which he had made with his father, a sociology professor. It had been made from a block of wood with wheels glued to the sides. Hoiberg's car sat stuck on the ramp; it hadn't even reached the finish line. Fred took it outside and chucked it across the parking lot.

"I was a very competitive kid," Hoiberg admitted. "Almost over the top."

When Fred was two years old, in 1974, his father accepted a job at Iowa State University as a sociology professor, and the family moved to a bright yellow home on Donald Street. His father would walk the few blocks to campus each day, and Fred would walk or ride his bike to Crawford Elementary School just a few blocks away. After school Fred would often stop at the Harold Nichols Wrestling shop to play Pac-Man. He strategically walked his dog, Bailey, around Sorority Circle. "It was a fun place to grow up," Fred said.

Iowa State had never really had a ball boy when it created the position for Fred in 1985. The next season, he made his first mark. In a game against Windsor, star Jeff Hornacek came down the court quickly and landed on Fred underneath the hoop. Hornacek sprained his ankle and missed the rest of the game. "Injuring the best player in school history isn't exactly how I want to be remembered," Hoiberg said later. There were better moments to be had.

When Fred was in high school, Iowa State assistants Jim Hallihan and Ric Wesley began attending games at Ames High to watch the hometown kid. Hallihan saw him as a junior and reported back to coach Johnny Orr.

"Coach, this kid is really good," he told him. "He could start for us now."

"No, no, no," Orr said. "He's from Iowa; he can't be *that* good."

"I'm telling you..." Hallihan persisted.

Hallihan and Wesley continued to watch and continued to be impressed. They watched Hoiberg at quarterback en route to becoming the state's Gatorade Player of the Year in football. They saw countless games on the hardwood. As Hoiberg and Ames prepared to play in a substate game against Indianola in 1991, the two

After serving as a ball boy as a kid, Fred Hoiberg became a hometown hero when he stayed home to play for Iowa State. Following a 10-year NBA career, the All-American boy saw his journey come full circle when he returned home to coach the team he grew up idolizing. (Photo courtesy of Iowa State Athletics)

convinced Orr to go watch. Johnny and his wife, Romie, got in the car and pressed through an ice storm to see Fred. He played three quarters and scored 51 points in a 108–60 win. The next day, Orr approached Hallihan and Wesley.

"That's the greatest player I've ever seen!" Orr exclaimed.

"Yeah, we've been telling you that for a while."

Hoiberg, who would lead Ames to a state title and be named Iowa's Mr. Basketball, held offers from Iowa State, Arizona, and Stanford. Nebraska was offering a football scholarship. He visited Stanford. Then he visited Arizona. On the side of his hotel in Arizona was a sign that read, *A Thousand Wildcat Fans Want Fred Hoiberg to Play for Arizona.* Fred looked at the sign and noticed some people had written snide remarks. "That's when I knew the best thing for me long-term was to stay home," Hoiberg said.

"He was good," Orr said. "We had to get him here, but we were lucky."

There were no growing pains when Hoiberg arrived in Ames. Orr joked with Hallihan and Wesley that he never had to tell Freddie anything. Just, "Go get 'em, Fred."

"It was funny, but it was so accurate," Wesley said. "Fred was such a *smart* player. He just gave great effort and did things exactly the way you were supposed to every single time."

During his freshman season, Iowa State was beating Texas-Arlington in a Tuesday night game, with a few minutes remaining. Next up would be Iowa on Saturday, and the fans were already yelling "Bring on the Hawks!" Suddenly, Fred went to the ground. The crowd fell silent. Hoiberg was helped off the court, putting little weight on his right ankle. On Wednesday and Thursday, Fred was on crutches. On Friday, he shot around some but didn't practice. "There was never a question that he [would] be ready to play in that game," Wesley said. "Even though he was quiet, his competitive spirit and his toughness were just unmatched."

Fred played, and even dunked on 6'10" center Acie Earl, as Iowa State upset No. 16 Iowa.

During Fred's senior season, coach Tim Floyd took the reins of the program. He needed to somehow get the attention of the team. If he got on Fred, he thought, it might work. There was a problem. "I couldn't find anything wrong about what he was doing," Floyd said. So one day, Floyd made up a story. He told the team he heard a rumor that Fred snuck a beer into the football game. If he heard anything about it again, Floyd told the team, Fred would be suspended. After practice, Hoiberg marched to his office.

"Coach, what are you doing?" Hoiberg asked. "I didn't have a beer!"

"I know, but Loren Meyer needed to hear that," Floyd said.

Fred looked at him, smiled, and walked out.

"He was your homegrown, All-American boy," Hallihan said. "You just don't get many of those. He never disappointed. He always did the right thing."

By Hoiberg's senior season, he was a star. He had become widely known as the Mayor, receiving write-in votes in the 1993 mayoral election. Hoiberg finished his career as the program's third-all-time leading scorer with 1,993 points and was named an All-American.

Hoiberg was selected in the second round of the 1995 NBA Draft by the Indiana Pacers, eventually spending 10 years in the NBA with the Pacers, Chicago Bulls, and Minnesota Timberwolves. When doctors discovered an enlarged aortic root in Hoiberg's heart in 2005, the man who had seldom faced adversity was at a crossroads. Hoiberg required immediate heart surgery and a pacemaker, but he still had hopes of returning to the court. There were workouts, but doctors advised against a return, and Hoiberg obliged. After all, he had married Carol, his high school sweetheart, years before, and by then had children and a family.

In 2010, after spending four years in the front office with the Timberwolves, Hoiberg was offered the head coaching position at Iowa State. The native son decided to return.

In the midst of his five seasons coaching the Cyclones, Hoiberg sat in his office, back in the town where it all started. He talked, still in disbelief, about his glued together Pinewood Derby car. He talked about his storied career. Most of all, he talked about the town he grew to love.

"It's a special place," Hoiberg said of Ames. "People realize that once they get here."

2011 Oklahoma State: The Perfect Storm

Peering through his face mask, Jeff Woody heard the restless crowd at Jack Trice Stadium. In mere seconds the ball would be handed to him, so he wasn't thinking about the outcome the fans so desperately desired. He didn't see the swirling yellow rally towels surrounding him. He didn't see the praying fans or the overwrought sideline. He saw the defense. He saw his linemen. He saw the ball laying on the painted white grass at the 25-yard line.

Before Woody had hustled onto the field, running backs coach Kenith Pope had relayed a message from the booth and offensive coordinator Tom Herman: *Hold on to the football!* Woody scanned the defense. Then he heard it: *"You have the hopes and dreams of every Iowa State fan in your hands."*

The Friday night of November 18, 2011, began inauspiciously. Iowa State was hosting second-ranked Oklahoma State on national television, and was given next to no chance to walk away with a bowl-clinching victory. Many of the 52,027 fans in attendance had undoubtedly come to see the Cyclones take on a national title contender and see what might happen. Vegas slotted Oklahoma State as 27-point favorites.

Yet as fans filed into the stadium, picking up their yellow rally towels along the way, and as the sun set and the moon peaked in the cold night sky above Jack Trice Stadium, there was a noticeable ambience. "Something special is in the air here," ESPN broadcaster Joe Tessitore proclaimed. Something special, indeed.

By halftime, the game was going as most had predicted. Oklahoma State was winning 17–7. But the 10-point deficit was certainly still manageable for Iowa State. Then the Cowboys marched down the field on eight plays to open the second half and extend their lead to three scores. This was where the BCS title contenders were supposed to take over.

Instead, the Cyclones responded with their own scoring drive, capped by a James White 32-yard touchdown run. Then Iowa State was suddenly ready to score again after recovering an ensuing surprise onside kick. As quarterback Jared Barnett rushed toward the end zone, the ball was poked loose at the 9-yard line. Oklahoma State, leading by 10 midway through the third quarter, had a chance to put the game away. On the Cowboys next drive, linebacker Jake Knott knocked the football loose and Leonard Johnson recovered. The Cyclones converted the turnover into a field goal to draw within seven.

It was with 5:35 remaining that Tessitore made his proclamation about the air and with 5:30 to play that ISU's Albert Gary dove to catch a seven-yard game-tying touchdown. With 1:17 left, Oklahoma State kicker Quinn Sharp's field goal sailed right, just over the top of the upright. Tied at 24, the teams were headed to overtime.

"There was a palpable excitement and confidence in that game," Woody said. "At no point during that game—down by 17 or whatever—was it in question that we were going to win that game. That's from the fans, the coaches, the players, the atmosphere. Everything."

In the first overtime of what turned into a double-overtime battle, Iowa State scored on the first play when White hauled in a 25-yard pass on a wheel route. Oklahoma State forced a second overtime with their own touchdown. On the first play of that second overtime, Knott tipped OSU quarterback Brandon Weeden's pass into the air and Ter'Ran Benton intercepted it.

Now, Woody stood in the huddle on the sideline.

"Look at me now," Pope told the 240-pound bruiser. "I want you to go two-hand lock the whole time. Those guys have one choice to win the game, and that's to create a turnover."

With any score Iowa State would upset the nation's No. 2 team. It would clinch a bowl game. It would be the biggest win in school history. The Cyclones preferred a touchdown. "I *did not* want to kick a field goal," coach Paul Rhoads said.

Tabbed as 27-point underdogs against No. 2 Oklahoma State, a national title contender, Iowa State shocked the world on November 18, 2011, when Jeff Woody (pictured) scored a touchdown in double overtime to lift the Cyclones to a 37–31 victory. (Photo courtesy of Iowa State Athletics)

The offense huddled on the field and awaited the call: Trey Up Left 40-Z.

A variation of the read option, there was really *no* option. Woody knew he was getting the ball. This was the most basic, safest, easiest play Iowa State had in its playbook. Woody scanned the defense. He looked where his blockers would go. He would take the handoff and plow ahead. Then he heard the words Herman always preached: *"You have the hopes and dreams of every Iowa State fan in your hands."*

After Woody set up to the left and one yard back from Barnett, he took the handoff, tucked it between both hands, and lowered his shoulders, falling forward for a six-yard gain. The Cyclones were on the move. "Let's just run it again," Herman said.

The offense huddled: Trey Up Left 40-Z.

Woody set up just as before. He took the handoff, spun to break a tackle, and kept pushing. Then he spun again, carrying three defenders to the 4-yard line for a 15-yard gain. Suddenly, he was suspended in the air *by the ball. Get to the ground!* he thought.

Fans slowly crept down the aisles, with Iowa State four yards out and on the brink of history.

"Why not?" the coaches decided. "Let's run it again."

The offense huddled: Trey Up Left 40-Z.

Woody positioned himself for a third straight time, just left and one yard back from Barnett. He took the handoff, cut right, then back left before getting hit, crossing into the end zone.

"I threw my hands up, and I'm celebrating," Woody said, "and I turn around, and the entire field is just getting swarmed like somebody just broke a bathtub and the water is just running out onto the field."

Fans flooded the field, and Woody and the rest of the team were stuck. Suddenly Pope appeared around the 20-yard line. "I told you to hold on to the ball, and you did," Pope told him. "That was a great job!" Somewhere along the way, Woody had lost the ball. A manager had come over to take it, and caught in the moment, Woody relented. In an A&W restaurant in Indianola, Iowa, of all places, sits the only game ball Woody has seen since.

Woody and Pope sang "Sweet Caroline" with the 52,000 fans. "Woody," Pope said, "we've got to find our way out of here." He grabbed Woody by the shoulder pads and dragged him while pushing through the crowd until they reached the tunnel.

The scoreboard read: *Iowa State 37, Oklahoma State 31.*

Iowa State, which had entered the game 0–56–2 against teams ranked in the top six, had taken down the second-ranked team. It had clinched a bowl game. It had shocked the world.

"All those factors combined together, it combines into a perfect storm," Woody said later.

5 Cael Sanderson

To understand Cael Sanderson, you must first know what drove him. During the dawn of his wrestling career on the mats in northern Utah, it was a dream that preceded greatness. When Sanderson was only a first-grader, he scribbled three goals onto a small piece of paper.

He wanted to be a good person.

He wanted to be a good student.

He wanted to be an Olympic champion.

"When you tell [your parents] you want to be an Olympic champion and you're from some little town in the middle of Utah, that's just not something that people do," Sanderson said. "They [didn't laugh at me] or say to think twice. They believed in it as much as I did."

The story of the greatest wrestler of all time begins in Heber City, Utah, where Cael grew up the third of four brothers. If there was one thing the Sandersons did, it was wrestle. His grandfather wrestled. His father wrestled. His brothers wrestled. Cael was going to wrestle. "There was never any question," Sanderson said. "It was just how soon would my dad let me jump in there and start competing." When Cael was just a little kid, he began wrestling for his grandfather, Norman Sanderson, who had a youth wrestling club called the Little Mountain Grapplers in Pleasant Grove, Utah. As a freshman at Wasatch High School, Sanderson began wrestling for his father, who coached wrestling at the school.

Growing up, Sanderson watched his father's teams consistently get thumped by Uintah High School. The year before Sanderson started high school, his father's Wasatch High School team had beaten Uintah for the first time. When Uintah arrived at Wasatch during Sanderson's freshman season, it was standing room only, and fans stood shoulder-to-shoulder. Cael wrestled the reigning state champion and pinned him. Later that season in the state final, he drew the kid again. He pinned him again. Wasatch won the state title that season, and Cael's career was underway. By the time his senior season came to a close, Sanderson had posted a 127–3 record and collected four state titles.

The Three-Time Champs

There is only one Cael Sanderson in Iowa State history, and so there is just one four-time NCAA champion in the record books. Yet two other wrestlers in the annals of Iowa State have accomplished a feat that isn't far behind.

When Larry Hayes captured an NCAA title in 1961, capping a career in which he went 51–4–1, he became the first wrestler in Cyclones history to claim three national titles, a distinction he would hold for nearly two decades. Nate Carr finished his career in 1983 with his third national title, ending his ISU career with a 122–16–2 mark before earning bronze in the 1988 Olympics.

Cael was pretty sure he knew where he'd wrestle in college. When he was in grade school, he and his brothers would go to Arizona State youth camps, where coach Bobby Douglas saw them wrestle. Douglas had since moved on to Iowa State, and Cael's two older brothers, Cody and Cole, had already gone to Ames. He took a few visits elsewhere to make sure he was making the right decision. "I absolutely did, there's no question," Sanderson said. "I have not questioned that decision one time in my life."

After redshirting during his first year in Ames, Sanderson began his collegiate career in 1998. Cael had otherworldly quickness and unfathomable conditioning. He never got tired. He never stopped trying to dominate. During his freshman season, he finished a perfect 39–0 to win his first national championship.

Sanderson went 40–0 during both his sophomore and junior seasons, claiming his second and third NCAA titles. Cael wasn't just winning, he was dominating the college wrestling world. "When I was in college, I wasn't just trying to win," Sanderson said. "I felt like I had to dominate every time I competed, and if I didn't, it felt like a loss."

When Cael arrived at Iowa State, there was a plan. He wanted to win an Olympic title eventually, but he also wanted to win four national titles. "I wasn't trying to go undefeated in college," Sanderson said. "That wasn't my goal going in." Yet people started talking after his freshman season about the daunting task, and talk only heated up as his undefeated seasons mounted. When he did an interview, he was asked about the streak. When he went to Walmart, people asked too.

By the time the final day of the NCAA championship arrived on March 23, 2002, Sanderson remained undefeated and in position to complete the perfect career. His closest win all season had been in January when he beat Jon Trenge 6–1. As the season progressed, all eyes locked on Sanderson and his unblemished career. "I didn't read anything, any of the articles," Sanderson said, "and I didn't look at message boards." One day, early for lab, Sanderson sat at the computer and clicked into a message board. He saw his name up and down the page and quickly shut it off. He didn't want to see.

"The important thing was to keep people away from Cael," Douglas said. "Let Cael be Cael."

The entire sporting world was talking about Cael by the time the championship match arrived. Could Sanderson make history? He tried to block out the noise.

"That last day, there were a few long moments where you start thinking about it," Sanderson said. "The problem was I felt like I was good enough to win, and if I didn't win, it would [have been] a big letdown. I had to catch myself a few times thinking about what could go wrong instead of what I wanted to do."

One way or another, the streak would end in the title match, a rematch against Trenge. The match went no differently than many of the 158 that preceded it. Sanderson dominated for a 12–4 victory. He had claimed his fourth NCAA title. He was 159–0. He became the only undefeated four-time champion in history. The crowd offered a standing ovation as Cael raised his arms after the victory.

"It was just peace," Sanderson said. "I think that's the greatest feeling in the world. You don't have anything to worry about."

During Cael's senior campaign, 34 of his 40 matches ended in either a pin or technical fall for Sanderson, and only four lasted the full seven minutes. Of his 159 career college victories, Cael collected bonus points in 139. He won an unmatched four Most Outstanding Wrestler Awards at the NCAA tournament. His streak was named the No. 2 most impressive college sports feat *ever* by *Sports Illustrated*. No win was more significant than the last.

"It was one of those moments that was frozen in history," Douglas said. "I don't know if anyone could ever really realize what

When Cael Sanderson capped his Iowa State career with an unblemished 159–0 record and four national titles, he etched his name in history as arguably the greatest wrestler of all time. (Photo courtesy of Iowa State Athletics)

was taking place. When you're making history, you tend not to recognize it. That was a historical moment for wrestling."

There was still that Olympic dream. So two years later, Sanderson arrived in Athens for the 2004 Olympics. "At the time it was all business," Cael said. "There was no other option other than winning the gold medal." Since he had scribbled on that small piece of paper as a first-grader, Sanderson had dreamed of this moment. Ultimately, he claimed Olympic gold.

"The reality of actually getting it done and making it happen is a little more than just dreaming," Sanderson said. "I always thought I was going to be an Olympic champion, and [the realization of that dream is] just a tribute to the people in my family and other people that were around."

There are nights now, all these years later, when Sanderson falls into a fitful sleep and dreams again. In those dreams, Cael still has one or two years remaining to go undefeated. Then he wakes up and feels the relief. *Oh, I already did that*, Sanderson thinks. *Good.*

6 Troy Davis

From the first day he arrived in Ames as a freshman in 1993, Troy Davis wanted to return to Florida. He would call home crying. He packed his bags and was finally going to leave in 1994, following his freshman season. The short kid with dreadlocks sat in Dan McCarney's office with one foot out the door, ready to quit.

"I was ready to go," Davis said. "There was nothing left for me to accomplish."

Davis had arrived in Ames in 1993 to play for Jim Walden but hardly saw the field. In the final game of his freshman season, he returned a kick 99 yards for a touchdown against Colorado. He had only been given 35 carries as a freshman. He was homesick. After McCarney replaced Walden, Davis decided he was going to transfer. McCarney told Davis he would be a focal point of the offense and that Iowa State would run upward of 30 times a game. He asked for a chance.

"That put a smile on my face," Davis said, "and that's really why I came back."

"It wasn't like I was sitting there looking at a two-time Heisman finalist at the time, because he hadn't even hardly played," McCarney said. "He showed some faith and trust in me, and the rest is history, as they say."

When Davis arrived in Ames from Miami on his recruiting trip, he was mesmerized by the snow. "I tried to put some in a cup and take it back home," Davis said. In the early stages of his

After choosing to stay at Iowa State following his freshman season, Troy Davis rumbled into the program's history books over the course of the next two seasons, setting virtually every rushing record on his way to being a two-time Heisman Trophy finalist. (Photo courtesy of Iowa State Athletics)

recruitment, the Florida schools backed off when Davis failed to pass the ACT. Iowa State kept pushing for him, and when he passed the exam in May, he stood by the Cyclones even when Florida State and Miami came calling. "I wanted to go to a school that hadn't been known and make them known," Davis said. While the NCAA clearinghouse waited to approve the highly touted running back's transcript, he missed practice. By the time he joined the team, he had fallen behind in the playbook. Then he hardly played.

"What do you think?" broadcaster Eric Heft asked a coach.

"I don't give a shit if he knows the plays or not," the coach responded. "Just get him the ball, because we can't tackle him."

People wondered why Davis wasn't playing, but Walden was on the way out as Iowa State went 0–10–1 during that 1994 season, so the answer didn't matter much. Then McCarney came in and talked Davis into staying on.

"That first spring we knew we had a heck of a running back," McCarney said.

The 5'8" 185-pound bruiser burst onto the scene during his sophomore season as Iowa State handed him the ball more than

Player Profile: Darren Davis

With his brother already at Iowa State, schools might as well not have wasted their time recruiting Darren Davis. Dozens went after the running back, including Florida State and Miami, but Darren was going to Ames to play alongside Troy.

The 5'8", 190-pound running back certainly didn't disappoint. Just like Troy, Darren became a workhorse for the Cyclones. He holds three top-10 single-game rushing marks and by the time his career came to an end, Darren had rushed for 3,763 yards and had gained 5,008 all-purpose yards, both second only to Troy in Iowa State record books.

"That's the first thing people think about once they think about Iowa State: Iowa State, that's the school Troy Davis and Darren Davis went to," Troy said.

30 times per game. "Getting the ball that many times," Davis said, "you have to get something out of it." He did, becoming the first sophomore in major college football history to run for 1,000 yards in a combined five games. By season's end Davis had become the first sophomore, and only the fifth NCAA player, to rush for 2,000 or more yards (2,010) in a season.

After being invited to New York for the Heisman Trophy ceremony, where he finished fifth, Davis readied for his junior season. In the third game of the season, Davis was handed the ball a school-record 53 times for 241 yards and five touchdowns. "When the game was over, they said, 'You carried the ball 53 times,'" Davis recalled. "And I was like, *Wow, who could do that?* But I did it." The next week, Davis rushed for a school-record 378 yards on 41 carries, at the time the third-highest single-game rushing total in NCAA history.

By the final game of his junior season, Davis had racked up 1,960 yards. Iowa State lined up late in the first half on fourth-and-goal at the Kansas State 1-yard line. Offensive coordinator Steve Loney huddled the group. "Who wants the ball?" he asked. Troy raised his hand. "Give Troy the ball," Loney said. Troy dove across the goal line, got up, and did the Heisman pose. "Hey," Davis explained, "I [was] going for the Heisman."

Davis finished the season with 2,185 yards. He became the first player in NCAA history to rush for 2,000 yards twice in a career. "It was a blessing because nobody had ever done that before. Nobody else is there," Davis said. "I don't think that'll happen again for decades."

Davis was invited to New York for the second time as a Heisman Trophy finalist. Upon his arrival, Davis met 6'3" Heisman Trophy winner Eddie George.

"How does a little dude like you run for all those yards on the big guys?" George asked.

"I got a heart, and I want to prove a small guy can make big things happen," Davis said.

Davis might have been small, but he was a force to be reckoned with. One year against Texas A&M, linebacker Dat Nguyen came through the hole on a blitz. Davis picked it up and knocked the future All-American out. "Nobody worked harder," McCarney said. "He was a man's man."

In New York, Davis finished second to Florida quarterback Danny Wuerffel in the 1996 Heisman Trophy voting. Still, Davis had become not only the best player in Iowa State history but one of the best runners in college football history. He was a two-time consensus first-team All-American. His 4,195 yards in back-to-back seasons remains the most in NCAA Division I history. He put his name atop the Iowa State record books for career rushing yards (4,382) and touchdowns (36). The kid who wanted to make Iowa State known did just that.

"The fans there, they loved [me]," he said. "Whatever [I] did, they were behind me. It's a dream come true, because every athlete that I know who goes and plays football, they want to be the top name of that school. When they mention Iowa State, they mention [me]. That puts a smile on my face."

The 2000 Cyclones

There is a possibility that the defining moment of what would become arguably Iowa State's greatest team *ever* was not found in some big game or moment, but rather in a loss. Don't be mistaken, a win for Iowa State against No. 1 Cincinnati was hardly expected anyway, and a 15-point defeat, on the surface, yields few positives. Except there was more to it.

You see, that loss appeared as a 15-point defeat, but sometimes looks can be deceiving. In reality, the Cyclones had trailed the nation's top-ranked team by five with less than two minutes remaining. Then the top-ranked team did what top-ranked teams do and held Iowa State scoreless while connecting on 10 free throws down the stretch when the fouls came.

Afterward, Cincinnati coach Bob Huggins walked over to shake Iowa State coach Larry Eustachy's hand as Eustachy sat with headphones over his ears during a postgame radio interview.

"What do you think of my team?" Eustachy asked. "Where do you think we are in the league?"

"No worse than third," Huggins said.

"Really?" Eustachy responded.

"Yeah," Huggins replied, "you've got all the pieces."

This was in stark contrast to what pretty much everybody else had been saying. Iowa State had finished 15–15 the season before, and the preseason predictions didn't figure much was about to change. The Big 12 coaches voted the 2000 Cyclones sixth, and the writers had them seventh. One magazine's preseason poll slotted Iowa State dead last in the conference.

"It pissed me off, extremely," said Marcus Fizer, who was the Big 12's returning leading scorer. "I knew where we were as a ballclub, and to be picked so low was blatant disrespect not only for the coaching staff, but my teammates and us as a whole. We approached that season with that chip on our shoulder. We knew how good we were."

Knowing and proving are two separate things, however, and an early season loss to Drake did little to squash lackluster expectations from outsiders. "Honestly," Fizer said, "we just lost that game. Drake beat us." But that fight, against Cincinnati? "That proved to us how special we were," Fizer said, "and how good we could be."

Following that loss in Hawaii, Iowa State rattled off a then–school record 13 consecutive wins, including the first four games of its conference schedule. A double-overtime loss halted the streak, but then the Cyclones won six more games. That streak included a win *at* Kansas (the first since 1982) and put Iowa State in the polls. Another overtime loss on the road sent them to 10–2 with conference title hopes hanging in the balance.

Part of the reason the expectations had been set so low was that Iowa State, in its first two seasons with Fizer, hadn't done much. He couldn't do it alone. But before the 2000 season, Jamaal Tinsley had arrived from junior college, and so too had Kantrail Horton. These were the guards Iowa State needed. Combined with Fizer, Paul Shirley, Stevie Johnson, Mike Nurse, and Martin Rancik, the group had come together. Kind of.

"Interestingly enough, I don't know that we liked each other all that much," Shirley said. "That didn't hinder us on the basketball court, because our interests were lined up. We knew that in order to achieve the things we were going to do, we needed to put aside any personal differences we might have in order to play well on those Wednesday and Saturday nights."

By the time Iowa State reached the second-to-last week of its Big 12 schedule, the race for the conference title was about to run through Hilton Coliseum. On the final week of February 2000, No. 14 Texas and No. 10 Oklahoma State would arrive in town to play Iowa State. One of the three teams would win the league.

"I just remember a lot of people talking about how much we needed to win those games and how big they were and how we realized that that didn't matter to us," Fizer said. "We never had any thoughts in our mind that we were going to lose the games."

After all, Iowa State *did* have Marcus Fizer. The eventual Big 12 Player of the Year scored a then–career high 35 points to knock off Texas. Then he scored 29 to beat Oklahoma State. Iowa State had completed the tall task but still needed to close out its regular-season schedule with two wins to clinch. Fizer scored 35 against Texas Tech and then 34 against Baylor to help Iowa State win the

No team in Iowa State history has experienced as much success as the 2000 Cyclones, who won a school-record 32 games while claiming both the regular-season and postseason Big 12 titles on their way to the Elite Eight. (Photo courtesy of Iowa State Athletics)

outright regular-season Big 12 title, its first regular-season conference championship since 1944-45, when it won the Big 6.

Even when many thought the Big 12 regular-season winner wouldn't likely win the postseason conference tournament, the Cyclones did. As a No. 2 seed in the NCAA tournament, they cruised past Central Connecticut State and Auburn to the Sweet 16. Then they dispatched UCLA to reach the Elite Eight, where the eventual national champions, Michigan State, halted them five minutes short of the Final Four, having won a school-record 32 games.

Those preseason polls? Sometimes looks can be deceiving.

"This team," Eustachy said, "will be remembered forever."

The Dirty Thirty

Through this portal pass the hardest nosed football players in the world.
They walked onto the field each day, with the sign above the locker room door reminding them that they were the hardest-nosed football players in the world. Quite frankly, being anything else wasn't an option. As the smallest college football team in the country in size and number, they had to be tougher than their opponents in every sense of the word. And nearly every single Saturday, they were.

The Dirty Thirty—an affectionate moniker for the 1959 Iowa State football squad—is quite possibly the most hard-nosed and toughest group, mentally and physically, the Cyclones have ever produced. Not given a chance for success in 1959 with just 30 players on the roster (down from 55), they took on all comers anyway, finishing with a 7–3 record. To appreciate the achievement, you must know how this collection of footballers was assembled.

Iowa State coach Clay Stapleton was hired on February 1, 1958, and in his first season that fall, the product on the field left a lot to be desired. "The first year was a disaster," Stapleton said later. The Cyclones lost all six Big 8 games, and were the laughingstock of the conference. However, in the fall of 1959, Iowa State College became Iowa State University, and with the change in name, a change in the football program was also hoped for.

Roughly 9,000 students arrived on campus that fall, and they began hearing rumblings that the Cyclones football team only had 41 players on the roster. Because of the low numbers, the Big 8 threatened to kick Iowa State out of the conference for not producing a more filled-out roster. Nonetheless, Iowa State stayed put.

Pegged as the toughest, most hard-nosed players in school history, the Dirty Thirty overcame players quitting and injuries en route to a surprising 7–3 finish in 1959. (Photo courtesy of Iowa State Athletics)

But staying put meant having to put in essentially double the work of its competitors.

"We were not allowed to have water, never allowed to take our helmets off, these sort of things," team member Tom Graham said. The harsh practice environment was all in the hopes that it would make guys tough. "It was a boot camp about every day," team member John Cooper said. Well, it did make guys tough, but it also caused a lot of injuries, and players to quit. As players dropped like flies, Stapleton began wondering if his hard-nosed coaching philosophy was worth it, but he stuck to his guns.

"Even if everyone quit, it was better for me as a coach to do what I believed in," Stapleton once said. As the practices got tougher, the number of team members got smaller. As the season opener approached, the Cyclones were down to just 30 players. Players had to play both ways in those days, so team captain Dwight Nichols asked the coaches if he could have a meeting with the team.

"If anybody else is going to leave," Nichols told his teammates, "leave now so we know what we're going to deal with, because if we end up with 11, we'll play with 11."

Many of the 30 guys remaining on the team were playing hurt but still found a way to push on. Whether playing through a separated shoulder, cuts, or otherwise, letting their teammates down would be worse. "You had to stay healthy," Cooper said.

Fortunately, those 30 players stayed healthy and were ready for their season opener at Drake. The field at Drake Stadium on September 19, 1959, was as muddy as ever, but that didn't slow down the shorthanded Cyclones. Behind the strength of the single-wing offense, run to perfection by Nichols and running back Tom Watkins, Iowa State blew out Drake 41–0. Covered in mud, the Cyclones ran to the locker room victorious and were greeted by athletic trainer Warren Ariail.

"Here comes the Dirty Thirty!" Ariail exclaimed. The name was often looked at from the outside as Iowa State having dirty players, but nothing could be less true. Stapleton's squad averaged just 45 penalty yards per game. "These kids were damn nice kids who were willing to pay the price," Stapleton said.

With a new nickname and a 1–0 record, momentum was building. The following Friday, Iowa State traveled to play Denver, where they dealt with a new obstacle: the altitude. Oxygen tanks filled the ISU sideline, but by the end of the game, they weren't the ones who needed it. "By the fourth quarter, the Denver players were exhausted and we weren't at all," team member Jim Barr said. All of that conditioning paid off, as Iowa State left with a 28–12 win.

Player Profile: Tom Watkins

Speed, physical toughness, and intelligence are each a part of the formula to make a dynamic ball carrier. Unfortunately for Iowa State's opponents, Tom Watkins had all three qualities.

Hard to bring down and having breakaway speed, Watkins formed a deadly one-two punch with ball carrier Dwight Nichols on the famed Dirty Thirty in 1959. That season, Watkins led the team in rushing with 843 yards, which was the second-highest total in the nation. In his three-year career at Iowa State from 1958 to 1960, Watkins amassed 1,605 yards. He broke the school record for single-season touchdowns with 10 in 1960 and was a running back and returner in the NFL for the Cleveland Browns, Detroit Lions, and Pittsburgh Steelers.

Watkins, who passed away in 2011, was inducted into the ISU Hall of Fame in 2002.

"Tom Watkins was probably one of the best athletes we had on our team," Dirty Thirty teammate Tom Graham said. "He was not only that, but a very bright guy. Very successful. He had great character and was a neat guy."

In the home opener against Missouri, the Tigers handed the Dirty Thirty their first loss by a score of 14–0, but crossed communication signals gave birth to the Telephone Trophy rivalry between the schools. A 41–6 blowout win by Iowa State over South Dakota on the road set up the daunting challenge of playing at Colorado on October 17, 1959.

The Buffaloes had beaten the Cyclones eight straight years, and pitched shutouts in four of the last five, and the CU crowd was relentless. "These look like high school football players!" the crowd yelled. It was Iowa State who was all smiles that day, earning a 27–0 win to give Stapleton his first conference victory. "Why, there isn't a one of our Dirty Thirty who doesn't have more guts than five ordinary men," Ariail once told Nichols.

After a convincing win against Kansas State and a close loss to Kansas, Iowa State was paid a visit by Nebraska, who the week before had ended Oklahoma's 74-game conference winning streak. The Cyclones jumped to an early lead and never looked back, getting an 18–6 win. "I think we would have rather beaten Nebraska than walked on the moon," Graham said. "We didn't like those people from Lincoln. I sure as hell didn't."

A painfully cold thrashing of San Jose State in Ames set up a showdown with Oklahoma in Norman for the Big 8 title. Iowa State's chances of going to the Orange Bowl looked good early, but the Sooners handed the Cyclones a loss in the season finale, and the Dirty Thirty finished the season 7–3. That season set up future success for Cyclones football, and it all started with a mentality. It's that identity that all Iowa Staters can be proud of.

"There will never be another football team," Cooper said, "that was tougher than the Dirty Thirty."

9 Dreaming of an Upset

When Bob Lamson eased his head onto his pillow on an unassuming night in January 1957, he could just as well have had a nightmare. Two days before Wilt "the Stilt" Chamberlain was set to arrive at the Armory with No. 1 Kansas, nightmarish thoughts were certainly to be expected. Instead, the Iowa State assistant shut his eyes, fell into a fitful sleep, and dreamed.

Earlier that season at the Big 7 Holiday Tournament in Kansas City, Iowa State had met Wilt for the first time and had played rather admirably. Even before Wilt became eligible as a sophomore, coaches were already worrying about the wunderkind. In his collegiate debut in 1956, he gave more reason to worry, scoring 52 points while grabbing 31 rebounds. In Kansas City the seven-footer scored only 12 points against Iowa State, and it took a last-second shot for the Jayhawks to secure a 58–57 win and send the Cyclones into the loser's bracket.

Iowa State had slowed Wilt in its first meeting with a 1–3–1 zone defense, sure, but coach Bill Strannigan felt that strategy allowed the other Kansas players too many open shots. On that fateful night two days before the Monday showdown in Ames, Lamson had dreamed up the perfect solution. As the story goes, the next day Lamson diagrammed his idea and presented it to Strannigan. The team practiced it for 30 minutes on Sunday and decided to use it.

At the early season tournament, Iowa State's 6'8" center, Don Medsker, had played behind Wilt while one of the forwards, Chuck Vogt or John Crawford, stayed in front. Then one of the guards, Gary Thompson or Lyle Frahm, sagged to create a barrier around Chamberlain. When Lamson shut his eyes, he dreamed that Medsker would instead play *in front of* Wilt while the two forwards pinched him, leaving the guards chasing three guys in a zone up front.

Finally, game day arrived on January 14, 1957.

The anticipation for the matchup in Ames had been building since Iowa State narrowly lost in Kansas City. With Wilt aboard, many thought Kansas was destined to go undefeated. The Jayhawks arrived in Ames ranked No. 1 and with an unblemished 12–0 record. The Cyclones were ranked No. 7. For weeks, the 7,800-seat Armory had been sold out. There would be handfuls of newspapers and radio stations there, and the game would be broadcast on WOI-TV.

"The basketball menu here tonight is pure caviar," Maury White wrote in the *Des Moines Register* leading into the matchup. "Wilt Chamberlain & Co. against Iowa State, the only team to come within a point of undefeated Kansas in 12 games."

When the game had finally arrived, it did so on the heels of a blizzard that had descended upon Ames. Temperatures dipped to

15 degrees below zero, and yet fans navigated the snow-covered roads and waited outside in the bitter cold for admittance. Eventually, more than 8,000 people crammed onto metal bleachers inside the confined Armory.

To make Lamson's dream defense work, Iowa State would need to alter its offense. If the Cyclones took a normal number of shots, Wilt would just grab the rebounds. So Iowa State took only calculated shots (38 total), when it had good spacing. Otherwise, it moved the ball.

By halftime, the strategy was working, and Iowa State trailed 19–17.

"I thought Kansas did not play very smart," Thompson said. "Two guys aren't going to cover three if you move the ball and we're coming late all the time. They turned down a lot of good shots to try to get it to Wilt. They said we stalled, but we went for the good shots in our offense. A lot of the score holding down is the fact that they didn't shoot the ball, either."

Iowa State built leads multiple times in the second half, including one of 37–33 late in the game. Then Kansas made a shot to draw within two before Wilt, with nine seconds remaining, was fouled. Wilt was a notoriously poor free-throw shooter, and the game was on the line.

"Block off!" Thompson yelled from the side. "Block off!"

Wilt made the first. There was no way he was making both.

"Block off!" Thompson yelled again. "Block off!"

Then, unbelievably, Wilt hit the second. The game was tied at 37, and Strannigan called a timeout to draw up a play. On that night inside the Armory, there was not one soul who didn't know what Iowa State was drawing up. Thompson, who was outscoring Wilt 18–17, was getting the ball. Everybody knew that. Well, Kansas knew too.

Iowa State set two different screens to get Thompson free as Vogt inbounded the ball to Frahm, but Wilt towered above, and

Don Medsker became an unlikely hero on January 14, 1957, when he hit a game-winning shot at the Armory in Ames to help Iowa State upset No. 1 Kansas and Wilt "the Stilt" Chamberlain 39–37 before being hoisted by the court-storming crowd. (Photo courtesy of Iowa State Athletics)

another Kansas player helped double the Iowa State star. In making sure Thompson didn't get the ball, Medsker had been left open near the top. Frahm dished it, and Medsker quickly rose and fired. As the gun shot off, the 15-foot jumper sailed into the air. The ball swished through the net.

"The crowd just exploded," Thompson said.

Fans stormed onto the court and lifted players into the air. Wilt stopped in the Iowa State locker room afterward to congratulate the Cyclones. "You played a fine game and deserved to win," Wilt told them. Kansas would lose just one more game, in the national championship.

"Give Lamson credit for the defense," Strannigan said, although he later said parts of the story had been far-fetched. In his dream, Lamson would say, Thompson had taken the game-winning shot. Whatever the case, Iowa State had stunned the basketball world.

The dream had worked like a dream.

10 The Run

"Here's Wallace...pumping...looking...running to his right, looking... and he's going to be almost caught. Now he's running at the 25...and runs...down the sideline back to the 10! Now he's giving ground, goes around to the 10, to the left side, to the 5! Touchdown! Oh my goodness, what a run by Wallace!"

—Pete Taylor, Voice of the Cyclones

You probably thought the play was dead in the water. "There's no way he can make something of *this* situation," everybody said. Hell, even Seneca Wallace didn't know if he could get anything out of the play.

Not only did Seneca turn what appeared to be a hopeless situation into a scene of jubilation for Iowa State fans, he left an indelible mark on the history of Iowa State football in one snapshot of time. The Run, as it is affectionately called today, is a moment that has stood the test of time, ever since it unfolded on the night of October 12, 2002.

The story of Seneca Wallace is certainly more than just one play, but it was how the Run unfolded that mirrored the optimism surrounding the Iowa State program.

"It will [last] forever," former coach Dan McCarney said. "I hear from my players here at North Texas who still get it...on YouTube. It's one of those plays that goes down forever."

Iowa State was operating from the Texas Tech 12-yard line, facing second-and-11. Wallace took the snap under center, dropped back three steps, and looked to his left. Seeing a wall of Red Raiders defenders, he rolled back to his right all the way to the 32-yard line, and was nearly brought down by a defender for a devastating loss. *Okay, well, maybe I can try to scramble to pick up a few yards, maybe get a little bit of distance from the pocket and maybe try to throw the ball down the field,* Wallace thought.

But Seneca wasn't quite done. Instead, he continued to roll right, then got to the 20-yard line, where he sensed a change in the Texas Tech defense. He started to see the defense let up in its pressure, so he found the cutback lane, sprinting from west to east along the 10-yard line.

Red Raiders cornerback Ricky Sailor saw Seneca making headway in getting toward the end zone and knew he was essentially the last line of defense. What he didn't know—and what everybody else in Jack Trice Stadium *was* aware of—was that Iowa State running back Mike Wagner was setting himself up for a monster block. Sailor never saw Wagner coming and was met by a hard blow that brought an audible gasp from the crowd, sent Sailor to his back, and left Seneca free to walk into the left side of the end zone untouched.

"I saw him rolling back my way," Wagner told reporters following the game. "I knew everyone saw it but him. He was out there by himself on an island, and I had to take him home."

From the snap to when the touchdown was scored, the man in the No. 15 red jersey had zigzagged across the field an estimated 135 total yards in just less than 15 seconds.

"It wasn't like I was even tired after the play," Wallace said. "Normally you get a guy to run 100-something yards, he's going to be exhausted, a little winded."

Friends and family filled the stadium that day to watch Seneca in action, and the adrenaline was flowing. Wallace placed himself in the forefront of the Heisman race and vaulted Iowa State into the top 10 in the national polls.

"Sometimes we coaches just have to look at each other and shake our heads," then–offensive coordinator Steve Brickey later told *Sports Illustrated*. "He's that good."

Now more than a decade removed from donning an Iowa State jersey, Seneca still hears all the time about the Run. "That's what a lot of us athletes play the sport for," Wallace said. "It's about the memories, and when you have memories like that—that people still hold on to—it makes you feel good."

The Run is simply one of those plays that Cyclones fans love to hold on to. It lives on through YouTube and other highlight reels, but for those who were there that day, it's an image that just doesn't seem to fade.

"It's one of the most magical plays I'll ever remember, and I've been part of a national championship at Florida," McCarney said. "One of the most magical plays that I'll ever remember in my life."

11 The Lafester Game

It played out more like a Hollywood action film than a basketball game.

The pace was throttled up to breakneck speed. For 45 minutes, the floor inside Hilton Coliseum acted as a stage for some of the most dramatic, high-motored action in the history of Iowa and Iowa State basketball. The night was December 19, 1987. The game? It's known universally by three words: the Lafester Game.

On a night where a theatrical display of basketball unfolded in front of the 14,636 raucous fans, Iowa State's Lafester Rhodes was the hero, leading man, and just about the only thing most people talked about afterward. In school-record fashion, Rhodes poured on 54 points and played every single minute against the Hawkeyes. "It's great that I set the record, but that was not the main thing I wanted to do," Rhodes said afterward. "I wanted to win the game." And the Cyclones needed all of his 54 to earn their 102–100 overtime win.

Hilton Coliseum turned into a scene of frenzy. In fact, it's fair to say the energy in the building was frenetic from the beginning, so that's probably the best place for this story to begin.

Known for being a place of high energy, the Hilton crowd was enthusiastic when Iowa arrived. But this was different. Iowa State and Iowa were both nationally ranked, No. 20 and No. 7 respectively, and this was the first-*ever* ranked matchup between the two. The place was *loud* from the get-go.

"I can't remember a ton about the game except for it was so frickin' loud in there, I had a headache for like two days, and I had headsets on," said ISU broadcaster Eric Heft. "It was unbelievable."

The court was laden with future NBA talent, including Jeff Grayer on the Iowa State team and B.J. Armstrong and Roy Marble playing for Iowa, but it was a matchup between Ed Horton from the Hawkeyes and Rhodes that showed itself early. Iowa grabbed a 14–7 lead just more than four minutes in, and Rhodes and Horton were trading buckets. ISU coaches even thought about pulling Rhodes for defensive purposes.

"Coach, we've got to get Lafester out or [put] somebody else on [Horton], because the kid is killing us," ISU assistant Jim Hallihan told coach Johnny Orr.

"Let's let it go a little longer," Orr responded.

So Rhodes stayed in, and kept scoring. Eventually, Horton's production began to slow, while Rhodes' point total kept climbing. "We just couldn't find him defensively," Iowa coach Dr. Tom Davis said. Six straight points by Rhodes were followed by a Hawkeyes run, but Rhodes hit a three-pointer as time expired to take a 50–49 halftime lead. He had 26 first-half points.

In the first meeting between Iowa State and Iowa in which both teams were ranked, Lafester Rhodes (pictured) put on a show with a school-record 54 points in the fast-paced game to help the Cyclones to a 102–100 overtime win. (Photo courtesy of Iowa State Athletics)

Also known for his abilities on the track, Rhodes embraced the running philosophy of Orr, and he applied it directly out of halftime. He had five more points within the first minutes of the second half, and the Cyclones made six of their first seven shots. "The more they pressed us, the faster we played," assistant coach Ric Wesley said. Every defense Iowa showed, Rhodes found a way to score. "His quickness is hard to guard with big guys," Davis said.

Iowa State took its biggest lead of the game, 84–75, with 7:40 remaining, after a basket by Grayer, who finished with 28 points. That bucket came after two tip-ins by none other than Rhodes. "It seemed like every time he let the ball go, it was just going into the basket," Grayer remembered. After a quick run by Iowa, the Cyclones led 90–89 but turned over the ball. Horton was fouled with 12 seconds remaining, making the front end of the one-and-one to tie the game.

With Iowa State sitting on a 97–92 lead in overtime, Rhodes had played every second of the game. Hallihan suggested subbing. "Coach, Lafester needs a break," Hallihan said. Orr looked up at the scoreboard, then back at Hallihan. "Well, he's got 50," he reasoned. "Let's just leave him in there until he dies."

So once again Rhodes stayed in, and Iowa eventually took a 100–99 lead with 1:16 to go in OT. Rhodes then scored the go-ahead bucket off a steal by Terry Woods. A defensive stop on the ensuing possession turned into Rhodes catching the ball in the corner, where he was fouled on the shot. Rhodes' one made free throw, and 54th point, gave Iowa State the win and Rhodes the school record. He was 20-of-31 shooting and 5-of-8 from downtown. "It's a great feeling that I left a mark on Iowa State [when] I played there," Rhodes said years later. "My kids, they'll probably look at it as a big thing to them."

Emotions ran high after the game, and Iowa assistant Gary Close and Orr came to blows over a timekeeping situation that had occurred near the end of the game. Amongst the pandemonium on the court, in the stands, and between the coaches was US presidential candidate Jesse Jackson, who was in Ames for the Iowa Caucuses and witnessed ISU history; he spoke to Rhodes on the court after the game.

In the decades since that historic night, the Lafester Game is the only game Hallihan—who coached at Iowa State for 12 years—has sat down and watched again from start to finish. It's one game that has stood the test of time. After all, it did play out like a Hollywood classic.

"Get popcorn," Hallihan advises Cyclones fans. "Sit there, and get a pop. You'd enjoy it."

12 Dan Gable

Dan Gable has a direct, matter-of-fact rhythm in his voice. As he speaks, each word is chosen meticulously to get him to his next thought. His tone has a sense of purpose. That's how it's always been for Dan Gable. Each word or action is carried out with meaning behind it. That's what drives him, and what has always driven him, to be great.

Gable is considered to be one of the greatest wrestlers, if not *the* greatest, of all time. He had a 181–1 record in high school and college, the only loss coming in the final match of his career. The Olympic gold medal he obtained at the 1972 Olympics in Munich stands tall, as does his coaching career at Iowa.

It's that single loss that many remember about Gable's wrestling career. But that defeat does not define Gable, it has fueled him. This story must begin when Gable was growing up in Waterloo, Iowa, as a part of a wrestling family.

"When I was born, I was born a wrestler, because I was from a community [in which] everybody at that time wrestled," Gable said. "It was the best and easiest sport that I've ever done."

It might have been the "easiest" sport he ever did, but that was mostly a product of the work he put into it. By rule, he wasn't allowed to compete as a freshman for Waterloo West, but as a sophomore in 1964, his grittiness and focus pushed him to an undefeated season and a state championship at 95 pounds. The fire within him was high, but it was grief that put a bit more oxygen to the flames.

Along with his parents, Dan was on vacation on May 31, 1964, in Harpers Ferry, Iowa, when a phone call came in from Waterloo. Dan's older sister, 19-year-old Diane, had been murdered in the family's home. It was later learned the killer was a 16-year-old boy Dan somewhat knew. Upon returning home, backdropped by his grieving and arguing parents, Dan moved into his sister's old bedroom. Losing her made an already hungry wrestler hungrier.

Gable's high school dominance continued, as he won two more state championships and finished his prep career with a 64–0 record. Instead of sticking close to his parents and going to Iowa State Teacher's College, eventually known as the University of Northern Iowa, the self-professed "home kid" decided to go to Iowa State at the urging of family friends who were familiar with the program. It wasn't much of a sales job for coach Harold Nichols.

"I think he took me to McDonald's, and that was as much as he had to do," Gable remembered. "I was signed, sealed, and delivered. It was the best wrestling school in the state."

While redshirting his first year, there was quite an adjustment for the soft-spoken but often intense wrestling phenom. His grief surrounding his sister's death lingered, and he worried that being 90 minutes away from home would cause more problems. But Dan made frequent trips home that year, helping with the adjustment.

Although he is largely remembered for a loss, Dan Gable became arguably one of the greatest wrestlers in history with a 117–1 mark at Iowa State while later breezing through competition at the 1972 Olympics to claim gold. (Photo courtesy of Iowa State Athletics)

"I found out when I left to go to college, and especially 90 miles [away], that, wow, [my parents] really did like each other," Gable said. "They mended a lot of fences, and they pulled together and they became one."

The family dynamic was no longer his concern, but his performances on the mat were still driven by an intense desire to win. An undefeated season, culminating in a national title as a sophomore, followed. As a junior he registered 26 pins in 30 matches, five straight at the NCAA championships, to go undefeated again and win another national championship.

Gable was as focused as they come during his senior year. He was so dedicated, he ran from building to building on the Iowa State campus to attend classes. He didn't want to feel like he wasn't putting in work. "I sensed he was [intense] as a student and not just a wrestler once I got acquainted with him," said teammate Ben Peterson. "Everything sooner or later kind of wrapped around wrestling for him."

The Cyclones were on the brink of winning the 1970 NCAA team championship and Gable was going for his third straight individual title, attempting to cap off a perfect prep and collegiate career. He was 117–0 entering the March 28, 1970, 142-pound title match against Larry Owings of Washington.

A scrappy match with Owings found Gable down four points with three seconds remaining. Owings held on, and the streak had been snapped. It was the final match of Gable's Iowa State career. The crowd was stunned. "They just thought I was unbeatable and that type of thing," Gable said. Iowa State won the team title, but as Gable stood on the podium in second place, tears rolled down his face as he raised his head to the cheers of the crowd.

The soul-searching process was underway. Gable didn't want to have that feeling again. True to his nature, his focus intensified and his striving for perfection began anew. "I went back 365 days from the day I won the national title the year before and I studied every day," Gable said. "I found all these different days that I didn't do well."

It would be two years before he could attain his next goal of becoming an Olympic champion. He stayed and trained at Iowa State for those two years, not resting on his laurels. When he arrived in Munich for the 1972 Olympics, he had no outside thoughts in his mind.

"I pretty much knew I was going to win," Gable said. "I'm not saying it from a cocky point of view. I just trained, and every time I wrestled, I felt like I was going to be the winner."

Not only was Gable the winner, he flat-out *dominated* his opponents. Gable didn't surrender a single point en route to his gold medal, and thwarted the Soviet Union's goal of having one of its wrestlers beat him. "He kept saying, 'Put me down; I came here to win the gold medal and I did, so it's done,'" Peterson, who also won gold in Munich, remembered.

Gable's enthusiasm for his teammates on Team USA made it evident he would turn his focus to coaching in the future. Because there were no openings at Iowa State, he looked east, joining the staff at Iowa in 1972 before becoming head coach in 1976, leading the Hawkeyes to 15 NCAA team titles before he retired in 1997. Despite the Cy-Hawk rivalry, Gable tried not to get caught up in any hatred. "In fact, I love my six years at Iowa State," Gable said.

13 The Roland Rocket

When Gary Thompson was in junior high in Roland, Iowa, he and some of his buddies would make the short 15-mile jaunt to Ames, where they'd play pool at the local YMCA. Around halftime of the Iowa State basketball game, they'd head to the Armory and, because the crowds weren't very big at the time, they'd get in free to watch the second half.

As a scrawny 5'6" sophomore at Roland High School, Thompson became a star. That year, in 1951, the Rockets, as the team was named, advanced to the state tournament. Roland was a small town (population 687 in 1950), and Thompson was one of only 40 boys and 73 students in the *entire high school.* In those days, once you made the state tournament, all teams were thrown together. To win the state championship, Thompson and the

A Stint at Pitcher

When Iowa State reached the 1957 College World Series, they did so with the help of All-American shortstop Gary Thompson. Once there, the Cyclones picked up their first win with Thompson on the pitcher's mound.

Thompson hadn't pitched since high school (maybe, he says, he tried an inning in college), when Iowa State led Notre Dame by three runs in the bottom of the ninth with the bases loaded. The pitchers had been wild, and coach L.C. "Capp" Timm huddled the infield. He took the ball from the pitcher and looked toward Thompson.

"Little man," Timm told Thompson. "I know you'll get 'er over the plate."

Thompson threw a knuckleball, and the pitch didn't knuckle. The batter lined a hit to left-center to clear the bases and tie the game. After stranding a runner at third to end the inning, Iowa State scored three in the next inning. Thompson had become the pitcher of record. "So I'm 1–0 in the College World Series," Thompson said.

Rockets would need to beat Waterloo West, Des Moines East, and Davenport, three of the biggest schools in the state.

In March 1951, at the field house in Iowa City, Roland faced Waterloo West in the quarterfinals of the state tournament in front of 14,000 fans. After trailing early, Roland surrendered only nine second-half points in a 43–40 upset. Thompson had starred.

"Little Gary Thompson, a 15-year-old sophomore who measures just 5 ft. 6 in. in height, was fairly taking the breath of the onlookers with his exploits," Bert McGrane wrote in the *Des Moines Register*. "He hounded the opposition. He stole the ball from dribblers and captured rebounds in spite of his lack of height. And he pitched in baskets from anywhere."

In the semifinals, Roland dispatched Des Moines East 46–37 to advance to the title game. There, the Rockets led entering the fourth quarter. In the final three minutes of the game, though, Davenport used a run to surge to a 50–40 win. Yet Thompson had burst onto the scene. He began receiving mail from around the state.

"I kind of picked up the name of the Roland Rocket from there," Thompson said.

In the next two years, Roland advanced to the semifinals in the state tournament twice more. By the time his prep career ended, Thompson had three times been named first-team All-State, scoring a state-record 2,042 points while Roland went 127–8 during his tenure. Recruiting was slow in those days. Thompson was contacted by Kansas, and there was a guy bulldogging him who didn't care where Gary went so long as it was Baylor, SMU, or Rice. Thompson wanted to stay close to home. One day, he went over to coach Clayton Sutherland's house in Ames and they ate hamburgers in the backyard. That was the extent of recruiting. The Roland Rocket chose Iowa State.

Thompson arrived on campus in 1953, and while Sutherland had recruited him, by the time he began his varsity career as a sophomore, Bill Strannigan had replaced Sutherland. The Cyclones were on the heels of six consecutive losing seasons leading into Thompson's first year with the varsity, and he started from the onset. That year, Iowa State posted a winning record.

The rise of the program with Thompson aboard began his junior season. In December, Iowa State hosted No. 8 Vanderbilt at the Armory, and Thompson put on a show. With the Cyclones leading by double figures late, Vanderbilt kept pressing. Thompson gave a signal to go deep. His defender bit, and Thompson put in a layup for his 39th and 40th points, becoming the first player in program history to score 40. The Cyclones won the Big 7 Holiday Tournament in Kansas City, the school's first conference tournament title, and won a then-school-record 18 games. Thompson was named Iowa State Athlete of the Year.

As a senior, Thompson outscored seven-foot phenom Wilt Chamberlain to help Iowa State upset No. 1 Kansas in Ames. By season's end, he had been named the 1957 Big 7 Player of the Year, ahead of Chamberlain. "That's a pretty nice thing to have on your résumé," Thompson said. He went on to add more accolades to his résumé. Thompson had become the first 1,000-point scorer

Iowa State's first multisport All-American made a name for himself at Roland High School just north of Ames before becoming the first 1,000-point scorer at Iowa State and ultimately one of the greatest players in program history. (Photo courtesy of Iowa State Athletics)

in program history and the first athlete to win multiple Iowa State Athlete of the Year awards. He was also named an All-American.

"Inch for inch," legendary Kansas coach Forrest "Phog" Allen said, "Gary Thompson is probably as good a player as the Big 7 has ever seen—and it's seen some fine ones."

Thompson, who also played shortstop for three seasons at Iowa State, leading the team to its first College World Series in 1957, was later named an All-American on the baseball diamond, becoming the first multisport All-American in Iowa State history.

Following his collegiate career, Thompson was drafted in the fifth round by the NBA's Minneapolis Lakers but opted to play for the Phillips 66ers in AAU basketball before embarking on a 34-year broadcasting career until 2005.

Today the crowds have grown, and Thompson's No. 20 hangs in the rafters.

14 Dwight Nichols

It's hard to imagine how different Iowa State football history would be without Dwight Nichols. His production on the field speaks for itself, certainly. Nichols led the Big 7 in total offense three times in his career, while his leadership as the captain of the famed Dirty Thirty is still remembered by loyal Cyclones fans more than 50 years later. Nichols' illustrious career came to fruition after quite a bit of doubt, however.

Nichols' reputation at Knoxville (Iowa) High School preceded him. He was the most fierce and fiery four-sport athlete around, captaining each of those teams before joining the marines after graduation. After serving for three years in the marines and returning home as a Korean War veteran, Nichols was looking for something else, and turned his eyes toward playing football at Iowa State.

The uncertainty about playing collegiately was ever-present. During his time in the service, Nichols had been getting letters from Knoxville football coach Ray Klootwyk, who had played for Iowa State in the 1940s, assuring him there would be a roster spot if he wanted one. Dwight ultimately decided he wanted to give it a shot, and he was accepted into the program in 1956 with the stipulation that he would have to prove himself to earn a roster spot. One of the most revered players in Iowa State history had to start his career as a walk-on.

As a 5'10", 164-pound freshman, Nichols spent the year practicing with the team, trying to find the right spot for his unique skill set. He was a hybrid of sorts between quarterback and running back, but there wasn't really an offensive system at the time that fit that mold. It was Iowa State coach J.A. Myers who decided to break the mold. He made Iowa State a single-wing offense, meaning the ball would be snapped directly to the running back. It was the perfect fit for Nichols, who said it was one of the best things ever to happen to him.

"I don't want to sound vain, but there was only certain people that had that," Nichols told the *Des Moines Register*. "The guys who played had to have certain talents… pass long, pass short, run, and be durable as hell."

"Durable as hell" doesn't begin to describe what Nichols brought to the table. He was an absolute workhorse for the Cyclones as a sophomore in 1957, leading his team to a surprising 7–7 tie at Syracuse, while garnering All–Big 7 accolades. It was the next season that started to cement Nichols in Iowa State lore.

Under new coach Clay Stapleton, Nichols broke out in Iowa State's single-wing offense, rushing for 815 yards (third in the nation) and gaining 1,172 yards of total offense in 1958 while being named Big 7 Player of the Year. Pound for pound, Nichols was one of the most efficient, and toughest, players that teammate John Cooper had ever seen.

Cooper roomed with Nichols during Iowa State road games and remembered that as they would each lay down to go to sleep, Nichols would begin spitting out statistics of what he had done the last time he played at that opponent's stadium.

"We might be down at Missouri, for example, and he'd start telling me, 'Two years ago I carried the ball against Missouri 14 times and got 184 yards and averaged 6.5 yards a carry,'" Cooper

Captain of the Dirty Thirty and a veteran of the marines, Nichols' toughness and durability were his trademarks as he ended his career as the all-time Big 7 rushing leader with 2,232 yards.
(Photo courtesy of Iowa State Athletics)

said. "He could tell you what he did when he played there the last time and what he did in the game. He was a student of the game, if you will."

During his senior season in 1959, Nichols captained the Dirty Thirty, one of the most memorable teams in school history, and one that was defined by toughness. Dwight Nichols had plenty of that.

"By the end of the season, the lack of numbers and depth were taking a toll on us," Nichols said later. "It was a great team, and it seems that most of the guys on that team went on to great success outside, after college."

Nichols found success in his own right following that season. He chose a business career over professional football, but his numbers at Iowa State are as impressive today as they were back then. Nichols ended his career as the all-time Big 7 leading rusher with 2,232 yards on 638 carries. The 638 carries ranked second in NCAA history at the time, and he ended his playing days second in Big 8 history with 3,949 yards of total offense. He was named to the All-America first team as a senior and finished eighth in the Heisman Trophy race. Dwight Nichols changed Iowa State football.

15 Jeff Grayer

The banquet was about to begin, and Jeff Grayer was nowhere to be found. It was going to be huge that year, having been moved from a hotel ballroom to Hilton Coliseum to accommodate the crowd, which was expected to be as big as it ever had been—roughly 5,000 people. Iowa State players were all set to line up above the curtain on the concourse and walk down into view of the audience. All but one player was there.

"Coach, Jeff's not here," a manager told assistant Jim Hallihan.

"Jeff's not here? What do you mean he's not here?" Hallihan asked.

"He said he's sick," the manager replied.

Hallihan hustled as fast as he could to dial Grayer's dorm from an office phone. Finally Grayer answered, and the freshman told Hallihan he was sick and just couldn't bring himself to go to Hilton Coliseum. Hallihan let Grayer know what he thought of that idea. "You get your butt…. Unless you're dying, you get your clothes on and get over here," Hallihan fired at him. "They're here to see you!"

Grayer reluctantly made his way to Hilton Coliseum thanks to the persistent prodding by Hallihan, showing up without a hint of an illness. The reasons for his desire to skip out? Nervousness and shyness. The very thought of speaking in front of that many people made Grayer uneasy, but reassurance that he was only going to be recognized made the difference.

As nervous as he was about speaking in front of thousands of people, playing in front of a crowd twice the size of the one gathered at the banquet didn't faze Grayer. After that day at the banquet, he turned it up a notch for his sophomore season, and… *boom!* Jeff Grayer wrote a big chapter in Iowa State basketball history.

He finished his career as the Cyclones' all-time leading scorer (2,502 points), scoring a school-record 811 points as a senior. Grayer was a second-team All-American in 1988 and a three-time All–Big 8 performer. And to think, we might never have seen Grayer in an Iowa State uniform had it not been his connection to Flint, Michigan, and a former Iowa State great.

It was Jeff's close relationship with ISU standout Barry Stevens—who had starred at Flint Northwestern—that made him more than aware of Iowa State, but it was the dedication by coaches in the recruiting process that really made an impression on him.

"The thing I remember the most is seeing [Iowa State coaches] in the stands," Grayer said. "Just about every time we played, they were here."

"I gave a big part of my life to that effort, there," said former Cyclones assistant Ric Wesley, who estimated he saw 20 of Grayer's

A quiet kid from Flint, Michigan, Jeff Grayer was anything but quiet on the court at Iowa State, where he became a force to be reckoned with and the all-time leading scorer during the rise of the program. (Photo courtesy of Iowa State Athletics)

games. "I just kind of spent a lot of time in Flint. We knew he was good."

Grayer *was* good. And the level of competition he was playing with in Flint was enough to prove it. Glen Rice, Roy Marble, Trent Tucker, and Stevens all hailed from Flint, and all had tons of talent. It was during summer league games that Wesley got to really see Grayer's talent against top competition, and he'd constantly relay that back to Ames. Grayer and those guys he played ball with all had the same goal in mind: get out of Flint and play collegiately. For Jeff, that meant joining the Cyclones.

When Grayer arrived in Ames, it was a bit of a culture shock. He looked around upon arriving and saw (and smelled) nothing but farmland. All it took for the quiet ballplayer to feel comfortable was to start meeting some of the people in Iowa, but it was that first impression that made his eyes go wide.

"My first year here, I was just stunned," Grayer told *Sports Illustrated*. "The farm smells, the sky, the look of the country."

After spending the first season conceding to Stevens as the leader of the team, Grayer prepared to take on some of those responsibilities and settled in. He became *the guy* and someone his teammates listened to. Grayer might have been quiet, but when he had something to say, guys around him took notice.

Grayer was as fierce a teammate as they come. One year, Jeff Hornacek was on the receiving end of a sucker punch against Nebraska, and Grayer went after the Cornhuskers player who had hit him, resulting in an ejection. Nothing about what Grayer did was malicious; it was just what he felt he had to do to defend his teammate.

Intensity even happened within the Iowa State squad. It was more than 100 degrees one summer day in State Gym, where the Cyclones held summer scrimmages. Grayer, as usual, was busting his butt up and down the court and threw a pass inside to Darryl Spinks. Spinks fumbled it, the ball was stolen, and Grayer was the lone player to fly up the court to try to recover on defense, only to watch the other team score. After the same sequence played out two more times with Spinks—the last allowing the game-winning basket—Jeff had seen enough. *Whack!* The ball sailed out of Grayer's hand and into Spinks' head and was followed by Jeff's fist.

"Every guy on that team knew if you didn't come to win, he was going to kick your butt," Hallihan said. "He wouldn't say much. But boy, he was a leader."

Jeff backed it up on the court too. He led the Big 8 in scoring average his senior season (25.4 points per game) and added 9.4 rebounds per game. Grayer's explosiveness and speed set him apart from most other players he shared the court with. Even though he was probably shorter than his listed height of 6'5", his athleticism stood tall.

"Jeff was one of those guys, when you got him the ball anywhere around the lane, he was going to score," Hornacek said. "He was a smart player in the fact that he knew how to get open."

Grayer's dedication to being successful as a senior at Iowa State ran so deep he rarely went out to do much else. "My total focus and my total level of dedication was on basketball," Grayer said. "I knew that was the time in which I really had to give it my best shot. The focus was there from start to finish." Sure, people would come to his apartment, but after having his car towed because of problems it was having, he decided staying in and focusing on basketball was what he wanted.

The Milwaukee Bucks selected Grayer with the 13th overall pick in the 1988 NBA Draft, and that same year he played on the US Olympic team that won a bronze medal in Seoul, South Korea. Just like at Iowa State, Grayer—an NBA journeyman—did whatever he could to make an impact during his nine-year professional career.

Jeff Grayer was all about winning. As a player he could set the tone without saying much, letting his play speak for itself.

"That's the perfect kind of guy," Hallihan said. "Mild-mannered off the court and a warrior on the court."

16 Bill Fennelly

The plan was all laid out. The first order of business for Bill Fennelly was to graduate from William Penn with a business and economics degree. Law school was the step after that, so he began studying for the LSATs. But all of a sudden, this feeling came over him that he couldn't ignore. Fennelly didn't want to go to law school. He wanted to be a coach. "I remember telling my dad that, and it got really quiet," Fennelly said.

"So you're going to get a job and put your paycheck in the mouth of an 18-year-old kid?" the elder Fennelly asked.

"Yes, sir," Bill replied.

"Okay, good luck," his dad, also named Bill, offered.

Growing up in Davenport, where his father operated a gas station, Fennelly always loved sports. As an undergrad at William Penn, he wanted to get involved with coaching to go along with his business studies.

When he was set to graduate, knowing he would forgo law school, he was offered a job right there at the college to be the head coach of the softball team and an assistant with the women's basketball team while working in admissions. "The first softball game I ever coached was the first softball game I ever saw," Fennelly said. He felt like he didn't know what he was doing out on the diamond, but he knew that being in the arena of sports was the right fit.

"I liked that every day was different," Fennelly said. "I love competition and everything about it. I was drawn to it."

Fennelly was also drawn to stops at Fresno State and Notre Dame as an assistant women's basketball coach before he got his first big break as the head coach at Toledo. In seven seasons with the Rockets, he led his team to the NCAA tournament three times and posted six 20-win seasons. It was going great for him and his family in Ohio, but Fennelly always caught himself glancing at a possible return to his home state.

The opportunity to return to Iowa wouldn't be easy because of the low number of Division I openings. But on one trip back to Davenport he took with his family, Fennelly opened up the

Player Profile: Lyndsey Medders Fennelly

Notorious for arriving at places early, Iowa State coach Bill Fennelly showed up at the high school gym on a recruiting trip well ahead of tipoff for the game he was scouting. As he settled in, he watched the game that point guard Lyndsey Medders was just finishing.

"You need to tell No. 14 to keep working; she's going to be a really good player," Fennelly told the team's coach after the game.

"Why don't you recruit her?" the coach responded.

Medders, a Los Angeles native, was open to going anywhere to play college basketball, so former ISU assistant Robin Pingeton started the recruitment immediately. Medders arrived in Ames in 2003 and embarked on a career that saw her end her college playing days as the all-time leader in assists at Iowa State (719) and ranked seventh in scoring (1,449 points). "She saw the game like a coach," Fennelly said. "She led and administered her teammates like a coach would want to."

Medders' and Fennelly's relationship didn't end after her senior season, though. Lyndsey married Fennelly's oldest son, Billy, and gave birth to a son, Will, in 2014.

"There's nobody I would rather [Will] be with than his grandfather," Lyndsey said. "If you would have told me that I'd say that 10 years ago as I signed on the dotted line to play for him, I'd have called you crazy."

"I got lucky to get a great player," Fennelly said. "I got even luckier to get someone who is now part of my family."

newspaper (on his birthday, no less) and saw the headline about the Iowa State women's program. *Theresa Becker Resigns*, it read. "I decided at that point we'd kind of look into it," Fennelly recalled. Fennelly started discussions with then–athletics director Gene Smith about a move to Ames.

Fennelly and his wife, Deb, are both Iowa natives, and their sons, Billy and Steven, were in fifth and first grade at the time, so the possible move was coming at a great juncture.

"You've got to have people that want you," Fennelly said. "One thing led to another, and I was very fortunate that they offered me the job. I took it and moved home."

Moving home didn't mean moving to a big-time program right away, though. The Cyclones had gone 8–19 in 1994, the year before Fennelly arrived in Ames, but the roster wasn't lacking talent. Janel Grimm, Jayme Olson, and Tara Gunderson would all be with the program in 1995–96, but a culture would need to be established. Fennelly's intense personality on the court had to set a standard for how his teams would play. People hadn't looked at Iowa State women's basketball favorably in the past, and in a lot of cases, people weren't looking at all.

"Not just that we hadn't won a lot of games, but everything," Fennelly said. "People didn't view us in a very positive way. I think it was, from day one, 'This is how we're going to do things.' We didn't come in with this five-year plan."

The plan was to build credibility from the ground up in a state where women's sports matter, and with a fan base that was already latched on to other teams in the university.

Iowa State women's basketball won its first 12 games of the season in Fennelly's first year, but it was that first victory—against Idaho State—that stands out. Fennelly isn't one to hold on to things from throughout his career, but that first box score still sits neatly in a frame in his office. Aside from the score, the framed paper shows the number of people in attendance: 310. The fans

When Bill Fennelly took over as head coach at Iowa State in 1995, he took the reins of a struggling Iowa State women's basketball program that had never been to the NCAA tournament. In his first 20 seasons at the helm, Fennelly took the Cyclones to 16 NCAA tournaments. (Photo courtesy of Iowa State Athletics)

didn't flock to games initially, but the foundation was beginning to take shape.

"I swear we knew the other team better than they knew themselves," Jayme Olson said of Fennelly's preparation. "We went into every game so well prepared. He knew exactly what we needed to do. We didn't always execute it, but you never walked in feeling that you weren't ready."

The Cyclones advanced to the program's first NCAA tournament in Fennelly's second year, but it was in the 1997–98 season that the women's basketball team started climbing out of the lows of pre-Fennelly futility. Finally, in 1997, after promotions through the Cyclone Club that summer, Iowa was scheduled to play in Ames after Iowa State lost by 11 the year before in Iowa City. So many fans attended that some had to sit in the balcony. They witnessed a 17-point Iowa State win.

"We played a great game, we beat Iowa for the first time in a long time, and I think that night didn't make our program, but we kind of took a quantum leap forward," Fennelly said.

Iowa State returned to the NCAA tournament that season and won its first game in the Big Dance in program history. Things have only gotten better since then. Fennelly has taken Iowa State to 16 NCAA tournaments in his first 20 years, has gone to two Elite Eights, and has won a Big 12 regular-season championship and two Big 12 tournament titles. Iowa State now averages nearly 10,000 fans per game and is consistently in the top five nationally for women's basketball attendance.

"I think when someone lists the great things about this university—the Campanile, the engineering, what you want—I honestly believe women's basketball is going to be in that pie somewhere," Fennelly said. "It'll be a really, really tiny piece, but it's in there. That was not even considered 20 years ago. I think that's kind of cool."

17 Marcus Fizer

Beverly Floyd hopped in her car, preparing to make the four-and-a-half-hour drive to Arcadia, Louisiana, from New Orleans, just like she always did. The wife of Tim Floyd—then the men's basketball coach at the University of New Orleans—was on her way to see her grandmother, Ruth Hudson, in a nursing home facility in Arcadia, and decided to take with her a New Orleans college basketball media guide to look through.

As Beverly sat down with her grandmother, flipping through each page of the Privateers' booklet, one of the employees of the nursing home, Sheila Frazier, stopped in the room. Frazier couldn't help but notice that Ruth and Beverly were flipping through the book, and she had to know what it was.

"What are you showing Miss Ruth?" Frazier asked.

"My husband is a college basketball coach at the University of New Orleans, and they put this brochure together," Beverly replied.

"My little nephew loves basketball," Frazier said. "Would you mind if I called him and asked him to come over and meet you?"

"Well, sure," Beverly said.

Her nephew, a little 5'8" seventh-grader named Marcus Fizer, hopped on his bike after his aunt gave him a call, pedaling as hard as he could to get to the nursing home where Beverly Floyd had the media guide that would ultimately set the course for his future. He clutched that media guide Beverly gave him like a Bible after that day, never quite putting the Floyd name out of his mind.

Fizer had moved to Arcadia from Detroit as a child to be raised by Frazier and her husband, and he always held a love for basketball. In 1994 Floyd moved on from New Orleans to coach at Iowa State, where he continued to hear about Fizer as he matured. Clippings from the *Ruston Daily Leader* would occasionally find their way into Floyd's hands while he was at Iowa State. His mother-in-law, Pat Byrnside, was the one to make sure Tim saw what Fizer was doing in his high school games. Fourteen points in a game as a freshman for Fizer? Into the trash the clipping went. Twenty-five points as a sophomore? Floyd trashed that too. "You know," Floyd said, "it's your mother-in-law sending you something."

But then he got one from Fizer's junior year of high school that said Marcus had scored 48 points in the Louisiana state championship game. That caught Floyd's attention. "I got real close to my mother-in-law at that point," Floyd said.

Although Floyd didn't give Fizer much thought until he started hearing what a special player he was becoming, Fizer didn't forget about his connection to the Floyds. Little did Tim or Beverly know, that day in Arcadia when Marcus had laid his eyes on the media guide, he had essentially made up his mind who he would play for.

Everybody started calling about Fizer as he became a hot commodity on the national recruiting scene. Kansas, Kentucky, Georgetown, North Carolina, and Cincinnati all called, among others.

"I remember I was in high school and I was shooting around in the gym and my coach came in and told me somebody from Kansas and somebody from Kentucky called," Fizer said. "And the first thing I told him was, 'I don't want to go to those schools. I want to play *against* those schools.'"

Fizer stayed true to what his heart told him as a seventh-grader and pledged to join Floyd and the Cyclones in Ames. He became the first McDonald's All-American in program history, and to this day was one of the easiest recruiting jobs in Floyd's career.

"I was hopeful when we signed the No. 3 player in the country that he would come out in the *Des Moines Register* and tell

It was a media guide that helped bring Marcus Fizer to Iowa State, but it was his All-American play on one of the Cyclones' best teams, in 2000, that has him regarded as one of the best in program history. (Photo courtesy of Iowa State Athletics)

A Conversation with Bob Huggins

When coaches could finally call recruits, Tim Floyd came in as about the 10th caller when he reached Marcus Fizer around noon. About one week later, he ran into then–Cincinnati coach Bob Huggins, who had a story to share.

"Tim," Huggins said, "do you know I was the first guy to call Marcus Fizer?"

"No," Floyd responded, "I didn't know that."

"Yeah, I called him at 8:00 AM," Huggins said. "We talked for 45 minutes, and at the end of the conversation, I asked him…two questions. 'Is there a school you grew up wanting to go to school at?' Without hesitation, the kid said Iowa State. After I picked myself up off the floor, I asked the kid, 'Why Iowa State?' And he said, 'Because of Mrs. Floyd.'"

everybody he was coming because of me and the great program," Floyd said with a laugh, "but he was coming because of my wife."

Once Fizer stepped foot on campus, it didn't matter to Iowa State fans *how* he had gotten there. All that mattered was that he was there. He averaged 14.9 points as a freshman, the only season he played under Floyd—who left to coach the Chicago Bulls—and carried the team as a sophomore offensively for new coach Larry Eustachy, averaging 18 points per game. As a junior, it was without question Marcus Fizer's team.

Fizer averaged 22.8 points and 7.7 rebounds per game in his third season, which earned him All–Big 12 first-team (for the second time), Big 12 Player of the Year, and consensus first-team All-America honors. He led the Big 12 in scoring his sophomore and junior seasons, leading Iowa State to a regular-season Big 12 championship, a Big 12 tournament title, and an Elite Eight appearance.

In the second-to-last game at Hilton Coliseum in his junior season, Iowa State played host to Texas, and the stage was set for the Cyclones to make a statement as they worked toward securing a Big 12 championship. Fizer took it upon himself, loudly and clearly, to make that statement.

Leading by 12 with just more than two minutes remaining, the Cyclones were still fighting to fend off the Longhorns. Fizer made sure they did just that with an exclamation point. With the ball in the corner on the right side of the court, Fizer faked a pass on the wing, and took one dribble toward the hoop.

He was met by Texas center Chris Mihm (the eventual No. 7 pick in the NBA Draft), but Fizer's 6'9" frame wasn't about to give way. He extended his right arm above the rim, keeping Mihm at bay with his left, and threw down a dunk so powerful that it is etched in the memories of Iowa State fans more than a decade later.

After Iowa State's controversial loss to Michigan State in the Elite Eight and finishing as the runner-up in the race for National Player of the Year, Fizer declared for the 2000 NBA Draft, where he was selected fourth overall by the Chicago Bulls, reuniting him with Floyd.

"I would have much rather stayed my senior year to fight back to win what we felt...was taken from us," Fizer said. "But my parents, the home that I grew up in, caught fire and burned down. We were basically homeless at the time, so it was more of a family decision to do that at that moment."

Despite his years spent in the NBA, it's the road that led Fizer to Iowa State that he remembers most fondly, and how one little college basketball media guide changed the course of his life's path.

"I don't think I could ever sum it up," Fizer said of his college career. "Once a Cyclone, always a Cyclone."

18 "Struck by a Cyclone"

On the chilly fall afternoon of September 28, 1895, the Iowa Agricultural College football team arrived at the grounds in Evanston, Illinois, as heavy underdogs only hoping to score against well-regarded Northwestern.

Led by legendary college coach Glenn "Pop" Warner, Iowa Agricultural College had begun that 1895 season against the Butte Athletic Club, a team made up of miners from Montana. While traveling to Butte, Montana, via train, for the season opener on September 15, the team encountered a blizzard, and players were forced to forage for food.

Upon arrival, the rough ride continued. After Butte scored two early touchdowns, IAC—as Iowa State was then known—drew within a score of 12–10. Officials, intimidated by miners who shot their guns into the air in distaste of particular calls, negated a late IAC touchdown. "We drove…Butte over the ground as though a cyclone had struck them," a member of the team told the *Ames Intelligencer* after it withdrew from the game.

It was nearly two weeks later that the team traveled to Evanston, Illinois.

The Midwest had been ravaged by tornadoes throughout 1895 by the time the Iowa Agricultural College football team arrived to play Northwestern for its second game of the 1895 season. IAC quickly took the Wildcats by storm.

With about 50 of its own fans in attendance and the wind howling, the Iowa group took the field against a Northwestern squad missing four players. Iowa used weight to its advantage in building a surprising 30–0 halftime lead before finishing off a 36–0 rout.

The Traditions

Away from Jack Trice Stadium and Hilton Coliseum, and even far from the spectrum of Cyclones athletics, there are a few Iowa State traditions worth knowing about.

Campaniling

As legend has it, a student officially becomes an Iowa Stater when he or she is kissed under the Campanile at the stroke of midnight. There is also mass campaniling on homecoming, and hundreds of students gather at the Campanile for a midnight kiss.

The Zodiac

Inside the entrance to the Memorial Union on campus rests a zodiac on the ground. In 1929 the myth started that students who walk over the zodiac will fail their next test. Because of this supposed curse and a lack of walkers, the zodiac remains risen above the ground.

The Swans

At VEISHEA in 1935, a large float shaped like a swan emerged from a smoke screen in the middle of Lake LaVerne. Four swans were set free, and two were named Lancelot and Elaine. Over the years, there have been numerous swans named Lancelot and Elaine.

The next day, the *Chicago Tribune* headline read, "Struck by a Cyclone: It Comes From Iowa And Devastates Evanston Town." The story began: "Northwestern might as well have tried to play football with an Iowa cyclone as with the Iowa team it met yesterday. At the end of fifty minutes' play the big husky farmers from Iowa's Agricultural College had rolled up 36 points, while the 15-yard line was the nearest Northwestern got to Iowa's goal."

The nickname stuck, and Iowa State has been known as the Cyclones ever since.

19 Experience Hilton Magic

Hilton Magic /hɪltən maj-ik/, noun. **1.** The ability to do things on the hardwood at Hilton Coliseum that might not be possible elsewhere. *"[Hilton Magic] is something that if you've never experienced it, then you can never really understand it."*—Marcus Fizer

Okay, so maybe you won't find that in a dictionary. But what exactly is Hilton Magic? For years players, coaches, fans, and announcers have made attempts at explaining the phenomenon, and for years the attempts have come up rather empty. You can look at the pictures of a filled Hilton Coliseum, watch the raucous crowd on television, and read the stories of the shaking floor and buzzer-beating shots, and yet the allure of Hilton Magic will still elude you. The only way to understand Hilton Magic is to experience it.

Of course, that doesn't mean Hilton Magic doesn't have a story.

In February 1989, as Iowa State prepared to face Missouri—a team they had fallen to by 25 when they played on the road earlier in the season—Buck Turnbull of the *Des Moines Register* wondered in his game preview, "Will the magic of Hilton Coliseum work one more time for Iowa State's basketball team?" On February 14, 1989, the Cyclones answered that very question with an 82–75 upset of No. 3 Missouri. Two days later, on February 16, a headline appeared in the *Register*: "Hilton Magic Spells 'Upset' One More Time."

"Whatever it is about the mystique of Hilton Coliseum, playing there sure works wonders for Iowa State's basketball teams," Turnbull wrote. "Year after year, no matter how badly the Cyclones might lose on the road, they come home to the rafter-rattling cheers of their vocal fans and respond with some amazing results."

Iowa State was preparing to face Oklahoma State, a team that had also dismantled them on the road, and Turnbull ended his article calling for more magic. "The Hilton magic will be needed," he wrote, "because the Cowboys drubbed Iowa State in Stillwater three weeks ago, 102–74." Then the Cyclones delivered, defeating the Cowboys 90–81 in a 37-point reversal.

Just like that, Hilton Magic was born in February 1989. Though, "It was before that," former assistant Jim Hallihan said.

In fact, Hallihan is right. Hilton Magic took off thanks to Turnbull and Iowa State's performances of February 1989, and the

There's no place like home, and there's certainly nothing like Hilton Magic, the phenomenon created inside Hilton Coliseum dating all the way back to 1983 when Barry Stevens helped usher in the home-court advantage. (Photo courtesy of Iowa State Athletics)

phrase was coined then, but the legend goes back further. Six years further, to be exact. When Johnny Orr arrived at Iowa State to resurrect the program in 1980, he brought an exciting brand of basketball. They ran, they pressed, they scored. In 1983 they began to soar. On February 8, 1983, Iowa State trailed No. 10 Missouri by one with nearly 12 seconds remaining in overtime. Barry Stevens, who scored 40 points in the game, caught a pass and swished a basket at the buzzer for a 73–72 upset. He rushed off the court as fans rushed on.

"Barry Stevens started Hilton Magic that night," Hallihan said. "We just had a spectacular, magical game. People were saying, 'You can't beat them. You can't beat them.' And we did it. It was just amazing how we could do things at Hilton Coliseum. Couldn't do them other places, but you could do them there."

The Cyclones have been doing those things ever since. There was the memorable 102–100 overtime thriller against Iowa in 1987. There was the upset of No. 2 Oklahoma State in 1992 when the crowd grew so loud the floor shook and two Darwyn Alexander free throws fell off the rim to secure an Iowa State upset. There was the win against No. 5 Kansas in 2012 as fans stormed the court and ushered in a new era of Hilton Magic.

"The great thing about our fan base is, through the good times and the bad, fans will continue to come out and support and still make it a very difficult place to win a basketball game [against us]," Fred Hoiberg said. "It's been a fun thing to be a part of."

So back to that definition. "Bottom line, it's just the fans," Iowa State great Jeff Grayer said. "We would come out there, and they would give us that extra boost, that extra energy. I never played in an arena, whether that's in the pros or anywhere else, where it has been that loud."

Pete Taylor: Voice of the Cyclones

On a sunny fall Saturday afternoon, a farmer would sit in his combine, busting through bushel after bushel of corn while he listened. On a dark night, driving through the lonely roads of Iowa, a woman would watch the yellow center line zoom past and listen. On a late school night, a kid would sit in his bedroom, refusing to go to sleep, and listen. Across each barrier, they all heard the same thing. They all heard the voice of Pete Taylor.

More than a voice, when fans turned the dial to an Iowa State broadcast, they heard the work of an artist. "Gets it to Elmer for a breakaway, and he slam-dunks it!" Taylor exclaimed over the airwaves when the Cyclones beat Michigan in 1986 to advance to the Sweet 16. "I've seen it all today," he proclaimed after he had described each Troy Davis juke, trudge, and yard in his record-setting 378-yard performance. "He's down the sideline..." he started during Iowa State's first bowl win in 2000. Followed by, "He might go! Touchdown, JaMaine Billups! How about that?" He shouted, "What a run by Wallace!" on Seneca Wallace's famous run in 2002. For 33 years, Taylor painted the pictures of some of the greatest players creating some of the greatest moments in Iowa State history.

When Pete was in eighth grade, his teacher asked all the students in his class to write about what they would like to do for a career. Pete filled notebook page after notebook page with writings on a career in radio broadcasting. He knew exactly what he wanted to do. In 1963, Taylor graduated from Roosevelt High School in Des Moines and traveled east to the University of Iowa, where he eventually graduated with a journalism degree in 1967. Then he settled in at KRNT-TV (KCCI). For the next 22 years, Pete

As Voice of the Cyclones for 33 years, Pete Taylor (left) became the familiar and comforting broadcast voice for Iowa State around the state of Iowa, calling some of the greatest moments in school history. (Photo courtesy of Iowa State Athletics)

became an Iowa television figure, four times being named Iowa Sportscaster of the Year.

In 1970 Pete began his connection with the Cyclones, covering Iowa State events for KRNT radio while working as KCCI's sports director. He was the Voice of the Cyclones.

"He described games very, very vividly," said John Walters, whom Pete hired out of college. "During those years when Pete was broadcasting, he was it. Iowa State was almost never on TV. The thousands and thousands and thousands of fans across the state that love Iowa State, it was Pete and them every Saturday."

Those who listened embraced Pete. He brought no catch-phrases with him to the broadcast. "One of the things I liked about Pete was he never had anything scripted," said Eric Heft, who was Pete's color man for 24 years in basketball and 19 years in football. "Every call that he made was spontaneous." Another thing about

Pete was that there never was any question about who was winning. For one, Pete was as vivid with his details as anyone out there. If he said it happened a particular way, it most certainly did. For another, the guy who had attended Iowa came to love Iowa State, and it often showed. "He got excited over good things," Heft said. "Sometimes disgust came through [in] his voice when things didn't go well."

It was 1984 when Heft began calling football games with Pete, and in their first game, on an early September day, they traveled to Iowa City for the season opener against the Hawkeyes. It was 85 degrees that day, but with no air conditioning, it had swelled to 110 degrees in the booth. By the time halftime arrived—after more than two hours—the two were sweating and watching Iowa State struggle in an eventual 59–21 loss.

"What the hell did you get me into here?" Heft asked Taylor.

"Look," Pete said, "if I have to sit here and take this shit, so do you!"

That was Pete. He had a sense of humor and a way of treating people that made them want to stick around. His voice made them want to keep listening. "That was their guy," Walters said. "It was a special relationship between he and the fans."

In 1990 Pete left KCCI to take a full-time position at Iowa State as director of athletics fundraising. Through the years he hosted the football coaches' television show, the *Cyclone Replay Show*, and radio call-in shows for both football and men's basketball. In 2003 Pete died at the age of 57 following complications from a stroke. John Walters succeeded him as the Voice of the Cyclones.

"One of the things I always thought about Pete was, he had a chance to go somewhere else, and he didn't care to go anyplace else," Heft said. "He was an Iowa Stater. He loved it here. He loved Iowa in general, and he especially loved Iowa State."

21 Clyde Williams

Rarely will you find Iowa and Iowa State fans who agree on anything. But when it comes to Clyde Williams, you're probably not going to find many differing opinions. What he did for the Hawkeyes as a player has him placed as an important part of early athletic U of I history, but what he did for the Cyclones as a coach and administrator changed the landscape of Iowa State athletics forever.

In 1879 he was born Samuel Clyde Williams—preferring his middle name since he was young—on a farm near Shelby, Iowa, but he moved into town when he was eight years old. He graduated high school—where he also served as a janitor—in 1897, with three boys and three girls. Clyde was an A student, but sports were a big part of his life.

Williams was a gifted baseball and football player, but action on the gridiron was in its infancy in the small Iowa town. Without a lot of resources in high school, the boys who wanted to play football tossed around an old catcher's mitt as the ball. Work boots and padded winter jackets rounded out the uniforms. "The principal bought us a football and rule book and acted as a referee," Williams' teammate Ray "Buck" Morton once said. "He divided the boys into two six-man teams to scrimmage."

"Clyde was a lovable character, a good student, full of life and fun," classmate Arthur Buckley said later. "We nicknamed him Wildcat and later shortened it to Wiley. He played baseball and football every chance he got."

Learning the nuances of the positions back then was crucial, and Williams (a quarterback) and Morton (a running back) did it so well that both made their way onto the football team at the

University of Iowa. As the quarterback, Williams was not permitted to carry the ball (per rules), so most of his scores came through kick returns. Iowa nonetheless saw monumental success with Clyde running the show.

The 5'10", 175-pound Williams led Iowa to two unbeaten seasons and was an All-American as a junior (he was considered to be the first player with such an honor in Iowa history). "Only the great Nile Kinnick, later, of Adel could rank with him," Iowa teammate Willis Edson claimed. Williams played part of the 1901 season but did not finish because he had played summer baseball in South Dakota under the name Wiley, which disqualified him for the Hawkeyes.

Williams did earn his degree from Iowa, and went on to practice dentistry in Knoxville, Iowa, for two years, but he wanted to get back to his love: athletics. He moved to Marshalltown, where he coached high school sports and played baseball in Des Moines, Marshalltown, Minneapolis, and St. Paul before making his most substantial career move.

Clyde arrived in Ames as an assistant football coach and head baseball coach in 1906, and at a football practice that year, he changed the game forever. President Theodore Roosevelt was trying to outlaw dangerous play in football with the flying wedge formation, so Williams came up with the idea of an overhand forward pass at a practice. Players practiced the move and at the end of the first workout were throwing the ball as far as 30 yards.

When Williams became head coach in 1907, the forward pass became legalized and Iowa State completed 16 of 17 passes against Nebraska to earn a 14–2 win. Williams had guided football as we know it today onto fields all across the country, and established himself as a true innovator of the game. He also developed the kickoff formation we see today, as well as the running punt, which was later outlawed.

In 1908, Williams organized Iowa State's first basketball team and began planning for an arena in 1909, which he saw completed in 1914. He served as Iowa State's football coach until 1912 and as athletics director from 1914 to 1919. Williams went into the auto business in 1919 and passed away in 1938, but his legacy was honored at Iowa State just weeks after his death when State Field in Ames—which he lobbied to have built at the corner of Lincoln Way and Sheldon Avenue—was renamed Clyde Williams Field. He is in Iowa *and* Iowa State's Halls of Fame.

"There are two plaques to the entrance of our football field," Iowa State assistant athletics director Merl J. Ross, who served under Williams, said in 1969. "One reads *Clyde Williams Field* and the other *Honor Before Victory*, which is typical of the immortal Clyde Williams."

22 Angie Welle

Angie Welle stood in the lane with defenders flanking her on each side and went through the usual motions: a spin, a scoop, and a flick of her left wrist. The ball swished through the net, the Iowa State faithful who had made the jaunt to Nebraska erupted, and an unassuming Welle made her way back on defense.

This sequence must have played out a hundred times before, so it would be difficult to blame Welle for treating it like all the rest. Yet this particular spin, scoop, and flick of her left wrist were different. With this particular sequence Welle became the all-time leading scorer at Iowa State.

"I'm just really happy to be done with it and move on, to be honest," Welle told reporters following the game, after she had learned of her feat only moments before in a television interview. "It's an honor, don't get me wrong, but it's kind of a relief. With the way Coach [Bill] Fennelly recruits shooters, it isn't going to last very long. I've got to enjoy it while it's there."

There it was: Angie Welle being Angie Welle.

"She breaks our school scoring record, and they could not get her to talk about herself; she just wouldn't do it," Fennelly said. "She was just that kind of kid."

Before Welle could ever imagine breaking any records at Iowa State, she was drawing attention to the hot, muggy gym on fall nights at Shanley High School on the north side of Fargo, North Dakota. Welle had started playing basketball in third grade—largely because her older sister did—and she blossomed.

She was tall and lanky at 6'4", but she wasn't exactly prototypical. Her long frame was thin, and she had this unorthodox, self-described "scoop" shot. Her left-handedness made her hard to guard, and she could run unusually well for her size.

Around Welle's sophomore season in high school, a call came in to Fennelly from a high school coach who had seen her play. So Fennelly made the seven-hour trek to Fargo to see for himself. It took all of five minutes for him to know. "We were going to recruit her," Fennelly said. In the seasons that followed, Fennelly wore through his tires driving to Fargo.

"I spent a lot of time in Fargo, North Dakota," Fennelly said these many years later. "I heard of Fargo before the movie."

And did those trips ever pay off. Welle received offers from Iowa, Georgia, Penn State, and Creighton—where her sister starred—in addition to Iowa State. She narrowed her options to the Cyclones and Nittany Lions. During Welle's junior season in Fargo, Fennelly took Iowa State to the NCAA tournament for the first time in program history. The team went again during Welle's senior season, and because she didn't have cable, Welle went to her neighbor's house to watch the Cyclones win their first NCAA tournament game.

Welle knew she wanted to be in Ames. The program appeared to be on the rise, she would have the chance to play right away, it was a drive and not a plane ride from home, and, most of all, she felt wanted.

"Whether he really, really wanted me or not, he made [me] feel like that. 'We have to get you,' is kind of how I felt," Welle said of Fennelly. "He just really, really, really made a huge effort."

Welle made a huge impact. During her freshman season at Iowa State, she started all but one game and quickly drew attention for the way she ran the floor in transition. Every time her teammates would look down the court, Welle was running and searching.

"The way she could run the floor was incredible," Fennelly still marvels. "She got six points a game just by running in a straight line, catching the ball, and making a layup."

After Iowa State cruised to a third consecutive NCAA tournament appearance in her freshman campaign, Welle recorded a double-double—one of 54 during her illustrious career—in the second round to send the Cyclones to the Sweet 16, where they eventually upset No.1–seeded UConn.

Iowa State went to the NCAA tournament in each of Welle's final three seasons, including twice more to the Sweet 16. The Cyclones were ranked nationally in *every* poll during Welle's four seasons, won a regular-season Big 12 title, two postseason Big 12 crowns, and went 103–29 during her career.

By the time Welle's college days came to an end, she held Iowa State records for points (2,149), rebounds (1,209), blocked shots (155), free throws made (557), and free throw attempts (768). She was a Big 12 Player of the Year recipient and a three-time All-American. That scoring record that was supposed to quickly pass after that night in Nebraska remains both at the top and the lone 2,000-point mark in program history.

Angie Welle holds the distinction of being Iowa State's lone female 2,000-point scorer, and her name can be found not only in the rafters at Hilton Coliseum, but also atop many categories in the record books. (Photo courtesy of Iowa State Athletics)

Angie Welle was the best to don the Cardinal and Gold.

"When you're doing it, you just do it," said Welle, whose No. 32 hangs in the rafters. "I tried to play to my strengths and hope somebody wouldn't catch on to that."

There it is again. As predictable as that fluid spin, scoop, and flick of her left wrist is Angie Welle being modest and humble. Her coach didn't hesitate to put things in perspective, though. "We were really lucky she ended up here," Fennelly said. "There's kids that come and change things. She's didn't just change it for the four years she was here, she changed it maybe forever."

23 George Amundson

As George Amundson's freshman season neared an end in 1969 with a game against Missouri quickly approaching, Iowa State coach Johnny Majors had an idea. He wanted assistant Joe Avezzano, who looked after the freshman team, to install the option.

"Coach," the flamboyant Italian told Majors, "I don't believe in the option."

"Joe," Majors told him, "I'm going to put this in."

"Coach…" Avezzano resisted.

"I heard you say you don't believe in the option!" Majors interrupted. "I believe in the option. You put the damn option play in!"

That Friday night against Missouri, the option having been installed, Amundson accounted for three (maybe four, Majors says) touchdowns as Iowa State beat the Missouri freshmen. On Sunday morning, after the varsity team had lost to Missouri on Saturday, Majors and his wife, Mary Lynn, headed for the coach's show. Mary Lynn had watched the freshmen play.

Iowa State and the Heisman Trophy

There have been three players in Iowa State history who have been candidates for the prestigious Heisman Trophy. The first such instance was in 1959 when running back Dwight Nichols rushed for 749 yards and nine touchdowns and finished eighth. In 1972 quarterback George Amundson passed for 2,110 yards, rushed for another 508, and combined for 26 touchdowns on the ground and through the air to finish seventh.

Then there was Troy Davis, who finished in the top echelon not once, but twice. When Davis rushed for 2,010 yards as a sophomore in 1995, he was voted fifth. The next year he became the first player to rush for 2,000 yards twice in a career and was invited to New York, where he ultimately took second to Florida quarterback Danny Wuerffel.

"I thought it was mine all the way," Davis said. "But Danny Wuerffel, he was on a winning team and he was going to the big bowl game. I came up short. I'm not mad about it."

Year	Player	Place	Points
1959	Dwight Nichols	8th	126
1972	George Amundson	7th	219
1995	Troy Davis	5th	402
1996	Troy Davis	2nd	1,174

"Mary Lynn," Johnny told his wife, "Amundson is really something else."

"John," she replied, "I don't know how long you'll coach, but you may never coach a better athlete than George Amundson."

Amundson had arrived at Iowa State that fall from Aberdeen, South Dakota, where he was a highly touted athlete. Growing up, he was big for his age, so throughout junior high, coaches used him as a fullback and tight end. "I saw myself as a quarterback," Amundson said. His high school coaches saw the same thing, and during his sophomore year, he was asked to make the switch. By his senior season, Amundson was first-team All-State at quarterback.

It wasn't just football that made Amundson stick out, either. During his senior year at Central High School in Aberdeen, in the spring of 1969, Amundson tossed a discus 211 feet, 4 inches. He was the first high school thrower to break 200 feet and set a high school national discus record. Many schools called, including Indiana, Tennessee, South Dakota, and Iowa State. Amundson's father wanted him in the Midwest, and Amundson himself really wanted to continue with throwing. Majors signed a letter agreeing to allow him to do both.

As a multitalented athlete, George Amundson became Iowa State's first 1,000-yard rusher one year and its first 2,000-yard passer the next. When all was said and done, the Heisman Trophy finalist was one of the greatest football players in program history. (Photo courtesy of Iowa State Athletics)

Over the course of the next four years, Amundson would finish football practice, toss his shoulder pads aside, kick off his cleats— leaving his football pants on—and begin throwing the discus right on the field. On some weekends, he'd go to the Kansas Relays or another event, throw the discus, and jump in a car waiting for him to head back to Ames for practice. He set the Iowa State discus record and threw in two NCAA championships.

Football is where Amundson made his biggest mark, beginning in 1970 as a sophomore. Amundson started the first three games at quarterback that season but ultimately split time with junior college transfer Dean Carlson. In November Iowa State traveled to face Missouri, a team it hadn't beaten in 15 seasons. After Carlson started the game, Iowa State was pinned at its own 5-yard line to begin the second half. The Cyclones faced a stiff 20-mile-per-hour wind and Amundson was the better runner of the quarterbacks. "Amundson," Majors shouted, "get in there."

Amundson headed in and promptly ran for a 77-yard touch-down. The next time, he scored on a quarterback sneak and then once more on a 33-yard run. Iowa State got the ball for the final time with about 1:30 remaining, leading Missouri 31–19. Majors gave the sign to take a knee, but Amundson called for a quarterback sneak and pushed forward.

"George! George! Get on the damn ball, get on the ball!" Majors bellowed before dropping to the grass and, on all fours, smacking the ground. "George! George! *Get* on the *damn* ball! On the *damn* ground!"

"But Coach," Amundson shouted back, "it's going to hurt my average."

"That takes confidence to do that to the head coach," Majors joked more than four decades later. "He's the only guy that ever did that, either."

There was always a saying with Amundson at Iowa State: "Let George do it." That came to fruition during Amundson's junior season. With Carlson still in town, and Jerry Moses and a few other running backs injured, Amundson switched to running back. That year, Amundson became Iowa State's first 1,000-yard rusher when he ran for 1,260 yards and 15 touchdowns to lead the Cyclones to the first bowl game in program history.

Then he moved back to quarterback as a senior and became the first player in program history to pass for 2,000 yards, setting a Big 8 Conference record with 2,387 passing yards while leading Iowa State to yet another bowl appearance. That year, he was named the Big 8 Player of the Year (ahead of Heisman Trophy winner Johnny Rodgers) as well as an All-American before being a first-round selection in the NFL Draft.

"He was the most popular guy around," Iowa State broadcaster Eric Heft said. "People gravitated to him, he was a great leader and a hell of a good guy."

As for Mary Lynn Majors' prediction?

"She was right too," Johnny Majors said. "I've never coached a better athlete."

24 A Historic Night in the Desert

Sage Rosenfels remembers it perfectly. Preparing for his final year of college football, it was a message from offensive coordinator Steve Loney that rang the loudest in how meaningful the 2000 season could be.

"The difference between 8–3 and 3–8 is so small that if you blink, you might just miss it," Loney told him. "The key is not to blink."

Iowa State's long wait for the first bowl victory in program history was sealed as JaMaine Billups (pictured) rushed into the end zone on a 72-yard punt return to secure a 37–29 win in the 2000 Insight.com Bowl at Bank One Ballpark in Phoenix on December 28, 2000. (Photo courtesy of Iowa State Athletics)

Coming off a 4–7 season in 1999, the 2000 season presented one final chance for Rosenfels and the seniors to reach their dream of going to a bowl game. They did just that and took it one step further by winning the Insight.com Bowl against Pittsburgh, 37–29. The win gave the Cyclones their first bowl win in 100-plus years of program history and has made that 9–3 squad one of the most remembered among Iowa State fans.

The difference between 1999 and 2000? The blinks were all but eliminated.

"It's easy to be average in football, it's easy to be average in life. It's tough to be elite, it's tough to be special," said former coach Dan McCarney. "Sage and those guys believed they could be elite and be different, and they wanted to be remembered."

There were plenty of sleepless nights to get to that point for McCarney. He took over a winless program in 1995 and was

13–42 entering the 2000 season. It was time for Coach Mac to win or move along. He found a way to win.

Not only had Iowa State not been to a bowl game in 22 seasons, it had been 11 years since the last winning season. When the Cyclones rattled off eight regular-season wins in 2000, it made rising above futility mean so much more.

"I dreamed about this opportunity when I took the job," McCarney said prior to the bowl game. "That we could take a winless program that had really fallen on hard times and be representing our university at one of the best bowl games in the country."

Before the season, McCarney had a large thermometer made that could be put in front of the team. On it were a list of goals for the season, one of which was "to go somewhere warm in December." The team got its wish when it was designated to play in Phoenix.

The Cyclones were met in Phoenix by a football field set in Bank One Ballpark—home of baseball's Arizona Diamondbacks—and thousands upon thousands of Iowa State fans. Estimates placed the Cyclones contingent at more than 20,000, which didn't go unnoticed by coaches or players, who could feel their energetic presence throughout the night.

Holding a 27–20 lead early in the fourth quarter and without speedy returner J.J. Moses, who had suffered a concussion earlier in the game, Iowa State was looking for something to spark its sideline. Enter JaMaine Billups.

The freshman stepped into Iowa State's punt return formation as Moses' replacement. It was his first shot at punt-return duty, and he made it count. Billups fielded the punt and took it to the right—along the ISU sideline—72 yards for the touchdown.

Billups flipped the ball out of his hand in the end zone, and his teammates rushed him to the ground in celebration. The touchdown swung the momentum fully to Iowa State, and what ensued following the game trumped even that incredible play.

Coming Up Short

Iowa State had reached a bowl game for the second consecutive season in 1972, and with 1:36 remaining, they had a chance to claim their first postseason victory. That is when the Cyclones scored a touchdown on a pass from George Amundson to Willie Jones to draw within one, at 31–30, against Georgia Tech in the Liberty Bowl.

Iowa State called a timeout.

"What do you think?" coach Johnny Majors asked.

"Well, let's run sprint, draw 90," Amundson said.

The Cyclones could kick the extra point to tie the game, but there wasn't any overtime. Amundson wanted to run his favorite play and go for the probable victory instead. Majors obliged and let Amundson go to the field.

"Of course we ran my favorite play, and of course I guess Georgia Tech knew it was my favorite play too," Amundson said. "They were sort of waiting there for us, and I remember trying to hit Larry Marquardt in the back of the end zone, and he was about 6'5", 6'6", and I threw it above him. So I guess I thought he was 10 feet tall. We ended up losing by one, darn it."

Iowa State fans flooded the field after the win, jumping on the goalposts and celebrating what had never been done in program history: ending the season as a bowl champion. The win validated Coach Mac as a man who could lead the program, and to this day, it remains one of the most special games of his career.

"I took that bowl trophy—the Insight.com Bowl trophy—back with me to the hotel, and I've never taken so many pictures in my life: with the trophy, with family and friends and fans and players," McCarney said. "It was a pretty amazing thing."

The win didn't just validate McCarney, it validated the program, the players, and most of all the seniors. Rosenfels and the seniors took a chance on a struggling program when they signed with Iowa State. When he was named the offensive MVP in his last game as a collegiate player, Rosenfels thought back to how hard it had been at times to get to that moment.

"I think we just stayed the course and we played with a lot of heart and a lot of passion," Rosenfels said.

Most important, they didn't blink. Not once.

25 Waldo Wegner

The annals of Iowa State history might be different had Waldo Wegner not picked up a copy of the *Iowa State Daily* in 1931, and had an advertisement inside the paper for basketball tryouts not caught his attention. But Wegner did pick up the student newspaper on that day, and he did make the trip to the gym to try out.

Before Wegner saw the advertisement calling for students to try out, he was simply a kid from Everly, Iowa, enrolled at Iowa State as a civil engineering major. At 6'4" Wegner had potential as a basketball player, so when he spotted the ad, he and a friend, Frank Hood, decided to give it a shot.

"I remember when we tried out. I was just a clod," Wegner said in a 1997 interview with Iowa State. "We were all standing there and we must have just looked terrible."

When the tryouts were over, neither Wegner nor Hood were listed among the players who had been awarded numerals. Ray Cunningham, then the head of the Iowa State College YMCA, decided to go talk with head coach Louis Menze and assistant Carl Rudi. He told the coaches they had overlooked the pair of freshmen, that in time the two might be valuable. Both Wegner and Hood were given numerals.

When Wegner reported to the freshman team shortly after, Menze called him "without doubt one of the crudest cage prospects who ever appeared at Iowa State." Wegner certainly still had a lot of work to do, but he had a willingness to work that caught Menze's eye. "I really wanted to play. I just wasn't very good at the beginning," Wegner said. "I worked hard to be in great shape, because I wasn't a natural ballplayer."

After classes let out in the spring of 1932, Wegner readied to head to an engineering summer camp. He packed a basketball and hoop to take with him and, despite little level ground, spent hours practicing. By the time Wegner returned as a sophomore for the 1932–33 season, he had markedly improved. He didn't start the first game of that sophomore season, but he started the next time out and would start every game and play every minute over the course of the next three seasons.

All-Century Team

When Iowa State celebrated 100 years of men's basketball at the university during the 2007–08 season, it named 15 players to an All-Century team. Eight All-Americans were guaranteed admittance onto the prestigious team while seven others were added after a year of fan voting. The All-Century team included:

Zaid Abdul-Aziz (formerly Don Smith) (1966–68)
Victor Alexander (1988–91)
Kelvin Cato (1996–97)
Marcus Fizer (1998–2000)
Jack Flemming (1935–37)
Jeff Grayer (1985–88)
Fred Hoiberg (1992–95)
Jeff Hornacek (1983–86)
Hercle Ivy (1973–76)
Barry Stevens (1982–85)
Jake Sullivan (2001–04)
Gary Thompson (1955–57)
Jamaal Tinsley (2000–01)
Waldo Wegner (1933–35)
Dedric Willoughby (1996–97)

By the time Wegner reached his senior season, he had transformed into a dominant center and tip-in artist. With Wegner on the rise, so too were the Cyclones. The crowds had started small at State Gym, but as Iowa State neared the end of the 1935 season battling for the Big 6 crown, excitement was at an all-time high.

"There weren't very big crowds early on, but when we started winning and it looked like there might be a possibility of us being in the upper half of the conference, it started filling in," Wegner said. "The last half of the year, they were hanging from the rafters."

As the season neared an end on February 11, 1935, Iowa State traveled to Norman, Oklahoma, trailing Kansas by one game in the conference. It was a make-or-break game, and the Cyclones' chances appeared doomed after the Sooners hit a late basket to take a two-point lead. But with three seconds remaining, Wegner turned to shoot and was fouled. He hit both free throws to force overtime and then sunk three more baskets in a 50–44 win. "That kept us in the conference race," Wegner said. A week later Iowa State beat Kansas by two at a packed State Gym, and the Cyclones won their final two games to seal their first-ever conference title.

Wegner, whose No. 14 jersey was retired in 1992, led the Cyclones in scoring in all three seasons with the varsity squad, averaging 10.6 points per game in his final campaign while being named first-team All–Big 6 for the second and final time. And because he had answered that ad some four years earlier and was named to the Converse All-American team following the 1935 season, Waldo Wegner went down in history as Iowa State's first All-American.

26 1944 Final Four

It was almost the banner that never was.

High above the upper level inside Hilton Coliseum hangs a Cardinal and Gold banner reading: *Men's Basketball—Final Four—1944*. It represents the Cyclones' first—and only—appearance in the NCAA Final Four to this day. It was an achievement unlike any other for the school's basketball program, and it was one that came very close to never materializing.

Sure, the NCAA tournament was just beginning to grow and its format was different then, with only eight teams—four from the West region and four from the East—comprising the field. Heck, the NIT was considered the premier basketball tournament at the time. But postseason play was what teams across the country aspired to, and Iowa State was no exception.

In the 1943–44 season, the United States was amidst the Second World War, and college enrollment across the country was declining due to the rising number of military service members. Iowa State offered something most places didn't—a strong engineering program, which allowed it to have a naval training program. Those students would be available to participate in athletics, regardless of age or previous college graduation.

Of the 10 players on the Cyclones' basketball squad that season, eight were service members in the naval training program. Led by the 23-year-old Price Brookfield, who averaged 11.6 points per game in 1944, Iowa State finished the regular season 13–3 (9–1 in conference play) and were co–Big 6 champs with Oklahoma. "We thought we had, and we did have, a good team that year," starter Ray Wehde said years later.

Because there was a plethora of naval trainees on the Iowa State roster, school officials were uncertain whether they could accept the NCAA bid to compete in the West Regional in Kansas City. By rule, trainees were not permitted to be away from Ames for more than 48 hours, which would complicate the traveling process for the tournament. On March 7, 1944, athletics director George Veenker issued a statement saying the school had determined it would decline competition. "We do not feel it fair to start play when we know now we could not go all the way," Veenker said.

The uproar from players was immediate. Ray Wehde and his brother, Roy, from Holstein, Iowa, were starters, along with Gene Oulman, Robert Sauer, and Brookfield, and took the issue to Veenker. "We all went back and pleaded for them to let us go," Ray remembered. "And they did. Nice of them."

Veenker and the school reversed the decision after learning the navy would allow exceptions to the 48-hour rule under certain circumstances, and the team would be able to go to New York City (where the national championship was held) if it made it that far.

So the western Kansas City regional was set. It would be Iowa State, Pepperdine, Arkansas, and...Iowa. But upon hearing the news the Cyclones would indeed be playing, the Hawkeyes eventually backed out. Some say it was for academics, and some say it was to avoid a matchup with the Cyclones.

"The bitterness and hatred between the two schools in those days was unbelievable," longtime former ISU sports information director Harry Burrell said later.

Missouri was given the invitation to replace Iowa, but there was one more change to the regional yet to come. Utah, which lost to Kentucky 46–38 in the first round of the NIT, desired a berth in the NCAA. The action on the hardwood was finalized, and Iowa State played Pepperdine, while Utah played Missouri.

Not knowing at first if they would be allowed to compete in the NCAA tournament in 1944, Iowa State qualified for the West regional, where the Cyclones beat Pepperdine to advance to the program's first-ever Final Four. (Photo courtesy of Iowa State Athletics)

Utah handled Missouri 45–35. Iowa State would have no cakewalk to get to the Final Four. Pepperdine was 20–12 and averaged (what was considered at the time a fast-paced) 54 points per game while touting 6'7" center Nick Buzolich. After trailing 19–15 at halftime, the Cyclones roared back to hold Pepperdine to a season-low 39 points in a 44–39 win after key baskets by Roy Wehde and James Myers created separation.

Iowa State had reached the Final Four and was one win away from playing for a national title in Madison Square Garden. Utah came out of the gate firing, opening with a 12–2 lead. Then things went from bad to worse when Ray Wehde fouled out in the first half. Iowa State climbed back in the second half and held a 28–26 lead, but three straight buckets by the Utes eventually fueled a

40–31 Utah win. "One of our disappointments there, but it was a great year with a lot of really fine players," Ray Wehde said.

Utah went on to win the national championship in New York. After the game in Kansas City, Iowa State was informed it wouldn't have been able to go to the title game, even if it had won. The navy decided it would indeed uphold the 48-hour rule, and Utah was notified before the game that it would represent the West in New York regardless.

Although Iowa State was denied a shot at a national title, the 1943–44 team went down as one of the most significant. It is one of only four ISU teams to have an average win margin of at least 10 points, and the team's 9–1 conference mark is the best league winning percentage in school history. And don't forget about that banner in Hilton Coliseum recognizing what is now considered one of the benchmarks in college basketball.

27 Cy-Hawk Part I: Rivalry Renewed

On the front of the worn trophy, there were few signs a football rivalry existed. The Iowa State logo was on the left, and the word *Cy-Hawk* was etched into the middle, the prefix suggesting there might be something. Otherwise, there was simply nothing. Not one of the golden plates on the front of the trophy used to indicate the winner in past seasons included the words *Iowa State*.

By 1998 the trophy had been locked away in Iowa City for so long it could just as easily have been forgotten. The Cyclones were on their fourth coach since the last time the trophy had been hauled off to Ames for safekeeping 16 years before, in 1982.

The True Renewal of the Cy-Hawk Series

It may have been 1998, when Iowa State snapped Iowa's 15-game winning streak in the Cy-Hawk Series, that the rivalry was renewed, but to find the true renewal of the rivalry, you have to go back to the 1977 football season.

Iowa and Iowa State first met on the gridiron in 1894, but after the two schools faced off in 1934, the series went stagnant until 1977. The resumption of the rivalry didn't come easily. In the 1960s the Iowa legislature put pressure on the two universities to renew the rivalry, and administrators from both schools eventually met with the governor. With some reluctance, the Cyclones and Hawkeyes faced off again in 1977 and have every year since.

"There is no rivalry when someone wins it 15 times in a row," coach Dan McCarney said. "Sooner or later a football team, somebody, has to put their foot in the ground and say, 'This is enough!' Plant your feet, take a stand, and say, 'We're going to make this a rivalry, and this is going to be a heck of a game every year.'"

Few figured that stand would be made in 1998. For one, Iowa State had been smacked by Iowa to the tune of 63–20 the previous season in Ames. The Cyclones were 28-point underdogs in 1998, and at Kinnick Stadium no less. Also, the week before Iowa State was set to hop on a bus and travel east, they had fallen apart and blown a second-half lead in a loss to lowly TCU. The day before the game, things hadn't gotten much better.

"[I remember] practicing just awful on Friday before we left in our walk-through," said Paul Rhoads, who was a defensive assistant on McCarney's staff. "I mean awful. Couldn't have felt any worse about that last preparation before we got on the bus."

The rivalry game between Iowa State and Iowa had only been revitalized in 1977 after legislative pressure to have a game played between the state's premier football programs. The Cyclones won four of the first six meetings thereafter, including three straight, before Iowa won in 1983. For the next 14 seasons, it wasn't much of a rivalry at all. There were some close games. Iowa State lost by seven in '88, by 10 in both '89 and '90, and by three in '93. Then there were the big blowouts, as was the case the previous season.

"If you don't like the tradition, then build your own," McCarney said years later, as if he were talking to that '98 team. "If you don't like the history of something, then change it." That's exactly what Iowa State did in 1998.

On September 12, 1998, Iowa State arrived at Kinnick Stadium on a hot, muggy afternoon. The Cyclones quieted the Black and Gold crowd of 70,379 early when they blocked Iowa's first punt. Three plays later running back Darren Davis was scampering into the end zone. That was just the beginning for Davis, and for Iowa State, which led 20–3 by halftime.

That 17-point lead certainly didn't feel comfortable. There had been similar leads for Iowa State in recent seasons, and many had disappeared. The Cyclones, who entered that fall day on a dry spell of 0–30–1 on the road in past seasons, made certain this lead wouldn't evaporate. On its first possession of the second half, Iowa State marched 80 yards—helped by a 39-yard run from Davis—to take a 24-point lead.

Davis just kept running. When all was said and done, he had 37 carries for 244 yards, the eighth-best single-game mark in program history.

The scoreboard read: *Iowa State 27, Iowa 9.* The streak was over.

"There was just positive energy, positive vibes everywhere, no matter what the naysayers and odds and lines in Vegas and 15 years of getting embarrassed by Iowa said," McCarney said. "That football team was not going to be denied. It was one of the hottest games I ever coached in, but one of the most memorable ones."

McCarney was doused with ice water on the sideline. The band and cheerleaders stormed onto the field. Players ran across it to grab the trophy that had long eluded them.

"Finally," McCarney said afterward, "we've got something to take home."

The rivalry had been renewed.

28 Cy-Hawk Part II: The Comeback

Iowa State players and coaches heard it loud and clear as they ran off the field at halftime. Iowa fans were actually *laughing* as the Cyclones trotted toward the locker room. The giggles rained down like gunfire, and it was hard for Dan McCarney to stomach.

McCarney's squad was on a four-game winning streak in the Cy-Hawk football series dating back to 1998 (when the rivalry was renewed), but it didn't look like a rivalry at all on September 14, 2002. Iowa held a 24–7 lead, and McCarney had the task of leading a come-to-Jesus meeting as he spoke only to starters in a smaller locker room. "I got after them as hard and as tough as any time I ever have with a football team," McCarney remembered.

"I just kind of looked at everybody and just knew as long as we could keep competing and maybe steal a couple of turnovers in the second half, we could make our way back," Seneca Wallace said.

Well, whether McCarney used words of inspiration or a variety of expletives, the pep talk worked just like he hoped.

Iowa State took the ball following halftime and flew down the field—after a couple throws by Wallace across his body produced big gains—for a five-yard option keeper by Wallace for the touchdown. It was 24–14 Iowa, and it was the defense's turn to hold up its end of McCarney's halftime challenge.

Less than two minutes after Wallace's score, Iowa quarterback Brad Banks simply let the ball slip out of his right hand on a pass play, and an eager JaMaine Billups pounced on it. Jamaul Montgomery hauled in a seven-yard touchdown pass from Wallace shortly after, and Iowa State found itself down just 24–21 midway through the third quarter. Those laughs and giggles from Iowa fans were getting quieter with each snap of the ball.

The vaunted Hawkeyes offensive line was getting battle-tested by the Cyclones' big guys, and once again, the pressure got to Banks and he fumbled for a second time. Less than 10 seconds later, Wallace threw a 19-yard flag route to the right to Lane Danielsen over a defender as he was pushed out one foot short of the goal line. A Joe Woodley touchdown ensued to give the Cyclones a 28–24 lead.

Iowa State wasn't done yet.

Iowa started at its own 5 after mishandling the kickoff, and the Iowa State defense wanted more. Jeremy Loyd caught Aaron Greving behind the goal line for a safety on the first play, giving Iowa State a 30–24 lead and a 23–0 scoring advantage in the third quarter.

As Iowa State hoisted the Cy-Hawk Trophy in Iowa City in 2002 following a memorable second-half comeback, the Cyclones achieved a streak of their own, having won five straight rivalry games. (Photo courtesy of Iowa State Athletics)

Other Notable Cy-Hawk Football Games

2005: Iowa State 23, No. 8 Iowa 3

A week after struggling to an 11-point win against Illinois State, Iowa State's tenacity on defense took the top-10 Hawkeyes by surprise. Three fumble recoveries, two interceptions (one for a 28-yard touchdown by LaMarcus Hicks), and three sacks all aided a big day defensively for the Cyclones as Iowa never got closer to the end zone than the ISU 26-yard-line.

2007: Iowa State 15, Iowa 13

Limping into its home stadium 0–2 with a loss to Northern Iowa on its résumé, Iowa State's monster day in the kicking game saved the day. Bret "Shaggy" Culbertson tied a school record with five field goals, the last coming with one second remaining, after a 38-yard catch by freshman Phillip Bates set up the game-winning kick.

2011: Iowa State 44, Iowa 41 (3OT)

It was the first time Iowa and Iowa State played a game in overtime in the rivalry's history, and the drama was palpable in this triple-overtime match. ISU quarterback Steele Jantz led the charge late in the game to get to overtime and finished with 279 yards on 25-of-37 passing with four touchdowns. James White scored the game-winning touchdown on a four-yard option, sending ISU fans flooding onto the field.

Another fumble by Iowa with just more than five minutes remaining—sandwiched between two Iowa State field goals—locked up the eventual 36–31 win. As stunned Iowa fans trudged out of Kinnick Stadium that night, the contingent of people wearing Cardinal and Gold crept closer to the first row of the Kinnick Stadium stands as their team raised the Cy-Hawk Trophy high above their heads.

"To have one of those comebacks down in Iowa, which rarely happened at the time," Wallace said, "I just think everyone was riding so high."

Sure, the win was big because it was five in a row for the Cyclones, but it also happened to be the only regular-season loss for Iowa in 2002 and kept the Hawkeyes out of the national championship conversation. In a game some refer to as "the Comeback," McCarney thought it might just be the greatest comeback he'd ever been a part of.

"So memorable," McCarney said. "I'll cherish that memory forever."

29. 1986 Michigan: "JV vs. Varsity"

The greatest win *ever*.

That's what Johnny Orr called it afterward, and given the time and place and opponent, few would argue. Orr had coached at Michigan for 12 seasons and had taken the Wolverines to the national title game one decade earlier. Suddenly there he was, coaching in the NCAA tournament against his former team and against his understudy Bill Frieder, who had coached under him for seven seasons. And that was just the start of it.

To reach the March 16, 1986, game had taken heroics. Iowa State had been tied at 79 with Miami of Ohio, with two seconds remaining in the first round. The ball was inbounded to Jeff Hornacek, who collected and fired a 26-foot jumper at the buzzer. The basket had clinched Iowa State's first NCAA tournament win in the modern era. It had also set up a date with big, bad Michigan, the No. 2 seed in the Midwest with national title aspirations.

Before Iowa State left for Minneapolis for its first-round game at the Metrodome, it had one of its best practices at the old Armory in Ames. When the plane neared the airport, it circled and

Another Michigan Memory

On November 17, 2013, Johnny Orr created a little more magic at Hilton Coliseum when he emerged from the tunnel with his protégé, Fred Hoiberg, before Iowa State hosted No. 7 Michigan. Orr, the winningest coach at both schools, fist-pumped to the crowd before the Cyclones knocked off the Wolverines with a 77–70 win. It was Johnny's final appearance at Hilton before he died later that year.

circled—for an hour and a half—waiting to land. "We were so fired up, it didn't even bother us," assistant Jim Hallihan said. Everyone was fired up for Michigan. Everyone, that is, except Johnny.

"You know how you feel when you have the flu and you're in bed?" Hallihan asked. "That's what he had that day, and he had to coach the game. He was *so* sick."

"He could barely make it out to the court for the game," Hornacek added.

Orr did make it out in time for the game, but the team was sitting below the raised court on the Metrodome floor, and Orr was slumped over. Michigan was monstrous. They had 6'11" Roy Tarpley. Iowa State had 6'4" Ronnie Virgil. The Wolverines jumped to a quick lead. "It already looks like the JV is playing the varsity," CBS broadcaster Dick Stockton proclaimed.

Iowa State needed to feel Johnny's presence and needed him to work the officials.

"Coach, I tell you what," Hallihan told him. "We're just going to take your stool and set it on the floor. You just be there so they can see. You don't have to do anything, just sit there."

They moved Johnny's blue stool onto the court and, in time, he got going. So did his team. Michigan was tall, plus they had a freshman named Glen Rice, a native of Flint, Michigan, who had played at the same school as Jeff Grayer. Rice, who would become a Michigan great, had nearly signed with Iowa State, but his high school coach didn't want him to sign early following his visit. Then Michigan called and offered, and Rice stayed home.

"They were so big, so strong, and so talented," Hallihan said. "But we were fast and quick, and we could dribble fast."

So while Michigan might have *looked* like a varsity squad against Iowa State, there was no such thing. The Cyclones' quickness was unmatched. Iowa State overcame its sluggish start to take a 40–31 halftime lead helped by a 61.5 percent clip from the field.

On three occasions in the second half, Iowa State built 11-point leads. The last such instance came with 16:17 remaining and the Cyclones up 46–35. Aided by 14 points from Tarpley in the final 16 minutes, Michigan twice drew within one point. The second occasion was at 64–63 with 1:25 to play, then Gary Grant missed an attempt to put the Wolverines ahead. When Iowa State moved past half court, Orr called a timeout with 1:20 remaining.

With the ball on the sideline at midcourt, Iowa State stacked four players in front of Hornacek. With each second feeling like an eternity, Hornacek held and held, looked and looked. "Elmer Robinson was kind of making eye contact," he said. Then Hornacek noticed something. "He was always five plays ahead of the coaches," Hallihan said. Rice had lined up on the wrong side of Robinson. Hornacek scrapped the play.

"Jeff, having trouble…" Pete Taylor started on the call. "Gets it to Elmer for a breakaway, and he slam-dunks it! A two-hand dunk! 66–63!"

"He just backdoored and he took one dribble and dunked it and kind of sealed that game," Hornacek said.

The teams went back and forth. With 11 seconds to play, Sam Hill went to the line with the Cyclones holding a 70–67 lead. He drained the first. "One more!" Orr yelled, hitting the table. Hill drained the second. Michigan got a meaningless basket at the buzzer, but Iowa State had advanced to the Sweet 16 with a 72–69 upset.

"It has to be my biggest victory," Orr said afterward. "Ever."

30 Harold Nichols

His presence was as stoic as they come. Harold Nichols carried himself as if he were a seasoned military general, and he would certainly be countercultural to the sport of wrestling today. What made him unique as the leader of Iowa State wrestling for 32 years makes him even more unique decades after he was at the helm of the Cyclones.

The soft-spoken, private guy known to many simply as Nick was a man of varied interests. In his retirement years, he was an entrepreneur of sorts, operating Nichols Wrestling Products in Ames. His business savvy and national respect made it a thriving operation.

"I think every [mat] in every high school in the state of Iowa was sold by Nichols Wrestling Products," former ISU wrestler and coach Jim Gibbons said.

Nichols' success in business could have been easily predicted by how he instructed his wrestling squads year after year. He was hands-on at times with his wrestlers but preferred the role of surveyor with a commanding presence when it came to his team. Nick let the assistants interact with the kids, but he was constantly analyzing and plotting. It was that dynamic that led Iowa State to six NCAA championships and 11 second-place finishes under his watch. But success growing up wasn't immediate.

Nick was raised near Cresco, Iowa, on an 80-acre farm where, as a freshman, he would have to walk five and a half miles home after practicing, leading him to—surprisingly—give up wrestling for a period of time. The next year, when his brother Don started high school, both were able to find rides, and Harold's career was back on track, but he had to play a waiting game. Nick didn't crack the lineup at Cresco until his senior year, but he finished second at the state tournament at 145 pounds that year, drawing attention from college coaches.

The Cresco boy found a home at Michigan, wrestling for legendary coach Cliff Keen and winning the national championship in 1939, still at 145 pounds. A Cresco pipeline to Michigan had been established, and Nick's brother Don won a title the next season.

"Don and I were the first pair of brothers to be national champs," Nichols once told Buck Turnbull of the *Des Moines Register*. "Later, I think this helped me as a coach, finding out what it took to be a national champion, and knowing it could be done."

Nichols earned his master's degree from Illinois and doctorate from Michigan as well as served a stint with the US Army Air Corps before starting his coaching career at Arkansas State in 1949. But he was not immediately the wrestling coach. Nick was the overseer of swimming and track and had to start his own wrestling program after two years. Iowa State came calling shortly after, in 1953. Iowa State coach Hugo Otopalik had passed away, and the 36-year-old Nichols was the only man interviewed to replace him.

Nichols' breakthrough at Iowa State came in 1965 when he and the Cyclones upended Oklahoma State for the national championship. Iowa State's one-point win ended an 11-year Oklahoma State–Oklahoma stranglehold on national titles. It was the arrival of Dan Gable a few years later that made Iowa State a wrestling destination.

Nichols and Gable were a perfect match. The aggressive style that was a trademark of Nichols' pupils was exactly how Gable wanted to compete. He became one of Nichols' 38 collegiate champions, and even though the interaction between the two wasn't constant, there was no question where Nick stood when it came to the care of his wrestlers.

"He made sure that that room was full of what was needed from a performance point of view, in terms of athletes," Gable said.

At the helm of Cyclones wrestling for 32 years, Harold Nichols' name became synonymous with national success as he guided Iowa State to six team national championships and 493 dual wins. (Photo courtesy of Iowa State Athletics)

"He was also very technical in his office as far as breaking things down, making sure you individually had what you needed."

While Nick was a supporter, he wasn't a cheerleader. Wrestlers knew not to look to him for a "rah-rah" kind of inspiration, but his matter-of-fact approach was complemented by assistant coaches like Les Anderson, who could relate to the athletes. "Les Anderson was the perfect partner for him, because of the personableness of Les," former wrestler Ben Peterson said. "He really made an effort in the places where Coach Nichols maybe [was] weaker."

And there weren't many places where Nick had a weakness. His Cyclones teams won their next five national titles in 1969, '70, '72, '73, and '77, and put Iowa State into the national consciousness for wrestling. His wrestlers also made an impact internationally with

Gable and Peterson winning Olympic gold in 1972 while Chris Taylor won bronze.

Nick finished his coaching career with an overall record of 493–93–14 and was inducted into the National Wrestling Hall of Fame. Nichols also left his mark with those he interacted with. While he never gave up on people he put his faith in, wrestlers returned the favor by sticking around after college to continue training. Those are things that leave an indelible mark.

"He got committed to guys, and I think everybody felt that," Gibbons said. "By the time I wrestled for him, coached with him, he was certainly much more of a father, if not a grandfather figure. He never gave up on people."

The Gentle Giant

Chris Taylor will go down as the biggest athlete in Iowa State history, weighing 440-plus pounds and standing 6'5". And he had the accomplishments on the wrestling mat to match his physical size.

Known as the Gentle Giant, Taylor was anything but nice on the mat, blazing through his competition in the NCAA tournament. He came to Iowa State after two years at Muskegon Community College and won the 1972 and 1973 heavyweight national championships, helping the Cyclones to team titles in those seasons. In 1973 Taylor became just the second wrestler in history to pin his way through the 32-man NCAA bracket to win the title, finishing his ISU career with an 87–0–1 mark, with 70 pins.

Taylor's international career was just as significant, as he was the heaviest competitor in Olympic history. In the 1972 Games in Munich, Taylor earned a bronze medal in freestyle competition after losing 3–2 in the semifinals to the eventual champion, Aleksandr Medved, in a controversial decision.

After spending time as a professional wrestler in the 1970s, Taylor died in 1979 at the age of 29 due to cardiovascular issues. In just two seasons in the Cardinal and Gold, it's the size of Taylor's accomplishments that are remembered most.

31 1992 Oklahoma State: An Assist from Hilton

Hilton Coliseum began to shake. Literally. Vibrations from the floor couldn't go unnoticed, and the crowd was alive.

The backboards also began to sway ever so slightly. Back and forth they moved as the contingent of 14,263 Cyclones fans roared to life. The ear-splitting noise Darwyn Alexander faced as he tried to knock home two free throws to give Oklahoma State a one-point win was unlike anything Hilton had seen before, and perhaps unlike anything since.

The loudest game *ever*?

"It was the most intense game I think I've ever been a part of," Fred Hoiberg, who was standing on the shaking court as a freshman, remembered. "The loudest gym I've ever been in, in my life, was that night at Hilton."

An 80 percent free-throw shooter entering the night, Alexander stepped to the line, stared at the shaking rim, and shot. *Clunk!* The noise turned up a couple notches. The next one was to tie. Again, he stepped to the line and fired. *Boink!* Off the rim it went, only to be tipped around with time finally expiring. Iowa State 84, No. 2 Oklahoma State 83. It was a signature victory, thanks to a boost from the Hilton crowd, that left everybody on cloud nine. But the game had been anything but euphoric in some ways.

Iowa State was coming off a 31-point beatdown by Kansas as they returned home to face the No. 2 Cowboys on February 15, 1992, and the team would not start one of its regulars. Frustration had boiled over for Justus Thigpen in the loss to the Jayhawks, and he began questioning the Cyclones' offensive strategy directly to coach Johnny Orr. That didn't go very well. "Me and him had never rattled off at each other like that before," Thigpen later said. Orr punished Thigpen by not starting him in the Cowboys game.

All was well between Orr and Thigpen, but the punishment stood, and he didn't start. Skip McCoy started in his place, and Thigpen didn't check in until 6:34 had elapsed. Things were getting ugly. Iowa State shot only 28.6 percent in the opening half and was down by 18 points going into the locker room. The lethargic nature of his team had Orr red-hot.

"I raised hell with the players in the locker room because we were so bad," Orr said afterward. "I don't think anybody thought we had a chance. We just wanted to save our pride."

The passionate halftime speech was an attention-grabber, for sure. "He quieted the waters," assistant coach Jim Hallihan remembered.

Iowa State still trailed by 18 with 16:39 remaining, but its offense was beginning to become otherworldly. The Cyclones shot an astounding 80 percent from the field in the second half to erase what looked like an insurmountable deficit. A driving layup by Thigpen, who scored 18 of his 22 points from the final 2:51 and into overtime, knotted things up at 67-all and forced an extra period.

The demons from earlier in the game caught up to the Cyclones, who quickly fell behind by seven in overtime. But Thigpen stayed in the zone. His two three-point baskets and a free throw by Oklahoma State gave the Cowboys an 83–81 lead.

With 15 seconds left in overtime, Thigpen dribbled to his right, near the three-point line. Hoiberg stood at the free-throw line, and Thigpen hit him on a roll to the basket. The seven-foot Bryant Reeves caught Hoiberg across the arm on the shot as it hit the backboard and dropped through the net. Tied ballgame.

Earlier in the night, Hoiberg's streak of 34 consecutive made free throws had come to an end, and he felt like the pressure was off to sink the go-ahead shot. *Swish!* Iowa State by one.

On the ensuing possession, a foul was called on Thigpen as Alexander went for the shot. Right on cue, Cyclones fans delivered with some of the loudest distraction noise Hilton Coliseum has ever seen. And it worked. Both free-throw attempts misfired, and the ball was tipped in and out of hands before the clock hit zeroes to the jubilation of the frenzied crowd. "That was Hilton Magic at its finest," assistant coach Ric Wesley said.

"I've been coaching for 42 years, and I've never had a greater comeback," Orr said postgame. "Actually, you saw the greatest comeback twice, once in regulation time, once in overtime."

The loudest game *ever*? Yeah, you could say that.

Barry Stevens

There was something special about Barry Stevens.

He talked fast (and *man*, could he talk). He ran even faster. He worked even harder. He could shoot the basketball like few others could. He was a jokester teammates laughed at. He was a leader who they followed. He was all of these things, and yet there was one other thing that truly made Barry Stevens special.

"Boy," former assistant Jim Hallihan said, "he had confidence in himself."

That confidence radiated from Stevens on the night of February 8, 1983, as the 6'5" sophomore stood in the huddle at Hilton Coliseum with around 12 seconds remaining in overtime. Iowa State was a program still searching for any sort of hope, and here was the chance, trailing No. 10 Missouri by one point. Stevens watched in the huddle as the play was being drawn up. He wanted the ball.

Barry had arrived at Iowa State in 1981 from Flint, Michigan. That was the first sign he might be unlike other players. "Flint guys are different," Hallihan said. Flint guys were known to work hard, and Stevens certainly did. His father was a construction worker, and at a young age Barry started going to some of the job sites and helping with some of the jobs. Then he became a star at Flint Northwestern.

In hiring Johnny Orr away from Michigan in 1980, Iowa State was in luck. Orr made it a point to recruit in the state of Michigan, a place he had become idolized. His eyes were set on Stevens. Barry thought about going to Minnesota, but he liked what he heard from Orr. His shooting ability and speed fit perfectly into Iowa State's up-tempo system.

"Barry might very well be the most exciting player that I've ever coached," former assistant Ric Wesley said. "I remember it feeling like you were at a racetrack, when those cars come around and you always have to move back a little bit. He was so exciting when he got it going, and he played with such enthusiasm."

From the outset of his arrival in Ames, Stevens made an impact. He averaged 13 points per game as a freshman, and his shooting began to electrify the fan base. "He would have days that he would just never miss," Wesley said. "It was just ridiculous. He never missed." Of course, there was that confidence too.

One summer, Stevens and Hallihan were having a conversation about Lafester Rhodes, an Iowa State player who had incredible speed. Hallihan was marveling about Rhodes and touting his numbers. Lafester could run a half mile in 1 minute, 50 seconds and a quarter mile in 47 seconds.

"You know," Stevens said, "I bet I can run a 50-second quarter."

"No, you can't, Barry," Hallihan responded, aware of the difficulty.

"Coach," a confident Stevens replied, "I can do that!"

So Hallihan and Stevens went out to the old Clyde Williams track across campus. Barry, staring down at his shoes as he so often did, sprinted around the track. Finally, he crossed the finish line. It had been a valiant effort, but his lap around the track had taken 60 seconds. To top it off, he puked.

If there was one thing Barry Stevens didn't lack, it was confidence. That showed more than ever on February 8, 1983, when Stevens' buzzer beater helped Iowa State upset No. 10 Missouri in the game many reference today as the birth of Hilton Magic. (Photo courtesy of Iowa State Athletics)

"Barry, you can't run 50 seconds!" Hallihan said.

"He thought he could," Hallihan recalled with a laugh. "He tried. Some guys would be afraid to try it, but not Barry."

That explains why Barry, in just his second season, was unafraid as he watched the play being drawn in the huddle with Iowa State down one point to Missouri. Barry and Ronnie Harris would start on the blocks with two forwards at the high post. If Jeff Hornacek came to his side, Barry would come off the pick, flashing to the top.

Hornacek went his way, and Barry sprinted up. He wanted the ball.

"Most guys either don't want the ball at the end of the game or they don't have enough confidence to make the shot," Hallihan said. "They'd rather not show a fault than show a fault. Barry was willing to put it on the line."

Harris had come up top and was running across the court as time ticked down. Hornacek adjusted. He waited for Barry to flash to the top of the key and then dished it to the middle. "He was one of those guys," Hornacek said of Stevens. "When games were on the line, he wanted to take the shot." Barry caught the ball 20 feet from the basket and turned and fired in one fluid motion with

A Game-Time Decision

Barry Stevens will forever be remembered for his game-winning shot against Missouri that jump-started Hilton Magic, but who knows what might have happened that night had Barry taken just a little longer to get his pregame outfit perfect.

When Paul Beene first met Stevens, his roommate at Iowa State, in 1981, Barry was decked out in light blue, patent leather gym shoes and a full Adidas sweat suit. He certainly was a slick dresser, but it almost caught up with him on the February night in question.

"We wore a suit and tie to the game, and we were worried about the clothes that we had on," Beene recalled. "We were almost late for the game, man, but we made it on time."

That outfit did the trick, and the rest is history.

a defender in his face. The buzzer sounded as the ball floated in midair. *Swish!*

"As I was fading away, I was just praying it would go in," Stevens said afterward, "and I had a gut feeling it would."

Behind Barry's 40-point effort, including the buzzer beater, the Cyclones had knocked off the No. 10 Tigers 73–72. Orr called it the greatest win in Iowa State history. Fans rushed onto the court. Barry ran off. Hilton Magic was born.

"That was the game," Wesley said. "It was such a big win."

The next season, as a junior, Stevens averaged 22.2 points per game as the Cyclones went to the NIT, their first postseason berth in four decades. Barry averaged 21.7 points per game as a senior, leading Iowa State to a then–school record 21 wins and its first NCAA tournament since 1944.

Stevens, a two-time first-team All–Big 8 selection, left Iowa State as the all-time leading scorer with 2,190 points (before the NCAA had a three-point line), which was later surpassed by Jeff Grayer, who played at Flint Northwestern and chose Iowa State largely because of his idol.

"We went from here as a program to here as a program," said Hallihan, spacing his hands, "and it was all because of him."

Stevens' No. 35 hangs from the rafters at Hilton Coliseum, having been retired one year after he suddenly passed away from a heart attack in 2007 at age 43.

He had that speed. He had that uncanny shot. He had that confidence. It was a combination of all three that helped Barry Stevens run off the court on that February night with an unforgettable legacy.

"Barry Stevens established Hilton Magic," Hallihan said. "That was the beginning. Everything changed after that. He was magical with the things he could do out there."

Sing "ISU Fights"

What might happen on any given play or during any given posses-sion is anybody's guess, but if there is one certainty in attending an Iowa State event, it's that you will definitely hear this Iowa State jingle. Over…and over…and over again. "ISU Fights" is one of the first things every student learns upon arrival on campus, and if there is one other certainty, it's that this song is one thing you *must* know, and one thing you *must* learn to love, to be an Iowa State fan.

There is a history, of course, and it doesn't hurt to log that to memory, too. As the story goes, Jack Barker, Manly Rice, and Paul Gnam were in a car when they came up with the tune and words to "Iowa State Fights" in 1930. Rosalind K. Cook, a member of the music department between 1921 and 1943, arranged the original version:

O we will fight, fight, fight for Iowa State
And may her colors ever fly.
Yes, we will fight with might for Iowa State
With a will to do or die, Rah! Rah! Rah!
Loyal sons we'll ever be
And we will fight for victory,
And when we hit that line
We'll hit it hard for ISC

If you're an Iowa State fan, you'll likely have already noticed that this version is a bit different from the one that is blared today. Eventually—in 1959, to be exact—Iowa State College became Iowa State University, and the fight song was tweaked, if ever so slightly:

O we will fight, fight, fight for Iowa State
And may her colors ever fly.
Yes, we will fight with might for Iowa State
With a will to do or die, Rah! Rah! Rah!
Loyal sons forever true
And we will fight the battle through,
And when we hit that line
We'll hit it hard ev'ry yard for ISU

Fight, Ames, Fight

In the early days, what was then Iowa State College was oftentimes referred to as "Ames." It wasn't until 1929, in fact, that varsity letter winners began receiving an *I* rather than an *A*. Because of this, when Jack Barker, Manly Rice, and Paul Gnam wrote "ISU Fights" in 1930, it actually wasn't the first pep song. In 1920 Charles Bassett had penned "Fight, Ames, Fight":

We're a bunch of loyal boosters for our Alma Mater Ames,
Best college in the USA, the one that wins its games,
We're here to help the Cyclones, with our yells and spirit too,
Just watch them while they buck the line, and see them go right thru.
Now a Cyclone's mighty dang'rous when it strikes a western field.
It tears up ev'rything in sight, what's in its way must yield!
Now watch OUR Cyclones "clean them up" in football, wrestling, track!
They do not know what 'tis to fail, for fight they NEVER lack.

Chorus:
Fight Ames, oh fight you warriors tried and true,
Fight Cyclones fight, we're proud of you,
For when you fellows take the field you start in right.
Before you're done the game is won for you can fight!
Fight Cyclones fight and we will win this game.
Fight fellows fight, fight all the time!
You're got the "rep" and "pep" boys, so keep on fighting,
Fight Ames! Fight all the time.

This is the version that is played and shouted at games today, but not without some added competition. With new uniforms and baton twirlers, the Iowa State marching band was beginning to take off in 1953, and a group of alumni set out searching to commission a pep song for it to play. Meredith Willson, a native of Mason City, Iowa, who went on to write and compose the famous musical *The Music Man*, was the perfect match. Willson had a strong interest in the state and set out to fulfill the request from alumni, compiling the words and writing a swinging melody.

The result was "For I, for S," which debuted as another Iowa State pep song on October 10, 1953, at halftime of Iowa State's game against Kansas State with Willson in attendance. The song was quite simple:

For "I," for "S," forever!
For Iowa State all the way,
Let's go! To show them what the gang's all here for
Go! To show them how the Cyclones cheer.
For "I," for "S," forever!
For Iowa State do it right!
It's time to climb upon the vict'ry wagon,
Fight! Iowa State, Fight! Fight!

"For I, for S" remains part of the marching band's repertoire as a pregame pep song played at Jack Trice Stadium, but the marquee song for the Cyclones is "ISU Fights."

"ISU Fights"—don't forget the fist-pump for each *Rah!* and the drawn-out *U* at the end—is just eight lines and 59 words, but it is the most essential bit of information for any Iowa State fan. Without it, you'll stand idle as the crowd welcomes the team or celebrates a victory. With it, you'll be fully equipped as the instruments blare it time and time again.

34 1987 Wrestling: Back on Top

The streak, while magnificent to some, had become unbearable for others, and the reminders were just about everywhere. Jim Gibbons would wake up every single morning in 1987 looking at his closet. There, hanging, was an Iowa wrestling poster with a Roman numeral *X* branded to the Hawkeyes' singlets. Day after day, Gibbons was reminded that for nine consecutive years, Iowa had dominated the wrestling world. He was reminded that the run of nine consecutive national titles for the Hawkeyes had begun his freshman year of college. He was reminded of the season before.

Gibbons had arrived at Iowa State as a freshman in the fall of 1977, after the Cyclones had claimed their seventh national championship. Since 1969, Iowa State had won five titles. "When you came to Iowa State, it was all about winning a national title," Gibbons said. Then, his freshman season, the Cyclones finished second to the Hawkeyes by *half a point*.

It would be that title for coach Dan Gable and Iowa that would begin the streak. For an unprecedented nine seasons, nobody could dethrone the Hawkeyes. Iowa State three times finished second and four times came in third. In 1986 Gibbons began his first season as the head coach. After beating Iowa in its dual meet weeks before the NCAA championship, including three of five eventual national champions, the Cyclones fell apart and finished a distant fourth. "We ended up peeing down our leg in the nationals that year," Gibbons said. The day after the season, Iowa State met as a teary-eyed team. This wouldn't happen again.

The reminders of Iowa's streak were everywhere. In addition to the poster on Gibbons' closet and the singlets pictured there, the team had made 10,000 buttons with a yellow Roman numeral X on a black background. The Hawkeyes were gunning for No. 10.

"Everybody wanted to see Iowa get beat," Gibbons said. "So actually, all the pressure was on the contender, surprisingly."

Iowa State entered the 1986–87 season disappointed with the previous year's finish but with a tough team made up of young wrestlers and veterans who had been recruited when Gibbons was an assistant under Harold Nichols a few seasons prior. In preparation for the postseason battle the Cyclones were sure to face, they wrestled a rugged schedule. They went and beat Penn State. They wrestled at Oklahoma State. They went to Arizona State. They wrestled Iowa. Name the top teams, and the Cyclones likely wrestled them.

"These guys were battle tested," Gibbons said. "There wasn't a gym in the country that we didn't win five matches in these dual meets."

By March 21, 1987, Iowa State was in position to end the streak.

When the finals rolled around on that fateful night, Iowa State had placed five wrestlers in the championship round to Iowa's four. In order to become the first team in college sports history to win 10 consecutive national titles, the Hawkeyes would need to win all their matches and have Iowa State lose all of its matches. It would be a difficult task, but three of Iowa's championship bouts were against Iowa State wrestlers.

With history on the line, ABC was airing the championship rounds. To accommodate its wishes to set the stage, the order of the championship matches was altered. "ABC basically changed the order of bouts," Gibbons said. Instead of starting at the lighter weights, the night would begin at 167, where Iowa's Royce Alger was favored against Iowa State's Kevin Jackson. By a score of 10–4, Alger started Iowa off in the right direction.

In the next Iowa State match, at 126, the Cyclones' Billy Kelly was up to face the Hawkeyes' Brad Penrith. With just more than

40 seconds remaining, Penrith led 3–2. But Penrith kept pushing for more, attempting a single-leg takedown. Kelly pulled him off balance and used his signature spladle to capture a sudden pin with 29 seconds left. Iowa State had clinched the title.

"I didn't know my pin clinched it," Kelly said that night. "One of our assistant coaches told me before our match that we had already clinched it. It would have put a lot more pressure on me if I'd known I had to win."

From there, Iowa State would get national titles from Tim Krieger (150), Stewart Carter (158), and Eric Voelker (190) in addition to Kelly's title and Jackson's runner-up finish. The Cyclones had four national champions, the most ever in a single season at Iowa State.

The streak was over.

"I've never not wanted the Cyclones to be an excellent team, and if they were in second place it was only because they were behind the Hawkeyes," said Gable, who won two national titles as a wrestler at Iowa State. "If the Hawkeyes happened to get beat by

The Wrestling Championships

The 1987 NCAA championship may be Iowa State's latest NCAA wrestling title, but there has been quite a legacy on the mat at Iowa State. In fact, before the Cyclones ended Iowa's streak that year, seven other teams in program history had won national titles.

Iowa State won its first NCAA title in 1933 (when it tied Oklahoma A&M), but it wasn't until the mid-1960s when the program built a legacy. Under the direction of Harold Nichols, the Cyclones won titles in six of 13 years between 1965 and 1977. That included two instances of back-to-back NCAA titles (1969/1970 and 1972/1973).

"Coach Nichols had labored for several years with teams that were getting second and third over and over again in the nation, and finally I think the chemistry and personnel were right, because he just kept working and coaching and recruiting guys and coaching them year after year," Ben Peterson said. "It was a fine-tooled machine, oiled and running well when it all goes like that."

somebody, and they were going to get beat by somebody, it was Iowa State."

In the years that Iowa had won championship after championship, Gibbons wrote a note of congratulations to Gable. In the summer of 1987, a few months after Iowa State halted the streak with its eighth national title in program history, a letter arrived in the mail for Gibbons. It was from Gable.

"I was not unhappy with my team's performance," Gable wrote, "which made your team's performance all the more magnificent."

"When you get a letter like that from Gable," Gibbons said, "that kind of says it all."

That letter hangs on the wall in Gibbons' office, and serves as a reminder.

No. 3 Nebraska 23, Iowa State 23

The fans began to flow from the stands as the Iowa State players rushed all over the field. There was no way this was happening. Iowa State wasn't supposed to beat mighty Nebraska, and yet it was on track to do just that. This was absolute pandemonium. Only problem was, Iowa State still needed to kick the extra point.

The day had started rather benignly. The Cyclones were 5–2, sure, but there was no way they were going to compete with the Huskers. This was *Nebraska*. This was the No. 3 team in the nation. This was the team with soon-to-be Heisman Trophy winner Johnny Rodgers. This was the team that had won the past two national titles. Iowa State was a 21-point underdog.

Yet everyone was excited. Well, almost everyone. The night before the game at Clyde Williams Field on November 11, 1972,

A Major Headline

The night before Iowa State was set to face No. 3 Nebraska in 1972, Johnny Majors had picked up the evening paper. Smack-dab in the middle was a picture of Dr. Don Hadwiger, a professor of political science and a member of the athletic council, saying football was being overemphasized. Majors was peeved. It was the night before a big game, and there was this.

After Iowa State tied Nebraska 23–23 the next day, *Des Moines Register* writer Jim Moackler was standing inside the door. "What did you think about the faculty advisor's article?" he asked Majors. "If he was here," Majors said, "I'd hit him right in the damn mouth."

The next morning, Majors went to his front door and picked up the newspaper. Next to the game story read a headline: *Majors: Like to Punch ISU Athletic Critic in Mouth.*

"Mary Lynn," Johnny asked his wife when he saw the headline, "can I be that stupid?"

"You must be," she said, "it's in the paper."

it had rained and rained. Iowa State didn't have a tarp, so by morning, the field had become wet and mushy. During warm-ups, Iowa State quarterbacks coach George Haffner saw Nebraska coach Bob Devaney and went over to meet him.

"Coach Devaney!" Haffner said. "I've always wanted to meet you. My name is George Haffner, the quarterbacks coach here."

"What the hell do you got here? A goddamn pigsty?" Devaney questioned, not acknowledging the introduction.

That pigsty would eventually cause an abundance of problems for Nebraska. During the course of the next four quarters, the Huskers turned the ball over eight times—six fumbles and two interceptions—as Iowa State kept the game close. The teams went back and forth. The Cyclones took a lead in the second quarter and the Huskers responded. Then Iowa State retook a lead in the third quarter and Nebraska pushed back ahead in the fourth.

With 1:03 remaining, Nebraska hit a 36-yard field goal to take a 23–17 lead. *Damn*, then-student Eric Heft thought, *it was a hell of an effort.* The ensuing kick return didn't get far, and Iowa State set up 74 yards from the end zone with 58 seconds remaining. The odds were against this Iowa State bunch battling the nation's No. 1 defense.

On that particular weekend Johnny Majors' father, Shirley Majors, then the football coach at Sewanee, a private college in Tennessee, had made the trip to Ames. His season was over, so he came to watch. He also brought his son some advice. Shirley had been watching Nebraska's film and noticed something in the defense, so he drew up a play he thought might work and gave it to Johnny. The team had 58 seconds to go 74 yards; there was no better time to try it.

Nebraska had a three-deep secondary, and the play called for split backs on each side of quarterback George Amundson. There was a receiver on the left side and a tight end and flanker on the other. Depending on where the safety went, Iowa State might have three options.

"Have you ever been playing basketball and you just throw it up and they go in?" Amundson asked. "That's the way I felt against Nebraska."

Amundson began the drive by hitting Ike Harris for a 12-yard gain. Then Iowa State called Shirley's play. The safety went deep, and tight end Keith Krepfle, who had already caught two touchdowns in the game, caught an 18-yard pass between the linebackers. The Cyclones called the same play. The safety went deep. Krepfle gained another 20 yards down the middle of the field. "Boom, boom, boom," Amundson said, connecting the passes in his mind.

Afraid Nebraska might be catching on, Iowa State called the same play but flipped it. Krepfle and the flanker instead went to the left side. This time, the safety bit on Krepfle, and Amundson heaved a pass to the southeast corner.

"Willie Jones, 24 yards in the corner of the end zone," Amundson said, "touchdown."

Amundson had taken Iowa State 74 yards in 35 seconds.

"The place goes nuts, I thought we won," Amundson said. "I looked up at the scoreboard, and it's 23–23. Extra point, that's no problem."

Complete and utter chaos ensued among the overflow crowd of 36,231. Students flowed onto the field and flocked Jones in the corner of the end zone while players rushed around the muddy field shouting. For two or three minutes, as the field was being cleared, Iowa State waited to kick the extra point. Majors pondered taking a 15-yard penalty to rush onto the field to tell the team to huddle and break the tension. Maybe he should have.

"I get it, hold it," Amundson said of the extra-point snap, "Tom Goedjen hooks it."

"It didn't even get as high as the crossbar," Majors added. "It went left of the goal post."

From pandemonium to stone silence. "I really feel bad," Goedjen said. "I wish I'd made it."

Instead, Iowa State settled for a tie with mighty Nebraska.

36 Jeff Hornacek

Give me a uniform, the 6'4", 145-pound guard thought, *and I'll make you keep me.* He heard what people said: He was too small. Too slow. Not athletic enough. Sure, he might not be flashy, but Jeff Hornacek knew he could play. He possessed this uncanny court awareness and intangibles that simply couldn't be taught. He just needed someone to give him a chance.

Growing up in La Grange, Illinois, Jeff was the son of a high school basketball coach. His father, John, coached at St. Joseph

High, but Jeff instead attended Lyons Township just outside Chicago. He didn't crack the lineup until his junior season, and that was because a teammate was suspended for taking a car off campus for lunch. He took advantage of his opportunity and averaged 20 points per game his senior season.

Few in Iowa State history have had the court awareness and passing ability of Jeff Hornacek, who started as a walk-on only to become one of the best players in program history after finishing his career as the Big 8's all-time assists leader with a school-record 665 assists. (Photo courtesy of Iowa State Athletics)

Western Michigan gave him a strong look but went with another player. He wanted to attend Cornell but waited until July to apply—too late for admittance in the fall semester—and was out of luck. He would have to wait until second semester. So there he was, rolling papers in the early morning hours for the Dixie Cup Company at a factory in Chicago.

Around Christmas, Iowa State assistant Gary Cook arrived in Chicago to scout a high school tournament. Jeff's father knew a lot of different coaches, and Gary, who had coached in the Chicago area himself, was one of them. Gary wondered what Jeff was up to. "Just waiting for second semester," John replied. Maybe, Gary told him, Jeff could be a walk-on. Iowa State wasn't very good and was having trouble with its guards, so the Cyclones could certainly give him a shot. If he proved himself, Jeff might even be able to earn a scholarship.

This was his chance. Jeff's family didn't have a lot of money, so the idea of a scholarship intrigued him. "Besides," Hornacek said, "I knew the two guards that were from the Chicago area, and in high school All-State rankings I was ahead of them. I just figured I could go there and at some point prove I could play." He enrolled and, without any knowledge of Iowa State, hopped in his car in January and drove to Ames.

"Every so often you get a gift from heaven," assistant Ric Wesley said. "That was Jeff."

It didn't take long for coaches to see something in Jeff that set him apart. He had an ability to see things on the court *before* they happened. Wesley ran the scout team and was tired of watching things get screwed up. "Jeff was just so smart that you just wanted him out there," Wesley said. "Everything just went better with him on the floor." So for the next several months, Iowa State had Jeff run the scout team while he sat out. When a scholarship fell through for a player that summer, it was given to Jeff.

Ten games into Hornacek's freshman season, Iowa State was in Chicago to play a talented Illinois team. By the second half, the Cyclones were being blown out.

"Look," assistant Jim Hallihan told coach Johnny Orr, "Hornacek has three busloads of people here, let's get him in the game." So Johnny put the hometown kid in. First he broke up a pass on a fast break, then he hit a teammate for a layup, and finally he made a jumper. In seven minutes, Hornacek had made an impression.

"You don't know what a coach is going to see in a minute or two at the end of the game," Hornacek said. "Instead of just jacking around, I played it like it was the NCAA championship."

A few weeks later, with the team still not improving and having lost six of its last eight games, Orr called Hornacek into his office.

"Can you play point guard?" Orr asked.

"Of course," Hornacek told him.

"All right," Orr said, "you're starting tonight."

Just like that, in about one year's time, Hornacek had gone from being a walk-on leading the scout team to starting in the Big 8. In that debut on January 26, 1983, he played all 40 minutes, scored eight points, and dished out six assists to help beat Colorado.

"The rest is history," Wesley said. "He never came out."

There was a learning curve, of course, and it was mostly for Jeff's teammates. While at St. Joseph High, Jeff's father had coached NBA Hall of Famer Isiah Thomas. One day when Jeff was younger, Thomas came back from college at Indiana and the two ended up on the same team in a pickup game. During the game, Jeff was cutting under the basket attempting to get out of the way.

"All of a sudden out of the corner of my eye I saw this pass coming," Hornacek recalled. "I just kind of put my hands up, caught it, and laid it in." The pass from Isiah caught Jeff's attention, and he took note. "I realized my defender wasn't looking at the ball, so you can just throw it right by him if the offensive guy is

132

Getting the call to the NBA

Jeff Hornacek became a mainstay in the NBA, but there was a point in time when he wasn't quite so sure he was going to make it at all. A few teams had called Johnny Orr for film, but Hornacek wasn't invited to the pre-draft camp in Chicago where some of the top prospects would have an opportunity to showcase their skills for scouts.

Hornacek's father, John, knew legendary coach Bobby Knight from Indiana because Isiah Thomas had played for the Hoosiers after starring for John in high school. He called Knight about the camp.

"Yeah, let me make a call and see what I can do," Knight told him. Five minutes later, the Indiana coach called back. "Okay," Knight told Hornacek's father, "he's in."

That was the turning point. It turned out, Knight's call had been to Phoenix Suns general manager Jerry Colangelo, who had in turn gotten him into camp. After a strong showing, the Suns eventually selected Hornacek in the second round to begin his 14-year NBA career.

ready. I think that's probably the part that I maybe had an advantage over other guys, because I saw things a little sooner."

The problem was, teammates initially weren't ready. Jeff would pass the ball past guys. Others hit them in the head. "Don't worry about the turnover," Orr told him. "Just keep throwing it; they'll learn to look." So he kept doing it, and the passes kept missing. "Keep doing it," Orr said. "Guys will get used to it." Suddenly they did.

Hornacek started every game during the remainder of his freshman season, and then every game for the next three years. He became an elite floor general for Iowa State, and under his direction the Cyclones were on the rise. His sophomore season, Iowa State went to the NIT—its first postseason appearance since 1944—and during his junior season they advanced to the NCAA tournament for the first time in four decades.

Then there was the encore in his final season. Iowa State had advanced to the NCAA tournament for the second consecutive year and found itself tied at 79 with two seconds remaining against Miami of Ohio. Hornacek hit a 26-foot game winner at the buzzer. In the next round against Michigan, Hornacek's memorable out-of-bounds outlet pass led Elmer Robinson to a dunk and sealed a trip to the Sweet 16.

When all was said and done, Hornacek, whose No. 14 hangs in the rafters at Hilton Coliseum, scored 1,313 points in his Iowa State career and became the Big 8's all-time leader in assists (665). "His court vision was off the charts," Iowa State teammate Jeff Grayer said. "All of his passes were on the money."

After being a second-round selection (46th overall) in the 1986 NBA Draft by the Phoenix Suns, the guy who was once deemed too small and too slow dished out another 5,281 assists during a 14-year NBA career that saw him become an All-Star and have his jersey retired by the Utah Jazz.

"When you're not necessarily the athlete that another guy is," Hornacek said, "you have to do other things that can make you succeed."

All Jeff Hornacek needed was a chance.

37 "I've Seen It All Today!"

Troy Davis always knew where to look, and he most certainly did look.

The night before the fifth game of Davis' sophomore season—in which the powerful running back was vying to become the first sophomore to reach the 1,000-yard mark in five games—a group of engineering students decided to start counting. They constructed a counter using cardboard, some paint, and duct tape. They named it the TD Yard-O-Meter. The yardage counter hung from Section O along the upper deck of the east grandstand at Cyclone Stadium, and the students would listen to the radio call, swapping numbers in and out with each carry.

After Davis rushed for 2,000 yards that season, the TD Yard-O-Meter received an upgrade. Gone was the cardboard, replaced with plywood and Plexiglas. The concept was the same: tally each and every single yard from Troy Davis.

"They kept up with every yard I did," Davis said. "Any time I wanted to know how many yards I needed to get to 2,000, I looked up there, and they had it up there."

Never was there a busier day than the fall afternoon of September 28, 1996.

When Dan McCarney had taken the Iowa State head coaching job the season before, he was up front with his coaches. "We're going to establish a good run game here," he told them. "We're not going to trick people or fool people, we're going to build this program on a great foundation, and that's running the football on offense." And run Iowa State did. The week before September 28, with Davis' parents in the stands for the first time ever, he had carried the ball a school-record 53 times for 241 yards against Northern Iowa.

When Missouri arrived in Ames on September 28 one week later, the TD Yard-O-Meter read: *539.*

Davis had already accumulated 203 yards on 25 carries by the time the fourth quarter came around, and he sat at 258 yards with just less than eight minutes remaining in the game with the score tied at 31. When you run the ball as much as Iowa State began to with Davis, any element of surprise was out the window. The Missouri defense—heck, every fan at Cyclone Stadium—knew Iowa State was going to run.

Sitting 40 yards from the end zone in the tie game, Missouri stacked the box with a 10-man front. Iowa State was *still* going to run.

"Here comes the blitz, it's the option," shouted broadcaster Pete Taylor. "The pitch to Davis.... He's around the left side, 35, 30, 25, 20.... He cuts back to the middle at the 15...to the 10, 5! Touchdown! Troy Davis on the option pitch from [Todd] Doxzon goes all the way for the touchdown. Forty yards running all over the field. He started left, came back across the center, and took it all the way."

Iowa State never looked back, and Davis kept on running. The 5'8", 190-pound Heisman hopeful went over the 300-yard mark on the next possession. The yards were piling up, and Davis wondered where he stood. Of course, the TD Yard-O-Meter was counting, and Davis and his teammates were watching.

"You're crazy," Davis told teammates.

"For real," they said, "you're over 300 yards."

"That put a smile on my face," Davis said. "The game wasn't over yet, so every time they called my number to carry the ball, I just tried to break another big one."

With 58 seconds remaining—and the line again stacked—the Cyclones were looking to run out the clock. Davis was looking for the end zone.

"It's off to Troy," Taylor started. "He cuts it back! He's at the 20-yard line, at the 15, at the 10, the 5! Touchdown! Oh my goodness. Troy Davis all the way on third down for another score. Add 30 more yards.... I've seen it *all* today."

The TD Yard-O-Meter read: *917*.

Davis had rushed for a school-record 378 yards on 41 carries, at the time the third-highest single-game rushing total in NCAA history. He had touchdown runs of 1, 38, 40, and 30 yards. And Davis recounted that he could have reached 400 if one of his runs—a 36-yard burst—hadn't been nullified by a penalty.

"I never thought I could run for that many yards, because I never did that in high school or little league," Davis said. "When I did it against Missouri, I was like, 'Wow, 378.'"

Davis again rushed for 2,000 yards by season's end, becoming the first running back in NCAA history to do so in back-to-back seasons. No game was bigger than that September 28 day, when Davis rushed off the field to chants of "TD, TD," each yard counted with the red painted numbers on the TD Yard-O-Meter.

"It was an amazing day," McCarney said. "It just seemed like every carry was almost a highlight reel for Troy Davis that day."

38 Sage Rosenfels

When Dan McCarney took over the Iowa State football program in 1995, he knew changes had to be made. Iowa State was continually losing the in-state battle for recruits to Iowa. So when McCarney rolled into Ames, he immediately went over a plan with his staff to turn the tide. The solution he suggested? Starting an annual seven-on-seven passing tournament on campus for high school teams from all across Iowa.

"We're going to do it on Father's Day, and we may get 50 kids that show up," McCarney told his staff. "I want to give Iowa kids and coaches a reason to come to our campus."

That number grew to what McCarney estimates to be 600 kids within the next couple years, and Maquoketa High School always had players in attendance. Mark Hildebrand brought his team on the nearly three-hour trip each season, and one particular year, he had a quarterback in tow who he thought possessed Division I talent. "You'll want to keep an eye on this quarterback that's a senior for me," Hildebrand told McCarney. "He's really a quality player."

Sage Rosenfels never really thought about playing college football up until that year, entering his senior season of high school. He always assumed basketball or baseball was what he was destined for, that is until the seven-on-seven tournament at Iowa State. Sage had grown up in Hawkeyes country and was never really exposed to the Cyclones, but when he heard there was interest in him at

Coming to Iowa State after getting noticed at a seven-on-seven football tournament, Sage Rosenfels quarterbacked the Cyclones for two years, leading the program to its first bowl win in school history before embarking on a 12-year NFL career. (Photo courtesy of Iowa State Athletics)

the tournament, his ears perked up. "More than anything, I think they saw the way I competed that day more than just my natural quarterback abilities," Rosenfels said.

Maquoketa went to the seven-on-seven finals in the tournament and played against West Des Moines Valley inside Cyclone Stadium, with McCarney checking in throughout the day. There were games going on across the facility, but McCarney made sure to pay attention to this kid from Maquoketa, watching his intangibles.

"Just the way he led that team, the throws he was making," McCarney said, "I absolutely knew then, 'We're going to recruit this young man.'"

A scholarship offer was finally extended around Christmas that year, and Rosenfels arrived on campus in the fall of 1996 as a true freshman, preparing to run the scout team while he redshirted. He earned his first two varsity letters by learning to be the holder during his redshirt freshman and sophomore seasons, while serving as the backup to Todd Bandhauer. Iowa State went 1–10 in 1997 and 3–8 in 1998 while Rosenfels played behind Bandhauer and "just tried to get better every day."

"I didn't come from a big high school with a big-time football program," Rosenfels said. "I had a lot to learn from the X's and O's of the game, but also physically. Over the first year and a half, I gained almost 30 pounds."

As a 6'4", 220-pound junior, Rosenfels jumped into a starting role, passing for 1,781 yards and 10 touchdowns. But Iowa State struggled to a 4–7 record. For his last go-around, Rosenfels and the seniors had big plans. The Cyclones hadn't been to a bowl game since 1978 and hadn't had a winning record since Rosenfels first arrived, but that was the goal: go somewhere warm.

Iowa State exploded onto the scene that season, finishing the regular season 8–3 and earning a berth to the Insight.com Bowl in Phoenix, Arizona. Rosenfels went 23-of-34 passing for 308 yards and two touchdowns to push Iowa State to a 37–29 victory against

Pittsburgh for the Cyclones' first bowl win in program history. Rosenfels called it his proudest moment at Iowa State. "For everything to work out our senior year to get to 9–3, it really was just an exclamation point and made it all worth it," Rosenfels said.

NFL watch lists of senior quarterbacks started to pop up in 2000. Drew Brees. Chris Weinke. *Sage Rosenfels*. The kid from small-town Iowa was suddenly listed by some as one of the three or four best senior quarterbacks in 2000. "That sort of really excited me," Rosenfels said. "I never really thought about the NFL until that moment."

Rosenfels was drafted in the fourth round of the 2001 NFL Draft by the Washington Redskins and went on to play for the Miami Dolphins, Houston Texans, New York Giants, and Minnesota Vikings in a run that spanned 12 seasons. As for a surreal career? Sage Rosenfels wholeheartedly believes it goes to show success is about the situations you put yourself in.

"I always thought that individual success only really occurs when the team has success," he said. "It's a good lesson for my kids that if they want to accomplish something, they can."

39 Down Goes UConn!

This was the women's basketball team everyone recognized versus the team nobody really knew. It was the team that made frequent national television appearances versus the team that never had. This was, albeit cliché, David versus Goliath. It was UConn versus Iowa State.

The players couldn't help but giggle as they prepared for their Sweet 16 matchup with vaunted UConn on March 20, 1999.

"No. 33…" coach Bill Fennelly began, reading the scouting report. "Coach, that's Shea Ralph," the players said. "No. 25…" he began again. "Coach, that's Svetlana Abrosimova," they said. And on and on it went. "We knew their names," center Angie Welle said. "These are unbelievable basketball players."

It wasn't as if this Iowa State team wasn't good, it was a No. 4 seed with 24 wins. But Iowa State wasn't *UConn*, the monster (as Fennelly called them) that the entire nation knew and the No. 1 seed that had a championship pedigree. Iowa State had only made its first NCAA tournament in 1997 and now had advanced to the Sweet 16 in just its third trip to the Big Dance. The Cyclones, who fittingly played the *Rocky* theme song before games that season, hadn't even fully unpacked at their Cincinnati hotel before they arrived at the Shoemaker Center.

"We've got to be like Rocky," Fennelly told the team before the game. "We've got to let 'em hit us and hit us, and hopefully at the end, we're still standing." Then the team walked out of the locker

2009 Elite Eight

Bill Fennelly sat on the bench thinking to himself. He kept going over the speech he would give to his team after the loss that was inevitable coming. Iowa State was hoping for its second-ever Elite Eight berth as it played Michigan State on March 28, 2009, and things weren't looking good.

The Cyclones were down 68–61 with 1:23 left, looking for a way to save their season. Fennelly called for a full-court press that worked to perfection. Nicky Wieben scored a putback, and an MSU turnover led to a Heather Ezell three-pointer to cut the lead to two with 50 seconds remaining. Another Spartans turnover resulted in a long ball from Alison Lacey, and the Cyclones defended three shot attempts on the other end to get the 69–68 win.

"That was certainly one of those games where you don't know how it happened," Fennelly said. "The game ends, and you're sitting around having a beer with your staff and are like, 'What just happened? Can anybody explain that?'"

room to meet the Huskies head-on. "Coach," the security guard said, stopping Fennelly outside the locker room, "if relaxed is good, you're in good shape."

The team *was* relaxed. After all, UConn was supposed to run away with the game. Everybody had counted Iowa State out, so what did they have to lose, anyway? *Well*, Stacy Frese thought, *we have a game that we could lose.* Nevertheless, the lone group that gave Iowa State much of a chance was constrained to the team bus that arrived at the arena that morning. And even then, remember those unpacked bags? By halftime, though, the game was tied at 28. *Heck*, Frese thought, *we're not even playing well, and we're still in it.*

The figurative first punch from UConn came five minutes into the second half. With the score knotted up at 39, the Huskies used a 7–0 run to begin to pull away as Iowa State went more than five minutes without scoring. It was a valiant effort, but maybe this was it. Then came another punch. The Cyclones had three players with four fouls.

The best answer to both problems—the deficit and foul trouble—appeared to be setting up shop with its long-range attack. After all, it was this trademark that had gotten the Cyclones this far. So with 5:26 remaining and Iowa State down six, Monica Huelman, who had been Fennelly's first recruit following his 1995 arrival, set up behind the arc, right of the key, and drained a three-pointer to cut the deficit in half.

"Mo's shot changed the momentum," Megan Taylor said later.

The next trip down, Tracy Gahan hit from the right. Then it was Frese from the left, Taylor from the top, and Frese again, this time from the right. In a three-minute span, Iowa State hit five consecutive three-pointers to surge ahead of a UConn team that had never lost in the Sweet 16.

"They all went in at the worst possible time," UConn coach Geno Auriemma said afterward. "And what makes it worse is that as they're going in, you can see the look on your kids' faces that was, *I don't know what to do."*

There was nothing to do as the last seconds ticked away. Iowa State won 64–58 and advanced to the Elite Eight. "You feel like you've been kicked in the gut," Auriemma said from the podium afterward, rubbing his temples. Welle rushed to a pay phone to call her parents, and Fennelly eventually headed back to the hotel. "I think most of us had to unpack," he said.

The Cyclones were still standing.

"If we played them 100 times we might have lost 99 times, but that's the great thing about sports," Fennelly said. "The rush of all these things that came together and all these things in the team concept. This kid did it, and this is her place in history. And this kid did it. And this kid did it. And you did it against *the* team in women's basketball."

40 Ben Peterson

As the 10-man wrestling team returned to Ames in the spring of 1969, Ben Peterson looked on in awe. The 190-pound freshman, who had practiced in the same room as these guys all season long, watched nine All-Americans, three of whom were national champions, stroll into the room having won the 1969 NCAA championship.

It's unreal what I am in the middle of, Peterson thought.

Peterson had arrived at Iowa State from the small town of Comstock, Wisconsin, somewhat by virtue of luck the previous fall. His prep career at Cumberland High School started inauspiciously as Peterson wrestled in seven matches as a freshman, only to be pinned seven times. By 1968, when he was a senior, his coach at Cumberland thought Peterson showed enough promise to go to the Olympic trials in Ames. He was pinned once and lost both matches there, but his raw talent caught Iowa State coach Harold Nichols' eye. Peterson was offered a partial scholarship and arrived in Ames later that fall.

One semester later, Peterson watched as Dan Gable returned as a national champion along with the likes of Chuck Jean and Jason Smith.

"It was the night I grew in my confidence as a wrestler more than any other time," Peterson said. "The confidence that built for me, to be able to do something similar, was just huge."

Some people initially wondered why Peterson had been brought aboard, but he worked in the wrestling room to get better. Freshmen weren't allowed to compete for the varsity, so there was little worrying about that. After Iowa State returned as NCAA champions in 1969, Peterson got back to work. He went home to Wisconsin for the summer and wrestled with his brothers. By fall, and the start of his sophomore year, Peterson had surprisingly captured the starting spot at 190 pounds.

"Ben was not a diamond in the rough," Iowa State assistant Les Anderson once told Buck Turnbull of the *Des Moines Register*. "He was more like a piece of coal. But when polished, he turned into a fine diamond."

The polishing didn't necessarily come easy. At the Midlands during his sophomore season, Peterson was whacked. Then he remembers vividly a night on the wrestling mat at the Armory in Ames. Peterson had been pinned, and he felt like the weakest link on Iowa State's 10-man team. So he worked harder in the wrestling room to improve, and by season's end he had won the Big 8 title at 190 pounds.

"I felt like that season, by the time I got to the end of it, working with the quality of athletes that were in that room and with the knowledge and experience of Harold Nichols and Les Anderson, I just saw myself improving every day and saying, 'I've got to stay at this. I could be a national champion myself,'" Peterson said.

He wouldn't be a national champion quite yet. After the conference tournament that sophomore season, Peterson ultimately finished fourth at the NCAA tournament as Iowa State won a second consecutive team title. His career was about to take off.

Peterson eventually won the final 52 matches of his collegiate career, capturing his first NCAA title in 1971 as Iowa State finished second. As a senior in 1972, he won a second title, helping the Cyclones capture their third team title in a four-year span. In addition to his two national titles, Peterson had become a three-time Big 8 champion and three-time All-American.

Following his senior season, Peterson qualified for the 1972 Olympics, making the trip with his brother John, Gable, and Iowa State heavyweight Chris Taylor. The expectations for Ben Peterson, as they had been years earlier, were set low.

"A sense I've gotten from Iowa State is just that you work hard and you keep working at it for a long time," Peterson said, "and then just wait and see."

In Munich, Ben Peterson pinned two opponents, won two decisions, and wrestled to a draw, ultimately winning the gold medal while his brother took silver. When the brothers qualified together for the Olympics again in 1976, John won gold and Ben took silver as the duo became the third and fourth two-time Olympic medalists in US history. Peterson had also become the only two-time Olympic medalist in Iowa State history, a mark that still stands.

Ben Peterson wasn't done making history. In 1980 he became only the fourth American wrestler to make three Olympic teams, although the United States boycotted those Games. Yet Peterson had come a long way from looking on as an awestruck freshman.

He was, and remains, among the greatest wrestlers in both Iowa State and US history.

41 Meet Cy

Whether you're young or old, a casual fan or the most loyal Cyclones follower, getting a picture with Cy is a must at any Iowa State event. Cy represents all that is Iowa State, and he is one of the most well-known mascots in the country. You may know that Cy was named the National Mascot of the Year in 2008, but what you might not be aware of is the history surrounding the famous figure, and that is just as important as that picture on game day.

Iowa State has been known as the Cyclones since 1895 when the name was coined by the *Chicago Tribune* after the football team scored 36 unanswered points in a rout of Northwestern. Cyclones was the undisputed nickname for the next 59 years, and Chev Adams, president of Collegiate Manufacturing, wanted to create a mascot in 1954. He contacted sports information director Harry Burrell to propose a nickname change, saying his business could create a mascot for the college.

Collegiate Manufacturing, an Ames business, was the top college souvenir company in the country and wanted to spearhead the project, but ran into a challenge regarding how exactly to depict a cyclone. After some discussion regarding a possible change in the school's nickname, history and tradition prevailed and Iowa State remained the Cyclones. Instead, the Pep Council was tasked with choosing a representation for the Cyclones, and a cardinal was eventually chosen because of the school's cardinal and gold color scheme.

The Pep Council solicited input from Collegiate Manufacturing for the design of the suit, with costs for the costume rounding out at $200 for the eight-and-a-half-foot suit. On October 16, 1954, the nameless bird was introduced to the Iowa State faithful at the homecoming game against Colorado.

A national Name the Bird contest was underway to name the mascot, and people responded. Roughly 350 submissions came in, including one from an alumnus in Pittsburgh. There were 17 people who entered, simply, Cy as the proposed name. Because the postmark date on the letters was used as the tiebreaker, Wilma Beckman Ohlsen of Ames was confirmed as the first to suggest Cy, and was credited with naming the mascot. She was rewarded with a personalized *I* blanket.

The new Iowa State mascot debuted on October 16, 1954, but it wasn't until a later Name the Bird contest was held that the name Cy was chosen. Cy, pictured here in the 1960s, has seen many transformations through the years.
(Photo courtesy of Iowa State Athletics)

Shortly after being cut from the varsity basketball team, Virgil Petty was chosen by the athletic club as the inaugural Cy. The original suit had strict requirements, as its core was made mainly of chicken wire and aluminum. Candidates needed to be between 5'11" and 6'2" and between 175 and 210 pounds, making practice in the costume before a game essential for Petty.

As time went on, the student performing as Cy changed, and in 1976 the first female to portray Cy was named. Then an ISU junior, 6'2" Betsy Thomas, shared Cy duties with two men and once told the *Des Moines Register* that someone in her sorority had conned her into trying out. "A lot of alums are shocked when they peek into the costume and find a girl inside," Thomas said.

In addition to the changes inside the Cy suit, the outward appearance of the mascot has changed through the years. Baby Cy was introduced in the late 1970s and early 80s to accompany Cy but was discontinued before Clone was introduced in January 1989 as a more agile performer. In 1995 Cy and Clone were merged to create a more menacing mascot than that of the cartoon-like suit worn in 1954.

Today, Cy wears a mischievous grin and is in the public eye more than 200 days out of the year, with four to six students performing the role. There are three suits, all different sizes, for Cy costumes today to allow a wider variety of performers, with the price of each greatly surpassing that of the 1954 version.

Although the appearance and the people performing the mascot's role have changed through the years, the spirit and passion Cy brings to game day is unmatched. So next time you're at an Iowa State event, be sure to get that picture taken with Cy.

42 One Heck of a Streak

The tales of Hilton Magic have been well documented. There was the shot by Barry Stevens in 1983 that maybe, just maybe, was the beginning. If that wasn't the beginning, then it certainly started with the game in 1989, when a local writer called for magic and Iowa State delivered it. The legend of the shaking floor and photos of the decibel meter climbing to unbearable levels certainly shed light on what Hilton Magic can produce. Yet it might not be one game, but rather a stretch of time—during which Iowa State was *literally* unbeatable at Hilton Coliseum—that makes the Magic most apparent.

To put this stretch in perspective, when Iowa State lost to Missouri on February 8, 1999, it would be another 1,027 days before the Cyclones would walk off the hardwood at Hilton Coliseum in defeat. If you're counting, that's two years, nine months, and twenty-three days between home losses. Jamaal Tinsley, who was on his recruiting trip on that February 8, arrived the next season and never lost a home game. In this stretch, which spanned parts of four seasons, Iowa State won *39 consecutive games* in front of the hometown faithful.

"The atmosphere of it all is just so dynamic," said Marcus Fizer, who played during part of the stretch. "When it was time for you or your ballclub to come into that atmosphere, it's something you probably never experienced before. There's just something magical behind it all, because a lot of times we hadn't been given the confidence of winning ballgames against the bigger clubs, and somehow, some way we always pulled it out."

In any streak of this magnitude there are bound to be close calls, and Iowa State certainly endured a few. There were two games—one against Kansas to close the 1999 season and one against Southern Mississippi in 2001—when the Cyclones won by two. Twice—once against Missouri in 2000 and another time in overtime against Morningside in 2001—Iowa State won by five. Maybe it was luck, maybe it was perfect timing, or maybe it really was magic. No matter what, the close calls stayed just that.

The streak included three wins against Kansas and two against Missouri along with wins against Oklahoma State, Oklahoma, Texas, and Iowa. Five were against ranked opponents.

"Part of it was we didn't know that we were on any sort of streak," Paul Shirley said. "It was sort of the perfect storm of athletics where the crowd has an impact on the game, the players know the crowd has that impact, and it served as this almost warm blanket."

There is a reason, though, that this is called a *streak*. Inevitably it did eventually come to an end. On December 1, 2001, after Iowa State had won its opener in the Cyclone Challenge, it faced off against San Jose State. The Spartans, who were coached by Larry Eustachy's close friend and longtime assistant Steve Barnes, had lost the night before to Division II Nebraska-Omaha. But Iowa State suddenly trailed by two as the final 15 seconds ticked away. Shane Power's off-balance three at the buzzer fell short. The streak—at the time the second-longest in the nation—was over.

"We've had a heck of a run," Eustachy said afterward.

Never has there been a more magical run in Iowa State history.

43 Jack Trice Stadium

The move couldn't have been more drastic. The excitement on campus in 1973 when students and fans learned there would be a new football stadium, which would eventually become Jack Trice Stadium, was palpable. But leaving behind the cozy and fan-friendly Clyde Williams Field would be quite a jump from what Iowa Staters were used to.

Clyde Williams Field seated about 35,000 people, had a track facility on-site, and provided an electric atmosphere that was well regarded in the Big 8. Construction for the new stadium, which began on October 26, 1973, was considered to be the crowning jewel of the Iowa State Center and would seat 42,500 initially. The $7.5 million stadium was also envisioned as a complement to the fairly new Hilton Coliseum just to the north.

The stadium was designed and built without the use of state funds, and the first game played was on September 20, 1975, when Iowa State took on Air Force. The Cyclones walked away with a 17–12 win, and got their first taste of what a wind tunnel the stadium could be. There was not much to be seen at the end of either end zone, and the two-level structure created almost a vortex of wind that made it a challenging environment.

Although relatively sterile in design, the color scheme of cardinal and gold seats brought the stadium to life. It was a much-needed upgrade from what Clyde Williams Field had to offer. "Of all the places I have been around the country, I can't think of one that has a better setup than we do now," Lou McCullough said at the time. "Our whole works is new." Everything was new and exciting in 1975, but there was one final piece left to decide: a name for the venue.

Jack Trice Stadium was built for $7.5 million and opened as Cyclone Stadium in 1975 with an original capacity of 42,500. Through the years, the stadium has seen a number of renovations, most recently in 2015 to enclose the south end zone and increase capacity to 61,000. (Photo courtesy of Iowa State Athletics)

After his tragic death in 1923 from injuries suffered in a game against Minnesota, Jack Trice was memorialized with a plaque that was placed in State Gym in 1924. After that, he was largely forgotten until around the time of construction for the new football stadium in 1973.

While rummaging around in State Gym, behind all of the dirt, grime, and bird droppings, university employees Charles Sohn and Alan Beals discovered the plaque bearing the name of Jack Trice. Upon more research into the man, they discovered an article written about Trice in 1957 by Tom Emmerson, a student journalist at Iowa State. After Emmerson's initial discovery of the plaque, and following his story's publication, Trice was forgotten. But Sohn and Beals were determined not to let that happen again.

During the time of the Vietnam War and civil rights debates, the story of Jack Trice became a hot-button issue on the Iowa State campus. Sohn and Beals began publicizing Jack Trice, with Sohn integrating the history into one of the English courses he taught in 1973–74. One of his students, who was aware of the need for the new football stadium's name, suggested naming it in honor of Jack Trice. That simple suggestion started a revolution in Ames.

When construction was completed in 1975, the Iowa Board of Regents filibustered, having reservations about naming the stadium after Trice, and voted to name the stadium once debts were paid off. Officials took a harsh stance not to have Trice be the namesake of the stadium, and the delay was done in part to force the story of Trice to die off, just like it had in the past. Only this time, Sohn and others persisted, and the debate raged on.

Finally, in 1983, it appeared the Trice supporters were making headway. The stadium debts were finally paid off, but ISU president Robert Parks, with the board of regents' support, proposed the compromise of Cyclone Stadium/Jack Trice Field. ISU GSB approved $500 for signs to have at football games that read, *Welcome to Jack Trice Stadium*, and supporters themselves began to raise funds simultaneously. On May 7, 1988, a $22,000, 6'5" bronze statue depicting Trice was installed on campus near Beardshear Hall.

After all of the publicizing by the *Iowa State Daily*, *Des Moines Register*, and celebrities such as Paul Newman, Ed Asner, and Senator Hubert H. Humphrey, ISU president Martin Jischke presented a proposal to the board of regents to finally rename the stadium. On August 30, 1997, Jischke fulfilled the dream of many by formally dedicating the venue as Jack Trice Stadium. "He has become a hero—not so much for what he accomplished, because his life was cut short—but for what he represented," Jischke said. The statue of Trice on campus was shortly thereafter moved to the stadium.

Jack Trice Stadium's appearance may have changed quite a bit since it burst onto the scene in 1975, but what the name represents is timeless. Iowa State University remains the only Division I school in the country with its stadium bearing the name of an African American.

44 The Late '70s: Flipping the Switch

There's no denying Iowa State football has experienced some pretty significant moments of success in its history. Beating No. 2 Oklahoma State in 2011 and the Cyclones' first bowl win in 2000 surely come to mind quickly, but what about significant seasons of *sustained* success? To find that, you'll have to turn the clock back a few decades to a time when you'll see the Iowa State football teams from 1976 to 1978 certainly stake claims as the best teams in school history.

Johnny Majors was on his way to Pittsburgh after taking Iowa State to the 1972 Liberty Bowl, and Earle Bruce was tapped to lead the program shortly after. And while Bruce had led Tampa to a 10–2 season in his only year there, his first three seasons at Iowa State produced several close losses and lots of fan disappointment. "Any time there was an opportunity to blow the game and lose, we did," Bruce said. From 1973 to 1975, the Cyclones were 4–7 each season, and fan patience was growing thin. "They were singing 'Goodbye, Earle' at one of the last games my sophomore year," former player Tom Randall remembered. "They were ready to get rid of him." Bruce needed to find a way to flip the switch.

It wasn't until a gig as a coach in the Hula Bowl before the 1976 season that the light finally flipped on for Bruce. He was coaching the players from the east in the game, and as players from the likes of Ohio State, Michigan, and Wisconsin walked onto the team bus, he couldn't help but think, *They're no better than my kids. I can't quite understand it.*

"The only thing I don't think they have, our guys, is they don't *think* they're as good," Bruce determined. "I said, 'We've got to make them think they're good.'"

Of course, there was doubt amongst the Cyclones players. Iowa State was riding a six-game losing streak heading into that 1976 season, but Bruce made it a point to set the tone early. "We've got to change the attitude of this team," Bruce said. That started with boosting the confidence of the entire team. Bruce kept preaching to the team what he saw from players on other teams. Suddenly, Iowa State started winning.

It was a toughness that trickled down from Bruce and his staff to the players, and that was no more apparent than on November 13, 1976. Iowa State hadn't beaten Nebraska in 16 years, and the Cyclones' hard-nosed defense came up big, recovering six fumbles. Highlighted by a 95-yard kickoff return touchdown from Luther Blue and the dynamic running of Dexter Green, Iowa State won 37–28 after the game had been tied at 20 in the fourth quarter.

"We won games instead of losing them because we finished the game," Bruce said. "We stayed with them, we didn't give up. We didn't make all the mistakes we made before and we were a little more confident in ourselves. It turned my life around."

The season was a monumental turnaround from Bruce's first three seasons, and the Cyclones awaited a bid to a bowl game for what would be the first time in four years. Iowa State was ranked 14th in the nation, possessed the No. 2 offense in college football, and had the Big 8 Coach of the Year and four first-team all-conference picks, but that bid never came, and the 8–3 Cyclones were left home. "It's unbelievable when you think about it," Bruce said.

"Kind of ironic that the best, if not one of the best, teams in Iowa State history didn't get to play in a bowl game," Randall said.

Despite the disappointment of missing out on the postseason, the Cyclones returned in 1977 on a mission. After starting 1–1, the squad rattled off four straight wins including another win against Nebraska, this time a 24–21 victory in Lincoln, where Iowa State had not won since 1960. "You don't beat them unless your defense plays well," Bruce explained. And the Cyclones did have some nasty defenders, especially in the trenches. Mike Stensrud and Tom Randall played up front, and both became future NFL linemen.

"We didn't want to let each other down," Stensrud said. "We also had great coaches. Earle Bruce had a great, fantastic staff."

Finishing 8–3 in 1977 for the second time, Iowa State got the bowl bid that had eluded it the year before, being invited to the Peach Bowl in Atlanta. A third straight 8–3 season in 1978—the only losses coming to ranked teams—had the Cyclones going to the Hall of Fame Bowl in Birmingham, Alabama.

Bruce left the Cyclones after the 1978 season to coach Ohio State, but that stretch of three eight-win seasons leaves a sweet taste in the mouths of Iowa State fans even decades later.

45 Louis Menze

Before Johnny Orr or Fred Hoiberg became synonymous with Iowa State basketball, there was Louis Menze. Rarely talked about, and often forgotten, it was Menze who began to build Iowa State into prominence in the Midwest. He took the program places it had never been. When he grabbed the reins in 1928, Menze began a 19-year coaching career in Ames that produced a little magic, long before Barry Stevens was even born.

A disciple of Forrest "Phog" Allen, Menze—who grew up in Kansas City—played for the legendary Kansas coach when the two were together at what was then Missouri State Teachers College in Warrensburg, Missouri. As a three-sport athlete in college, it was basketball where Menze developed a passion for coaching. Under the direction of Phog Allen, Menze became a great basketball mind in his own right, priding himself on thoroughness and perfecting the fundamentals. It was Allen's approach to the game that hit home for Menze.

"He inculcated in all of us the great virtue of never giving up no matter what the circumstances," Menze told the *Kansas City Star* in 1959.

Menze left Warrensburg to attend officer's training at Ft. Riley, where he worked with inductees and the infantry. After later working at a sporting goods company back in Kansas City for a short time, it was a call from the high school principal at his alma mater, Central High School, that set Menze on his life's path. "How would you like to go into coaching?" the principal asked. And so Menze began his coaching career.

Maybe it was the never-give-up approach to the game that he learned from Allen, but when Menze arrived in Ames after nine years at Central, he wasn't taking over a program with tradition. Iowa State had never experienced much success in basketball, going 20–69 in the five previous seasons combined, including 3–15 the year before Menze arrived. He wasted no time implementing his philosophies, though, as the Cyclones ended the 1928–29 season with their first winning record in seven years.

Iowa State forced its way into prominence in 1934–35, when Menze led the Cyclones to their first regular-season Big 6 championship. Waldo Wegner, the first All-American in ISU history, was a double-figure scorer that season, and gave credit to Menze for his ability to maximize potential from his players.

"If there's any man that's influenced my life, it was my coach," Wegner once said. "All the fundamentals I know about basketball, I learned here at Iowa State. Louie was the one who taught me the fundamentals that are still used today."

Program firsts continued under the direction of Menze. The Cyclones made their first postseason tournament appearance in 1940-41—after claiming their second Big Six crown and finishing with a then-record 15 wins—as one of 16 teams to play in the NCAA regional qualifying tournament.

At the time, only eight teams made the NCAA tournament, so a regional tournament was the only way to advance. Iowa State took on Creighton in Kansas City but fell to the Bluejays. It was that tournament, though, that set the stage for Menze to take his squad one step further.

Three years and another Big 6 regular-season championship later, Iowa State was *in* the NCAA tournament and ready to make a statement. Led by 23-year-old Price Brookfield—who came to Iowa State to be a part of the college's naval cadet program and eventually played in the NBA—the Cyclones defeated Pepperdine in the regional final, leading the program to its first, and only, Final Four.

Menze led Iowa State to one more Big 6 title the following season, which came to fruition thanks to a 61–39 drubbing of Kansas at State Gym. "If you get a bunch of guys that want to play defense and rebound, you can have a winner," former player Bob Mott once said. "Coach Menze always stressed that." It was the fundamentals of the game that always guided Menze.

After taking over as athletics director in 1945, a position he would hold until retiring in 1958, Menze stepped down as the basketball coach in 1947. He had taken Iowa State to new heights with a 166–153 mark and four conference titles. Casual fans may not think of Menze immediately, but he'll always have his place in ISU history and was inducted into the Iowa State Hall of Fame in 1998.

46 The Armory

The noise was deafening. Fans were sitting practically on top of the court, and the sound of the stomping feet on the metal bleachers at the Armory reverberated like a drum. The stomping would become so frantic and incessant that even the lights would be affected. Marv Stromer was there as a student in 1957 and noticed an odd flickering coming from the large glass globe encasing a lighting fixture above him. The energy in the building had caused the light to become unsteady, and Stromer was paying attention at the right time.

"The glass globe over the light let go and dropped—right on us!" Stromer later told Chuck Offenburger. "I reached up and caught it!"

The fixture was 10 or 12 inches in diameter, and Stromer's catch certainly saved fans in the surrounding area from getting injured, but nobody said much about the incident. They were too enthralled by the game to notice much else that day, when Iowa State beat No. 1 Kansas and Wilt Chamberlain. "We filled the place," Gary Thompson said. "There was Armory Magic."

The Armory, tucked away in the northwest corner of campus, produced many standout moments, but the history and the struggles for the venue to be built in the first place can grab your attention just as much as the action on the hardwood. There had been discussions of building a multipurpose armory at Iowa State since 1871, but it wasn't until 1920 that construction actually began for the 150-foot-wide, 210-foot-deep structure directly west of the Chemical Building. It was completed in the fall of 1921.

The Armory was intended to serve as a gymnasium, office space, and venue for commencement ceremonies, but in the winter

Originally opened in 1921, and reopened in 1924 after a fire burned it to the ground in 1922, the Armory, with its metal bleachers and deafening sound, became a major home-court advantage for the Cyclones until they moved to Hilton Coliseum in 1971. The building remains in use today. (Photo courtesy of Iowa State Athletics)

of 1922, a fire—which was suspected to be arson but was never proven—engulfed the structure, resulting in the destruction of the building. State legislature approved $125,000 to rebuild the Armory—this time with fireproof materials!—and construction on an identical building was finished in 1924.

An extension was added on the west side of the building in 1941 to mirror that of the east side, and in 1946 varsity basketball at Iowa State moved from holding games at State Gym to the Armory. The move was made purely because of space restrictions at State Gym, and the seating at the Armory (with a capacity of 7,500) allowed for a more raucous and intimidating home environment. "The other coaches would tell you that was one of the toughest places to play because it was so confined," Thompson said.

A remodel in 1956 improved the steel structure of the Armory, bumped the capacity to 8,500 seats, and added a crow's nest, which saw a change in the direction of the court from east-west to north-south. The hardwood on the floor of the Armory was portable and laid on dirt, truly allowing it to serve as a multipurpose venue.

When the Armory served as home for men's basketball, there were no dressing rooms for the players. Teams would dress in locker rooms at State Gym and *together* would ride a city bus the few blocks through campus to the Armory, where classrooms with chalkboards served as the meeting place for halftime. "There were no showers, so after the game we'd be wearing heavy overcoats over and back, and then you'd have to go back and shower over [at State Gym]," Thompson recalled.

The Armory was the home for men's basketball and wrestling until the construction of Hilton Coliseum in 1971 but still served ISU students as a place for general recreation. Today it is used by the university as classroom space, houses three Iowa State ROTC programs, and is the location for the school's Department of Public

State Gym

Originally intended to be an armory and primary athletic facility on Iowa State's campus, State Gym and its construction was debated from the 1890s until ground was officially broken in 1911 after the board of trustees approved the project with the condition it would be able to approve costs and materials.

Construction was completed in 1913 for $150,000 with the Iowa State's men's basketball team holding competitions in the facility that same year. It would be the home of Iowa State men's basketball from that time until 1946, when the team began playing in the larger Armory on the north side of campus. A cinder track was installed in 1915, and the facility also served as the dining center for military recruits on campus beginning in 1918.

State Gym was completely renovated in 2012, with a new addition built to the west, and serves as a recreation center today for ISU students, with five basketball courts, strength and cardio equipment, and an aquatic facility.

Safety. The noise in the building won't leave your ears ringing as it once would, but its legacy is sure to leave an impression.

47 Zaid Abdul-Aziz

Had it not been for a phone call Iowa State basketball coach Glen Anderson made to a former player out in New York, Hilton Coliseum might have one fewer retired jersey hanging from the rafters.

Hank Whitney enjoyed an All–Big 8 career for the Cyclones and a long professional basketball career, but his connection to his home state of New York paid dividends for the Iowa State program even after he departed. Anderson called Whitney one day in the mid-1960s, asking him to help out by going to watch a recruit in the New York area. All Anderson wanted was a simple report, so Whitney went and worked the kid out at a YMCA. "Hey, this guy jumps higher than me!" Whitney, known for his jumping ability, relayed to Anderson.

"I played one-on-one with him, and I came away so impressed," Whitney said later. "I told Coach, 'He is a hell of a ballplayer, you have to take him.'"

So Iowa State took that kid named Don Smith, who would become Zaid Abdul-Aziz in 1976. He really *was* one hell of a player. Smith would go on to earn All-America honors and be named Big 8 Player of the Year in 1968.

Abdul-Aziz grew up in Brooklyn, New York, in the Bedford-Stuyvesant area. Early home life was one of dysfunction for Abdul-Aziz, with people always coming and going from his home. Gang life surrounded the area. His home was right above a soul food restaurant and on days when things were at their roughest, Abdul-Aziz would make his way downstairs and, for 25 cents, he would play music from the jukebox. It was an escape and his first love.

Basketball was also a place to get away. Abdul-Aziz played basketball growing up, starring at John Jay High School in Brooklyn before his encounter at the YMCA with Whitney set him on the path to Ames. The 6'9", 235-pounder was a perfect combination of size and speed, but when he arrived at Iowa State, he had quite a culture shock, coming from Brooklyn. "When I got off the plane I was scared to death because I had never seen so many white people in my life," Abdul-Aziz once said.

While the shock to the system was hard to ignore, the environment in Ames was conducive to success. After sitting out his first year per NCAA guidelines, Abdul-Aziz burst onto the scene as a sophomore in 1965–66 and was named All–Big 8 and Sophomore of the Year.

It was during his final two seasons in Ames that Abdul-Aziz solidified his legacy. He led the Big 8 in scoring as a junior and senior (24.8 and 24.2 points per game, respectively) and led the league in rebounding each year he played. He was one of only two players in Big 8 history to score 600 points in a season *twice* (Wilt Chamberlain was the other), and he had 1,672 points and 1,025 rebounds during his career. In a matchup with Lew Alcindor—who later became Kareem Abdul-Jabbar—his senior year, Abdul-Aziz scored 33 points in a loss to UCLA.

Abdul-Aziz's indelible mark on the Iowa State program was so widely recognized that his jersey—initially bearing the name Don Smith—was retired *on his senior night* in 1968. The Cyclones had just fallen in the Armory to Kansas State, but fans still packed the metal bleachers to watch one of their favorites go into the rafters.

The No. 35 of Abdul-Aziz was put above the court and he was given gifts by the student body president, the mayor of Ames, and

Iowa State president Dr. W. Robert Parks. All that was on Abdul-Aziz's mind were his missed free throws at the end of the game that could have beaten Kansas State that night. "Everybody's telling him how great he is," an ISU instructor later told *Sports Illustrated*, "and he's apologizing for missing free throws." It was that drive to be better that took Abdul-Aziz to the heights of his career.

Abdul-Aziz was selected fifth in the 1968 NBA Draft by the Cincinnati Royals, and played for the Milwaukee Bucks, Seattle SuperSonics, Houston Rockets, Buffalo Braves, and Boston Celtics. He scored a career-high 37 points in 1971 against the defending world-champion New York Knicks and eventually retired from professional basketball in 1978.

A No. 35 jersey bearing the name Abdul-Aziz can still be found in the rafters today, honoring the two-time All-American. If not for that phone call between Whitney and Anderson, it's a jersey that would never have come to be.

48 Clyde Williams Field

All the waaaay to Lincoln Way!

There was a time when that chant was a crowd favorite in Ames. As George Amundson would lead Iowa State down the field and toward the south end zone at Clyde Williams Field, the crowd would go wild and proceed to scream its favorite chant.

Located on the corner of Lincoln Way and Sheldon Avenue, directly west of Friley Hall and south of State Gym, Clyde Williams Field first came up as an idea in May 1911. By December 1912, plans were in place for a new field with a concrete grandstand that would seat 5,000 fans. Iowa State's first field was built in 1893,

Iowa State moved to its new home at Clyde Williams Field next to Friley Hall on the west side of campus for the 1915 season and watched the stadium become a revered home-field advantage until the team moved to Jack Trice Stadium in 1975. (Photo courtesy of Iowa State Athletics)

west of Morrill Hall, and was called State Field, but the college was beginning to think about an upgrade. It wouldn't be until October 1914, though, when the board of trustees granted permission to build bleachers on campus property, that the new field, initially known as New State Field, began to sprout.

By the fall of 1915, Iowa State football had a new home at the cost of $32,000 raised primarily with contributions from faculty, alumni, and students. The "grandstand" didn't actually become recognized as a "stadium" until 1925, when plans were approved to create U-shaped seating and increase capacity to 14,000. Expansions in 1930, 1932, 1961, and 1966 eventually brought the stadium's capacity to 35,000, and the stadium was renamed Clyde Williams Field in 1938, only weeks following the death of the influential Iowa State coach and athletics director who had led the planning of the new field.

The allure of Clyde Williams Field, however, was not found in expansion details. As Iowa State rose to prominence on the gridiron, the stadium sitting tightly on Lincoln Way became one of the most revered in the Big 8 Conference. The praise for Clyde Williams Field didn't come simply from the aesthetics of the stadium—the seating was rather close—but was because of the raucous fans themselves.

The night before football games, Iowa State would stay at a hotel in Boone, and would arrive in town early the next morning for an early afternoon kickoff at 1:00 PM. Upon arrival, the bus would park on the corner and the team would walk to the locker room through the mostly empty stadium. "Except the student section," Amundson said. "One huge spot, and it was packed. It would be packed at 11:00 in the morning. The student fans would be going nuts."

Student tickets were general admission, and the line for admittance would begin at 9:00 AM. Then the students would push and prod their way through the gates.

"I remember the crush getting in," said Iowa State broadcaster Eric Heft, who was a student in the early '70s. "I remember one game I went at least 20 feet without my feet ever touching the ground just from the crush, and they stopped taking tickets. They just let everybody in because they thought somebody was going to get killed. But it was wild."

The environment itself was wild too. Students would form a tunnel for the team to run through before games and would then toss oranges onto the field following the Cyclones' first score (the Big 8 winner went to the Orange Bowl). They would also take a cheerleader and pass her up the student section. By the 1970s, the stadium had been around for parts of seven decades and had become somewhat rugged. But the atmosphere was unmatched.

"Game day at Clyde Williams, to this day, I've never seen a game day environment like that," defensive lineman Tom Randall

Honor Before Victory

When Clyde Williams coached at Iowa State in the early 1900s, he had a chance to put his motto to test. Known to preach "Honor Before Victory," Williams certainly proved the words had meaning when the Cyclones faced Iowa in 1912. Prior to the game, Williams had been given Iowa's signals from an anonymous source.

"Here are all of Iowa's plays and signals," Williams told assistant Homer Hubbard. "Here is what we're going to do." Williams proceeded to tear them up.

In 1938 W.G. Lane donated a plaque with the words *Honor Before Victory*. It was installed on the north entrance gate at Clyde Williams Field that year. In 2005 that plaque was moved to Jack Trice Stadium, where it now sits in the tunnel Iowa State runs through onto the field on game day.

said. "It was just a party. They were right down on the field and they were loud. It was amazing."

There were many noteworthy moments at Clyde Williams Field, from the Dirty Thirty team in 1959 to the game in which Colorado's buffalo, Ralphie, broke free on the field. But the best representation of the stadium itself might have come in 1972 when Iowa State faced defending national champion Nebraska. When the crowd would stomp its feet, the stadium would begin to shake. It undoubtedly shook more than ever before when Amundson hit Willie Jones in the southeast corner to tie the Cornhuskers at 23 in an eventual tie against the vaunted Big 8 foe.

The stadium was abandoned for a more modern Cyclone Stadium in 1975 and was eventually demolished in 1978, many years after fans had countless times cheered and willed the Iowa State offense all the waaaay to Lincoln Way.

49 Coach Mac

If someone were to tell you that a man could spend 36 years of his life in Iowa City, Iowa, smack-dab in the middle of Hawkeyes country, only to end up here, as an integral part of Iowa State history, you probably wouldn't believe them. And yet, here we are.

Dan McCarney was born in Iowa City in 1953. His father, an Irish police officer who eventually served as the city's police chief, was assigned to work security at Kinnick Stadium for football games. His mother worked as an employee at the University of Iowa's dental school. So there was little convincing to be done after McCarney starred on the Iowa City High football team. He'd take his talents across town to Kinnick Stadium and play for the Hawkeyes.

While the Hawkeyes struggled to find success during McCarney's tenure as a player, winning only six games in three seasons, McCarney became a team captain and a starting guard. When his playing career was over, he took a position as a graduate assistant on Bob Commings' staff at Iowa. Then Hayden Fry arrived in 1979, and McCarney was one of two coaches retained from the previous staff. For the next 11 seasons, McCarney, along with the other members of Fry's famed coaching tree, made Iowa relevant. "All of us were a bunch of young guns," McCarney said. "Nobody outside our friends and family really knew who any of us were in the coaching profession."

By 1990, with Iowa having advanced to eight bowl games, including the 1982 Rose Bowl, people knew who McCarney was. He was drawing interest across the country when his good friend Barry Alvarez left Iowa for the Wisconsin job. McCarney followed to be his defensive coordinator. "If I wanted to be a head coach someday, I knew I had to be in charge of half of a football team," McCarney said. At the time, McCarney became one of the youngest coordinators in the country, but in four years' time he helped guide the Badgers from 1–10 when he arrived to 10–1–1 and a win in the 1994 Rose Bowl.

Later that year, the Cyclones called.

It was, of all places, at a Denny's in Madison, Wisconsin, where McCarney made his first impression on Iowa State athletics director Gene Smith. Iowa State, which had been winless the season before, was searching for a new coach. McCarney left breakfast unsure where he stood. "Gene had a pretty good poker face," he said. On November 23, 1994, McCarney was named Iowa State's new coach.

"I didn't come here to be a cellar dweller," McCarney said. "I didn't take this job to apologize to people for not being able to get it done. I didn't come here for kids just to go out there and be competitive. I came here to win and help bring the respect back to this program."

With a sweat jacket on underneath another shirt, McCarney was intense. Back and forth from offense to defense he would go, and then back again. He walked, then paced, then jumped in with the defensive line. He would fly up and down the field in practice, bouncing off the walls.

"Mac was nonstop, on the go," quarterback Sage Rosenfels said. "He seemed like he had about 10 cups of coffee before practice. He'd get right in there. By the end of practice his shirt was as wet as most of the players'."

"He was just *so* intense," fellow quarterback Seneca Wallace added. "He had something about him to make sure he brought out the best in his players."

He certainly did that. McCarney slowly but surely took a program that had gone winless in 1994 to new heights. In 1998 Iowa State arrived in Iowa City having lost 15 consecutive games to Iowa. With the help of McCarney, the rivalry was renewed. The Cyclones rattled off five consecutive wins against the Hawkeyes (1998–2002). The success continued at the conclusion of the 2000 season when Iowa State advanced to its first bowl game since 1978. Then the Cyclones won it, marking their first bowl win in program history. McCarney led Iowa State to bowl games in five of six seasons between 2000 and 2005.

Iowa State fell on tough times in 2006, and McCarney resigned at season's end. But the guy from Iowa City, after 12 seasons in Ames, had become the longest-tenured and winningest coach in program history. He had brought respect back to Iowa State.

"I took that job with a huge chip on my shoulder, and I don't know that we ever went into a game without a chip on our shoulder," McCarney said. "Losing teams, you can be remembered as fine young men and a good student who practiced and played hard, but losing teams are forgotten easily. Successful teams are remembered forever. Especially when you do something that [has] never been done before in the history of Iowa State football."

50 Seneca Wallace

An astounding 10 yards deep into his own end zone, Seneca Wallace rolled to his left looking for his man downfield. He churned his legs and got to the goal line in Kinnick Stadium with a defender in hot pursuit. Under that heavy pressure, the right-handed Wallace squared up his shoulders on the run and flung a 30-yard pass to Jack Whitver for a first down.

It wasn't a scoring play, but it was one of many highlights for a Wallace-led comeback in Iowa State's 36–31 win against Iowa in

2002. More than anything else, it was an image burned into the minds of everyone in Iowa City that day. Certainly there could not be many quarterbacks around who could use those picture-perfect mechanics while on the run.

"That's an unbelievable play," ISU broadcaster Eric Heft remembered hearing from Hawkeye color commentator Ed Podolak after the game. "There's maybe three quarterbacks in the country that could make that throw, pro or college."

While Seneca Wallace proved himself to be a highlight reel and Heisman Trophy candidate early in 2002, the story really begins in 1998. It begins at the moment when Wallace didn't know if he even wanted to play football anymore.

A scholarship offer from Oregon State awaited Wallace out of high school, but an NCAA ruling that one of his classes would not be accepted stalled his chance to play for the Beavers. To make matters worse, his mother had just been diagnosed with cancer. The devastation of his mother's illness made Seneca question whether or not he wanted to pursue football.

"She means a lot to me," Wallace said at the time. "She's been there since I was little, so I wasn't sure." But at the urging of his mother, Seneca decided to strap up his helmet again, at the nearby Sacramento City College. Wallace shined at quarterback as a sophomore in 2000 as a dual threat but was not heavily recruited by four-year schools, who mostly wanted him as a receiver. But when Iowa State and Dan McCarney heard about this California kid, they jumped all over him.

"We saw him on tape and loved him. We thought we got a steal," McCarney remembered. "I was shocked there weren't more teams that were offering him." Wallace's decision came down to Iowa State and Kansas State, but witnessing the culture in Ames and seeing the Cyclones win their first bowl game in 2000 pushed him over the edge.

Though Seneca Wallace played at Iowa State for only two seasons, his dynamic running and passing ability made a permanent mark on the program. His play-making ability was no more evident than during his famous run on October 12, 2002, against Texas Tech. (Photo courtesy of Iowa State Athletics)

Wallace shot to the top of the ISU depth chart at quarter-back that spring, and replaced Sage Rosenfels, who had recently graduated, by leading Iowa State to a 7–5 record and a berth in the Independence Bowl while earning Big 12 Newcomer of the Year honors.

But it was as a senior in 2002 that Wallace left a lasting mark on the memory of Cyclones fans everywhere. Of course there was his 20-yard run against No. 3 Florida State in the waning moments of the season opener in Kansas City. It was an ending that longtime Cyclones fans remember well, as Wallace was ruled as coming a yard short of the touchdown that would have given Iowa State a chance to tie or win the game. Even through that loss, Wallace had put himself and his team on the national stage.

Following that loss, Wallace orchestrated a six-game winning streak that included the comeback performance at Iowa and an unforgettable win against No. 20 Nebraska. He was quickly establishing himself as one of the favorites to win the Heisman Trophy. "I don't know that anyone could have impacted our program more in a positive way than Seneca Wallace did," McCarney said.

But it was a play against Texas Tech that made the dynamic quarterback an Iowa State legend. Set up 12 yards from the end zone in a tie game, Wallace took the snap and dropped back. As defenders applied pressure, he zigzagged on the Jack Trice Stadium grass for an estimated 135 yards to finally get into the end zone, with the Cyclones ending their season in another bowl game at the Humanitarian Bowl.

Wallace went on to have a decade-long career in the NFL as a fourth-round selection, but it was the twisting and turning path to Iowa State that endears him to Ames, just as the fans are endeared to him.

"Thinking back on it, man," Wallace said, "it was an incredible time."

51 Return for Homecoming

They say you can always go home, and more than 100 years after its inception, there may be no better time to return to Iowa State (or simply make a trip there) than on homecoming.

As some colleges and universities around the country tried their hand at a homecoming in the early 1900s, professor Samuel Beyer suggested Iowa State start its own tradition. University president Raymond A. Pearson agreed, and in 1912, when the Cyclones hosted the University of Iowa on the gridiron at State Field, Iowa State held its first homecoming. The college at the time was only a glimmer of what it is today—with 1,830 students—but a reported 152 alumni returned, and classes were canceled for both Friday afternoon and Saturday. The tradition had only just begun.

Through more than a century worth of homecoming festivities, the traditions have evolved. There are the lawn displays—which started in the inaugural year with a blinking sign 55 feet long and 20 feet high that read, *Beat Iowa, Eat Iowa*—that continue today. There are the Yell-Like-Hell competitions that were first introduced in 1963 and allowed any residence hall to enter an original yell with finalists presenting at the pep rally. There is mass campaniling, which began in 1977, where students gather at the Campanile for a midnight kiss. There are pep rallies and tailgate parties.

Of course, there is also football, and through the years, homecoming has played host to many memorable moments both on and off the field.

Iowa State lost that first homecoming game against Iowa, and the four homecoming games that followed, before earning its first homecoming win in 1917 against Kansas State. The next year provided an easy-to-forget game because, well, there wasn't one. As the Spanish flu epidemic swept across the country, the game was canceled.

In 1953 homecoming garnered headlines for what happened off the field. After Iowa State defeated Missouri 13–6, students marched to the Knoll, where president James Hilton lived. They demanded Monday's classes be canceled. Hilton didn't come out (he wasn't home), so students marched to Lincoln Way and created a blockade. On Sunday and Monday they returned to the Knoll persistent with their demands for a day off school, but Hilton refused. A riot ensued, and tear gas was deployed. Students burned lawn displays and fought back against the tear gas. Another riot started in 1997 after Iowa State ended a 13-game losing streak with a win against Baylor. Students tore down a goal post, marched it to Lake LaVerne, and tossed it into the water.

The moments that have surrounded homecoming games are just as memorable: In 1954 Iowa State introduced Cy as its mascot during homecoming. The first night game was played in 1984 against Oklahoma. In 2012 Iowa State celebrated 100 years of homecoming.

There may be no moment more memorable than the one Seneca Wallace produced on homecoming in 2002 against Texas Tech. That night, Wallace turned a 12-yard touchdown run into the magnificent run remembered today, when he zigzagged an estimated 135 yards from sideline to sideline before finally finding the end zone.

Now, as the second century of homecoming continues, there are certain to be many moments and traditions worth catching in the years ahead.

52 Hilton Coliseum

Before there could ever be Hilton Magic, there first needed to be Hilton Coliseum.

Iowa State had been playing at the Armory across campus for more than two decades when James H. Hilton first conceived the idea for the Iowa State Center in the late 1960s. The plan called for a four-building complex, one of which would be an athletic field house. The first plans were proposed in September 1967 and showed a building much different from the one that ultimately came to fruition. That first bid was rejected because of excessive costs.

The next summer, in early June 1968, a new plan was proposed. This one called for an octagonal-shaped concrete structure that would cost $8.1 million. Within two weeks, on June 16, 1968, ground was broken just southeast of campus. On June 5, 1970, amid construction, the field house was dedicated and named James H. Hilton Coliseum after Hilton, the only graduate of Iowa State who has served as its president, and the man who had jump-started the project.

On December 2, 1971, Iowa State took the court for the first time.

"I remember coming out that first night, and the place [was] packed," Iowa State broadcaster and then–point guard Eric Heft said. "It was a rush. The buzz was great."

Hilton Coliseum, with an initial capacity of 14,020, was much bigger than the nearly 8,500-seat Armory, and was certainly much more spacious. Yet initially some wondered if the atmosphere could possibly be comparable. At the Armory, the metal bleachers and confined space created an electric environment.

"When you have a new arena, people say, 'Oh, it's not as loud as the old one,'" Heft said. "The Armory was loud, [with] metal bleachers, and people would stomp their feet. I remember people saying, 'Hilton's great, but it just doesn't have that atmosphere.'"

People certainly wouldn't be saying that years later.

Construction on the $8.1 million octagonal-shaped concrete building began in 1968, and Hilton Coliseum opened its doors for the first time on December 2, 1971. The arena has become home to some of the most memorable moments in ISU history. (Photo courtesy of Story Construction)

On that cold night in early December 1971, fans excitedly arrived at Hilton Coliseum for the first time. The game against Arizona had been sold out for weeks, and 14,510 fans packed into the newly christened building. The Cyclones overcame nerves in a 71–54 victory. "We had the jitters tonight," new coach Maury John said. "The large crowd had an effect."

The crowds would only get larger. Later that month on December 18, 1971, the rival Hawkeyes arrived in town. It was only the second year of the renewed rivalry after the series saw a hiatus from 1935 until the previous season when the Cyclones traveled to Iowa City. Now Iowa had come to Ames. The students were on break, so Iowa State sold their tickets. But students were still allowed to attend. "Students would come in, and [it was] like, 'Someone is in my seat,'" Heft said. Fans packed four-deep on the concourse.

Iowa State won 97–94 that night as an estimated 16,000 fans (or more) packed into the arena to create some magic long before the term Hilton Magic was ever coined. "It was a nuthouse," Heft said. "That was the biggest crowd ever there for a basketball game."

Hilton Coliseum became about more than just basketball. The new building housed both basketball teams, sure, but it also became home to the gymnastics, volleyball, and wrestling teams. Through the more than 40 years since its inception, that concrete structure has also been home to some incredible moments.

It is inside that building where Barry Stevens started Hilton Magic in 1983 and where countless other upsets took place thereafter. It was on that floor where Lafester Rhodes scored 54 points against Iowa in 1987. It was on a mat inside that building that Cael Sanderson won a number of matches during his unprecedented 159–0 career. The building has hosted the NCAA tournament and NCAA championships in multiple sports. The men's gymnastics team vaulted and swung to three national titles there in the early

1970s. That court has seen conference championship teams in both men's and women's basketball.

Now, more than four decades after its opening, those moments continue to build.

53. Nawal El Moutawakel

On the beach in Casablanca, Morocco, when Nawal El Moutawakel was young, her father would draw a line in the sand. When he moved his hand, Nawal would take off in a sprint, along with her brother and cousins. Time and time again, she beat them.

It was Mohamed El Moutawakel who encouraged Nawal, and who disregarded what society was telling them. Growing up in Morocco, the El Moutawakels lived in a society where women were required to be fully covered. They lived in a society where girls didn't compete against boys. Mohamed ignored what society was saying and pushed Nawal.

By the time she was 15, Nawal had been discovered by the Moroccan Track and Field Federation and was beating boys in Casablanca. When she was 17, Nawal began traveling with the national team, becoming the African champion in both the 100- and 400-meter hurdles in 1982. In August 1983, at the world championships in Helsinki, Finland, Nawal met Iowa State runner Sunday Uti from Nigeria. The two struck up a conversation. Sunday took Nawal's address and told her to expect to hear from a coach. She didn't think much of it.

One day later, Nawal received a big envelope from Iowa State. Assistant women's coach Pat Moynihan had offered her a scholarship. She initially put it away. Not long after, though, Nawal pulled the forms back out and took them to her father.

"Here," Nawal said, "I want you to sign this."

"You are going for real," he told her. "Now we go 100 percent."

When Nawal arrived at the Des Moines airport in January 1983, a runner on the women's team—holding a sign with Nawal's picture and name on it—was there to pick her up. Nawal was filled with questions. She wondered why the trip to Ames was so long. She wondered if the girl driving was Pat. She wondered where Iowa State was.

Six weeks after Nawal arrived in Iowa, as she adjusted to her new life, her brother called. He said he was coming to Iowa. Nawal was confused. When her brother arrived not long after, Nawal learned that her father had died in a car crash eight days after she had left. Her family had decided not to tell her. Her brother had come to Iowa to take her home to Morocco.

Nawal thought about her father. This was his dream for her. She wanted to stay.

The next year, in 1984, Nawal burst onto the scene. The tiny 5'2" sophomore started by winning the Big 8 440-yard dash. Then she became the second woman to win a relays triple crown, winning the 400-meter hurdles at the Texas, Kansas, and Drake Relays while setting the collegiate record. She later won the national championship in the same event.

Following that sophomore season, El Moutawakel qualified for the 1984 Olympics. It was the first time in history the 400-meter hurdles would be run as a women's event. Nawal was the lone woman in the Moroccan delegation and was summoned to visit King Hassan II. He had high hopes for her. Nawal arrived in Los Angeles, and Iowa State coach Ron Renko and Moynihan went over the strengths and weaknesses of each runner.

"I was very scared. Scared to maybe fall down. Scared to lose. Scared not to be at the level," Nawal said in a 2014 Olympic film.

"I spent the entire night not sleeping. Thinking about my race. Looking at it in my dream, in my nightmare. I was sweating and couldn't go to bed, and I was looking at myself running in slow motion going over the hurdle. Sometimes after passing the hurdle I would just fall down in a hole."

Finally, the race arrived. It was hot and humid, and Nawal was still scared. With a middle lane, she crouched down and focused. The gun sounded, and Nawal flew from her blocks. There had been a false start. "I thought it was me false-starting," Nawal said. "I was really disappointed." It wasn't Nawal. She reset herself. The gun went off again. Over the first three hurdles Nawal jumped with her left leg. Then she alternated left and right. *Where are the other ones?* she wondered. *How come I'm the only one running?*

She looked left, then right. The runners were there. They were well behind. As Nawal crossed the finish line, emotions struck her. With a time of 54.61, Nawal had become the first Iowa State track athlete to win Olympic gold. More important, she had become the first Moroccan, African, Arab, and Muslim woman *ever* to win Olympic gold. King Hassan II decreed all girls born on that day be named in Nawal's honor.

Nawal cried as she circled the track for a victory lap.

"I got a lot of support from my father," El Moutawakel said after the race. "He helped me a lot. He did everything he could to make me a champion. He had a lot of hopes for me."

54 Johnny Majors

Before Johnny Majors ever stepped foot on the hard, frozen soil in Ames in the winter of 1967 for his introductory news conference, he was told it was a coaches' graveyard. Then he arrived, and the questions continued. "Why would you come to *Iowa State?*" people asked. It was rather depressing. Here was this young and energetic 32-year-old coach, with his Southern drawl, who wanted to turn the program around. Yet all anybody wondered was why in the world he had chosen this place, in the center of Iowa, to begin his head coaching career.

As the 1968 season approached, Majors picked up a magazine. He flipped through the pages, stopping when he came upon a football article. *Failure Predictions of the Year*, the headline read. Off in the northwest was Washington State. Majors kept scanning the pages. *Failures of the Midwest: Iowa State*, he read. He grabbed a pair of scissors and proceeded to cut out the article. After practice every day around dinnertime before his first season, Majors met with the cheerleaders and, equipped with his cut-out article, went to every sorority and fraternity on campus. As a self-described vagabond preacher, Majors gave his spiel.

"Look, this is what they think about your school! Here's what people think about you in the country!" Majors told them, talking excitedly in his Southern accent while jumbling his words. "We're going to build a football program you can be proud of. We're going to play with *pride* and *enthusiasm*. We're never going to learn to lose! We will *practice* like winners, we will *dress* like winners, and we will *act* like winners and like champions, and then we can eventually *be* champions if we play with pride and enthusiasm and we never give up!"

Majors certainly knew football. "I was taught well by my daddy in high school," he said. He was a punter, passer, runner, and played defense, and Majors' high school teams won 30 of 31 games before he headed off to Tennessee. As a single-wing tailback for the Vols, Majors became a star. He was twice named Most Valuable Player in the Southeastern Conference and garnered All-America honors in 1956, eventually finishing second in the Heisman Trophy race that same year, to Notre Dame's Paul Hornung.

Out of college, Majors stuck around Knoxville, Tennessee, and became a graduate assistant. He eventually became a full-time assistant at Tennessee before moving on to Mississippi State and finally Arkansas before Iowa State came calling in December 1967. After 10 seasons as head coach, Clay Stapleton was stepping down to become athletics director. Majors was the final candidate Iowa State interviewed, but he was the Cyclones' first choice. The program had won two games in each of the previous two seasons, but Majors ultimately signed for $21,000 per season. "Johnny Majors has never known anything but success in athletics," Stapleton said at the time, "and I think he is the ideal man to coach Iowa State football."

The first few seasons took some work, as Iowa State twice won only three games. By the 1970 season, though, Iowa State had filled up Clyde Williams Field for the first time and won five games. It was 1971 when Majors jump-started both his career and Iowa State football.

Already with six wins, Iowa State hosted Oklahoma State on November 20, 1971. The week of the game, the Sun Bowl committee had told Majors if Iowa State beat Oklahoma State, it would get a bowl invitation. The Cyclones had never been to a bowl game before, and there were only 12 that season. If they won, they were in. If they lost, they'd be out.

"I really stressed that big with our players, and that we've got to concentrate," Majors said. "When you're here, you've got to concentrate. I'd never seen a team concentrate more individually in my whole life. It couldn't have been any better under that much pressure."

Before most games, Majors would write key points on the board. On this particular Saturday, he instead posted a sign: *Have a great day. You deserve it.* It was a great day, all right. The Cyclones scored 26 points in the first quarter alone, en route to a 54–0 win, the largest ever against a league opponent. They reached seven wins for the first time since 1960 (they would reach eight the next week) and received an invitation to the Sun Bowl that same night.

Majors took Iowa State to a second consecutive bowl game in 1972 before departing, after five seasons in Ames, for Pittsburgh (where he won a national title), and then Tennessee. He was inducted into the College Football Hall of Fame in 1987.

As the final seconds ticked away on November 20, 1971, against the Cowboys, assistant Joe Avezzano went over to players on the sideline. "You need to ride the coaches off on your shoulders," he told them. When the clock struck zero, Majors was lifted into the air. "That was a very special time," quarterback George Amundson said.

Into the night the band played while fans stayed and cheered. The Cyclones had reached prominence. And that is why Johnny Majors had come to Iowa State.

"People say, 'What was your greatest victory?'" Majors said. "No win in my career was ever bigger in the time and place than that win against Oklahoma State."

55 Triumph and Tragedy

With its newly acquired three-foot trophy packed into the rear compartment of the third and final plane, the excitement was palpable as the last group from the cross country team sped down the runway and into the evening sky as the sun began to set.

Mere hours earlier, the Iowa State women's cross country team had run to surprising success at the NCAA championship in

Milwaukee. The team had arrived hoping for a top-five finish but really wanted at least third place, which would garner it a trophy. That might be pushing it. The team was rather young and inexperienced. When Iowa State arrived on November 23, 1985, it headed straight for the Dretzka Park Golf Course, where coaches had cleared a 5,000-meter path on the snow-covered field. The course would be difficult and the weather worse. Coach Ron Renko provided instruction as his team jogged.

Two days later, on November 25, 1985, a Monday, the group of seven runners lined up with 9,000 spectators scattered across the course. It was 33 degrees and windy. The gun sounded, and the women took off. Finally, one by one, they began to cross the finish line. They had finished rather close together and must have performed decently, they thought. Assistant coach Pat Moynihan, a burly man with a mustache, figured third or fourth. They really wanted that trophy. Still uncertain where they stood, the runners took off for a cooldown. Suddenly one of Renko's friends ran across the snow. He held up two fingers.

"One minute we were all cold," runner Bonnie Sons later told the *Iowa State Daily*, "and the next we weren't." Behind five season's-best times, Iowa State had finished a surprising runner-up. The runners halted their cooldown and sprinted to the clubhouse.

At 3:17 PM, the third and final plane surged down the runway at General Mitchell International Airport in Milwaukee and lifted into the air. Some of the men's team had taken off in the first plane, and a combination of coaches and men's and women's runners got on the second. Pilot Burton Watkins was manning the third plane, and coaches Renko and Moynihan, trainer Stephanie Streit, and runners Susan Baxter, Sheryl Maahs, and Julie Rose giddily climbed aboard. Baxter, Maahs, and Rose had run the fastest times of their lives to help earn the trophy stowed in back.

"We pulled above [the clouds] and you could see this sunset.... And it was *gorgeous*," Sons, who was on the second plane, told the *Daily.* "The sun was out and you just forgot about everything else."

A freezing drizzle had begun not long before the Rockwell Aero Commander took off, but it was in the air. At 5:41 PM, Watkins turned on his radio to talk to the airport tower.

WATKINS: Des Moines. Five eight nine. I seem to be having some real trouble here. Ah, I'm ah...I'm in severe turbulence.

TOWER: Commander five eight niner, Roger. Ah, fly heading three six zero. If able, climb and maintain 3,000 feet.

TOWER: I think he's losing it.

WATKINS: I can't do anything. I'm in the trees now.

Then there was silence.

Only 28 seconds after Watkins had radioed the Des Moines airport tower, the Aero Commander had descended and crashed into the top of an oak tree, flipped over, and started on fire in a Des Moines neighborhood five miles from the airport. The seven aboard had died. Investigators later determined wing icing was to blame.

At the airport the rest of the Iowa State team waited. The third plane was supposed to be 20 minutes behind the second. A half hour passed. They wondered where the plane was. They were excited to see their coaches and teammates. They were excited to celebrate once again with their second-place trophy. Then they heard the news.

Some 5,500 people gathered at Hilton Coliseum for the memorial service. Seven Red Maple trees were planted at Veenker Golf Course, which was used for cross country events at the time. A rock was placed among them listing the names of the lives lost and reading, "We celebrate their talent and ambition which flowed from the excellence of their endeavors. We remember the grace by which they touched our lives."

As the sun sets on that rock, just as it did on that November day, it serves as a reminder. Not of tragedy, but of the triumph of a team and the remembrance of its fallen members.

56 1990 Oklahoma: In Their Own Backyard

History and tradition hit Iowa State like a ton of bricks every year. This was *Oklahoma*. The Sooners hadn't lost to the Cyclones since 1961, and had eked out a 43–40 win the year before. There wasn't much hope in Iowa State ever climbing over the hump to get a win. But when Iowa State went to Norman, Oklahoma, on October 20, 1990, everything changed.

With a brace on the left knee he had injured earlier in the season, Iowa State quarterback Chris Pedersen conducted a 10-play, 80-yard drive capped off by heroics at the goal line. Facing third-and-goal at the 1, the Cyclones offensive line pushed in, and Pedersen stretched his arms as far as they could go over the goal line. "Touchdown Iowa State!" Voice of the Cyclones Pete Taylor said over the radio broadcast. "Pedersen gets in!"

Three Cyclones swarmed Pedersen, who had fallen to the ground in celebration with Iowa State leading 33–31 with just 35 seconds remaining. It was a scene of disbelief as the squad from Ames, who had entered the day as 24-point underdogs, capped off its first win against the Sooners in 29 years. "Now I can die happy," an elated coach Jim Walden said afterward. "This puts me one up on a million coaches who've never been able to do this."

And to think, Walden almost didn't even make the trip. He had woken up Friday morning feeling sick, struggling with a 24-hour flu, and didn't make it to the Cyclones' final practice leading into Saturday's game. His team started the game just as sluggishly. Facing an early 14–0 deficit, it was a muffed punt by OU's Otis Taylor at the Sooners' own 19 that brought Iowa State to life. Three plays later, Pedersen was in the end zone on a quarterback draw.

A big sack on Sooners quarterback Cale Gundy set up Iowa State perfectly. Pedersen pump-faked, rolled to his right on the next play, and found a wide-open Blaise Bryant in the end zone. Touchdown Cyclones. Tied at 14. Oklahoma responded with two touchdowns—one on a Pedersen pick-six—and things appeared as if they were slipping away. It was 28–17 Oklahoma at halftime, and the Sooners were at home.

How could Iowa State climb back in? Bryant didn't return in the second half because of a rib injury. The Cyclones had to look elsewhere. All eyes fell squarely on running back Sherman Williams.

In the fourth quarter, Oklahoma was holding a 31–20 lead. A 23-yard fake punt pass by Marv Seiler to Troy Moore on fourth down kept a crucial 80-yard drive alive, and Williams made the defense pay with a seven-yard touchdown. He threw his hands into the air as he ran off the field, and the Cyclones knew they weren't done quite yet.

After a failed two-point conversion by Iowa State, Oklahoma could all but seal a win with 2:50 remaining when kicker R.D. Lashar trotted on for a 23-yard field goal.

The kick went up…and wide right! The Cyclones took over with some momentum. Iowa State soon faced fourth-and-8 with 1:58 to go, and needed a miracle. On none other than a quarterback draw, Pedersen ran for 20 yards for a first down, keeping hope alive. A 20-yard pass to Chris Spencer and a nine-yard quarterback draw had Iowa State knocking on the door.

Pedersen took it upon himself and finally pushed in with 35 seconds remaining for the final touchdown and a 32–31 lead. Amidst the pandemonium on the sideline, Walden sent out kicker Jeff Shudak for an extra point to give the Cyclones a two-point lead and Oklahoma a chance to win with a field goal. "That was dumb," Walden said later. "We should have gone for two points."

There was no worry in the end, as ISU defenders batted down Gundy's final heave short of the goal line, locking up the win. "The game is over! Iowa State has defeated Oklahoma 33–31!" Taylor shouted. "The Cyclones swarm onto the field! For the first time in 29 years, they have beaten the Sooners and have done it in their own backyard!"

And for Pedersen, the Ankeny native, who had heard stories about Oklahoma players laying down on the sideline in relaxation with their pads off during games against Iowa State in previous years, getting that win in Norman was pretty sweet.

"This win was for last year's Iowa State team, which we felt should have won," Pedersen said afterward, "and for all the other teams that kept getting beat by Oklahoma."

57 Blarge!

Five minutes.

That was how much time separated Iowa State from a chance at greatness. This was the *biggest* game in Iowa State history, and only five minutes stood in the way.

Holy cow, forward Paul Shirley thought, *we might be going to the Final Four.*

To be exact, there were actually 4 minutes, 51 seconds standing between Iowa State and the Final Four on March 25, 2000. That is when Marcus Fizer beat a double-team in the lane at the Palace of Auburn Hills just outside Detroit, some 90 miles southeast of Lansing, Michigan, to give Iowa State a 61–55 lead over Michigan State. The 21,214 fans, most dressed in Michigan State green-and-white, had fallen silent. The Cyclones, with their school-record 32 wins, had held leads with less than five minutes remaining 29 times that season and won each and every single time. "The whole team thought we were in control in the last five minutes," Michael Nurse said later.

Michigan State had already cut Iowa State's lead to one when Fizer took a pass on the right wing just more than one minute later. Shirley, streaking in a straight line from the top of the key down through the middle of the lane, turned his head, caught the pass, and lofted it toward the hoop in one seamless motion as he collided with Charlie Bell, knocking him to the ground.

Swish! Then came the whistle.

The clock froze at 3:43. Shirley clapped as he watched referee Lonnie Dixon call Bell for a block. *Oh, geez,* he thought. *I think I put us up by three and maybe four if I make this free throw.* Suddenly, though, referee Frank Basone rushed over to Dixon. He had seen a charge. *That's insane,* Shirley thought, *there's no way that's really what is going to be called.* Chaos ensued. Crew chief Curtis Shaw huddled the two as the pro-Spartans crowd went wild. *This is going to be clear once they talk about it,* was the next thought that crept into Shirley's head. *Obviously the guy who is calling a charge is an idiot.*

"Well," Iowa State broadcaster Eric Heft said, "is it a block or is it a charge?"

Blarge!

It was both. Officials had ruled a double foul. The basket was erased, and Shirley had instead fouled out. For Shirley, the rest of the game is a fog. Instead of shooting a free throw to put Iowa State up four, he was on the end of the bench. Iowa State got the ball back, but Nurse missed a shot and Michigan State took the lead on the ensuing possession.

"I just remember it being a snowball effect," Fizer said of the plays that followed. "Things happened to take place where you know there's nothing that's going to stop it once the ball gets going. We deserved better than that."

The Cyclones went four minutes, seven seconds without scoring—a span in which Michigan State went on a 12-point run to take a six-point lead—by the time Nurse hit a three-pointer with 44 seconds remaining to draw within 67–64. However, that was Iowa State's final basket.

Michigan State led by five with 9.9 seconds to play when Nurse was tangled in a scramble while going for an offensive rebound. He was called for his fifth foul. Larry Eustachy went ballistic. "That's bullshit!" Eustachy, still fuming from the double foul, screamed. That drew Eustachy his first technical, and another, coupled with an ejection, followed when he pushed past players and into the referee's face. The Spartans connected on all six free throws.

Michigan State 75, Iowa State 64.

"Everyone felt like the game was in our hands, and then before you [knew] it, the whistles start[ed] coming in and we were down and we lost the game," Fizer said. "At the end of the day, that was probably the most disappointing moment of my basketball career."

What happened afterward in the locker room is somewhat uncertain. "I was curled up in paroxysms of tears," Shirley said. Eustachy apologized to his team, but in reality his technicals hadn't made much difference. "It's been a long year, and everybody dreams of getting to the Final Four," Eustachy said afterward. "It just didn't unfold right at the end."

This matchup of No. 1–seeded Michigan State and No. 2–seeded Iowa State could just as well have been a national championship matchup, people said. The luck of the draw instead meant Iowa State was done in the Elite Eight. The Spartans went on to win the title.

"This was the most incredible game I've been involved with since I've been at Michigan State," coach Tom Izzo said. "Both teams battled and battled and battled."

Five minutes. That's how close Iowa State had come to the Final Four.

"We don't feel like we lost to Michigan State," Fizer said more than a decade later. "In 2000 we didn't feel like we lost to Michigan State, and to this day now, 14 years later, we don't feel like we lost to Michigan State."

58 Glen Brand

While he operated as a radioman in Guam during World War II, Glen Brand knew he wanted more. He had joined the US Marine Corps shortly after graduating high school in Clarion, Iowa, but it wasn't until he had been part of the war effort for three years that he realized what was important to him. "There was something better than digging ditches and things like that," Brand said later. "I decided to get an education and become an engineer."

That's not to say an education wasn't important to Brand before he left for the war, but it wasn't his focus. That belonged to wrestling. "By the time I was 10," Brand said, "it was drummed into my head that I had to wrestle." His first cousin, Dale Brand, was an alternate in the 1936 Olympics and coached Glen in high school, but only to modest success. Glen never won a state title and left for the war weighing about 145 pounds.

After three years in the war, Brand returned much bulkier, weighing 200 pounds, but education was his focus. His eventual career as an Olympic gold medalist was not even a glimmer in his eye when he arrived at Iowa State in 1946 to study engineering.

Famed ISU wrestling coach Hugo Otopalik knew the 22-year-old Brand had arrived on campus, and convinced him to watch a practice because of his background. Watching practice turned into *practicing*, which turned into Brand accepting a walk-on spot with the wrestling team. Freshmen were eligible to compete in varsity sports in 1946, giving Brand a chance right away. And boy, did he make the most of it.

Brand went on to win 51 of 54 matches in his Iowa State career, registering 30 pins. He endured two of his losses as a freshman, with the third coming in the NCAA final in 1947 against Joe Scarpello of Iowa. "After Joe beat me," Brand once said, "I spent the whole next year thinking about it. I decided I had wrestled a very dumb match."

All of the work Brand put in over the course of the year paid off. He treated wrestling like it was an engineering project.

"I always went immediately to work in every match. No stalling around," Brand once said. "I knew I was in better condition than the other guy. I wanted him to start expending energy immediately. By the clock, he would be tired, and I wouldn't be."

He went 11–0 in 1948, claiming a Big 7 title while working his way into NCAA contention again. A rematch with Scarpello was looming. This time, it wouldn't be in the finals. Always the tactician, with size and power to back him up, Brand won that rematch with Scarpello and eventually the national championship.

The victory made Brand one of Iowa State's first three-time All-Americans, and he was later named Iowa State's Athlete of the Year after the success of his junior season. But his biggest moment, and one of his proudest, was still to come. It was an Olympic year.

On paper, Brand's road to London was not supposed to be easy, even though he made it look that way once he stepped foot on the mat. He had to win 11 matches to get the coveted Olympic gold medal, and Brand handled the first six. Then came the rubber match with Scarpello. The winner would represent the United States in the Olympics while the other would be an alternate. Spectators were treated to the closest of the three matches, with Brand edging out Scarpello for a spot on the Olympic squad at 174 pounds.

After a close decision and a pin in his first two matches in London, Brand needed just two more wins to reach the pinnacle. Standing in his way was 31-year-old Adil Candemir of Turkey. Wrestling was the national sport in Turkey, and Candemir was one of its most celebrated athletes. After about 12 minutes, the Turkish veteran had enough. Brand picked him up and threw him to his back to move to the finals. "He was done," Brand said. "He was beat physically, mentally, and spiritually."

Brand went on to pin Erik Linden of Sweden to capture the first gold medal ever won by an ISU athlete, and the first Olympic wrestling title for an Iowa school.

"They played the US national anthem and raised the American flag as I was handed my medal in front of 95,000 cheering spectators," Brand said. "As the music played, I got goose bumps. It was the biggest thrill of my entire life."

Brand started 1949, his senior season, 7–0, but an appendectomy ended his collegiate career. After graduation, he founded Brand Hydraulics in Omaha, where he worked until he died at the age of 85 in 2008. Brand has been honored by the Iowa Hall of Fame, the National Wrestling Hall of Fame, and the Helms Hall of Fame.

"[Enrolling at Iowa State] was the best thing that ever happened to me," Brand said.

59 Jamaal Tinsley

The legend goes that Jamaal Tinsley, playing at Harlem's famous Rucker Park, once bounced the ball through his defender's legs with his left hand, brought it back with his right, and proceeded to hit a trey as the defender fell. And maybe that would be thought of as nothing more than a fictional tale had Tinsley not continued to exploit defenders for years to come.

When Tinsley arrived in Ames in the fall of 1999, Iowa State legend Gary Thompson sat and watched practices. Tinsley would put the ball through his legs. When a defender was close, he'd shake him and drive. When his defender sagged, he'd hit a shot.

"Tinsley was something else with the ball," Thompson said. "He could handle a basketball better than anybody here I can remember. You'd say, 'Did I really see that?'"

"Globetrotters have nothing on him at all," added broadcaster Eric Heft. "I've never seen anybody handle the ball better than Jamaal Tinsley."

Tinsley's story begins at PS 305 court in a desolate schoolyard in the middle of Brooklyn's Bedford-Stuyvesant. Ballers called it the Cage. Tinsley called it home. It was there where Tinsley would ball late into the night. It was there where he perfected his crossover, showed off his ball handling, and broke ankles. It was there where he earned the nickname Mel-Mel the Abuser because, he would say later, "I score whenever I want to." It was also from there, the place where Tinsley had crafted his game, that he needed to escape.

When Tinsley was six his father died of the flu. His stepfather passed away later that year. His mother was left to raise Tinsley and his seven siblings inside their cramped apartment. Tinsley attended three different high schools and left all three, never graduating. When he called it quits with school, his focus turned to basketball full-time. He spent his time on the streets and on the court, ultimately joining Brooklyn USA, an AAU team. During a tournament in Las Vegas, Tinsley impressed the recruiter at Mount San Jacinto Community College. California junior colleges didn't require a high school diploma or GED, so Tinsley went west.

The adjustment took time. Tinsley hadn't ever played organized basketball, he didn't understand the importance of practice, and he didn't know structure. In time, he learned. He averaged 22 points per game in his second season and became a two-time All-California Community College selection. Then Division I schools started calling left and right. Tinsley visited just one. On February 8, 1999, Tinsley watched as Iowa State was beaten 77–61 by Missouri in Ames. "You need guards so bad," Tinsley told coach Larry Eustachy. "I'm coming here."

He almost didn't stay long. He hated Eustachy's preseason practices and spent countless hours in his office. He packed his bags and almost left. Eventually he figured it out. Iowa State had been .500 the season before, but Tinsley was the point guard it needed. That loss Tinsley watched on his recruiting visit? It would be the last he would see at Hilton Coliseum.

With Tinsley as its floor general, Iowa State began to take off in 1999–00. Over the course of Tinsley's two seasons in Ames, the Cyclones went 34–0 at home. Tinsley and Marcus Fizer created a one-two punch that was difficult to counter as the Cyclones stormed to a Big 12 regular-season title in 2000 and then won the postseason conference tournament. In the Sweet 16 against UCLA, Tinsley fell one rebound shy of a triple-double as he scored 14 points, dished out 11 assists, and grabbed nine boards to send Iowa State to the Elite Eight.

Tinsley played unafraid. He once called Kansas' Allen Fieldhouse "just another gym" and then backed it up by winning there in back-to-back seasons. "He was pretty gifted, didn't back down from anyone," teammate Paul Shirley said. Behind Tinsley, and his career-high 29 points in the 2001 regular-season finale against Nebraska, the Cyclones clinched a second consecutive regular-season Big 12 title.

After growing up in Brooklyn's Bedford-Stuyvesant neighborhood and attending junior college in California, Jamaal Tinsley wowed onlookers with his dazzling ball-handling abilities during a two-year Iowa State career in which he acted as the Cyclones' floor general while guiding them through one of the best stretches in program history. (Photo courtesy of Iowa State Athletics)

"When it comes time to really, really put the hammer down and win the game, I have never had anybody close to his ability," Eustachy said after the second title. "He never comes up bad in these situations, and that's the mark of a champion."

By the time Tinsley's second season came to an end, he was named Big 12 Player of the Year, earned All-America honors, was named first-team All–Big 12 for the second time, and was runner-up for Associated Press National Player of the Year. He set Iowa State single-season records (which still stand) for assists (244) and steals (98) and became the first player in program history to lead the team in scoring, assists, steals, and blocks.

"I haven't seen every game that has ever been played here, but I don't know who ever in the history of Iowa State has impacted winning more than Jamaal Tinsley," Eustachy said after one game. "Some guys melt when it gets tough, and he just gets tougher."

That came from PS 305 court where, from dawn until dusk, people would come watch Tinsley ball while he crafted his game. "I would just try moves, try moves, and try moves," Tinsley once said. "I did things with the ball no one had ever seen."

And because he left the Cage behind, Tinsley became more than a playground legend. He became one of the best ballers in Iowa State history.

60 Mike "Mongo" Stensrud

The stunt had worked, and Mike Stensrud was running untouched and freely into the backfield, his eyes locked on Oklahoma's soon-to-be Heisman-winning running back Billy Sims. *Boom!* The monstrous 6'5", 270-pound defensive tackle struck as Sims took the handoff, knocking him back and jarring the ball loose.

Then there was nothing.

The man who had garnered the nickname Mongo from teammates lay on the grass dazed and confused. He had delivered such a punishing hit on Sims, with so much force and so much vengeance, that he had rendered himself unconscious. Stensrud rolled over on the ground just in time to watch Sims, apparently unaffected, pick up the ball and run for a 53-yard touchdown.

"That one individual hit, that was the worst one," said Stensrud, who went out so quickly he didn't see the fumble until a later film session in that 1978 season. "That was the only time I was ever knocked out. I just sat there dazed. I got my wits about me pretty quick, but it hurt."

More often than not during Stensrud's days at Iowa State, the hurt was being put on somebody else. A farm boy from Lake Mills, Iowa, Stensrud was the 1974 Class 2-A heavyweight wrestling champion and, of course, he played football.

From the moment Iowa State coach Earle Bruce saw Stensrud play, he knew he wanted him. Stensrud's brother, Maynard, was already on the team in Ames, and his girlfriend was there, too. So he made the trip south, picking Iowa State instead of Nebraska, Minnesota, and Iowa.

"I was so happy when we got him, because secretly I thought he was the best tackle in the country when I looked at him," Bruce said. "There was no doubt he was."

Stensrud stuck out from the outset of his arrival. He was massive and athletic with quick-twitch muscles, and he immediately started on the defensive line and was named the Big 8 Newcomer of the Year at the end of his freshman campaign. During that first season, Stensrud also picked up another title.

The night before every game—home or away—the team would gather to watch a movie. Before the Colorado game his freshman season, the pregame movie was *Blazing Saddles*, a film featuring actor Alex Karras as a character named Mongo. The character was a big, dumb cowboy who sat on a bull, taking down horses with a single blow and lighting his cigar not with a match, but by sticking his face into the fire. Offensive lineman Randy Young placed the moniker on Stensrud.

Stensrud wasn't dumb, but he admitted the name did sort of fit. The prime example came one December night when he and five friends gathered on the eighth floor in his Wilson Hall dorm room, located above the concrete entrance. It was around Christmas, and nearly all the students were home for break, but he and his friends were drinking, and Stensrud had this bowling ball.

"You know, I think this bowling ball would be like a Super Ball," he told his friends. "I think it would bounce."

So Stensrud took the screen off his window, sent two friends downstairs to make sure nobody would be hit walking out, and for the next two hours they tossed the ball out the window and watched it bounce as high as six floors up.

"I was a jackass," Stensrud admitted. "I really was."

Other superlatives were used to describe him on the football field. "He could be *mean*," Bruce said. Stensrud wasn't a dirty player—he didn't accrue any personal foul penalties, and he didn't step on hands or pinch in the pile—but he was mean in the sense of the punishment he sometimes delivered. He had a forearm shiver that jarred face masks loose, and his hits were often cringe-worthy.

"He was a crazy son of a bitch, I'll tell you that," Iowa State broadcaster Eric Heft said. "If he wanted to make a play, there weren't many offensive linemen who were going to keep him from making that play."

Then there was the other part of Bruce's description. Stensrud *could* be mean. Stensrud said he didn't always take football seriously. Of his freshman year, he said, "I didn't care if I was playing." He would have rather been farming. For the next few years

Stensrud got by mostly on pure talent until his senior season—after his first son was born—when Bruce called him out in the *Des Moines Register* and it sparked him.

Stensrud, who later used his newfound passion in an 11-year NFL career, anchored an Iowa State defense that went to back-to-back bowl games in 1977 and 1978, two seasons in which he was named an All-American.

In his four seasons at Iowa State, Stensrud racked up 306 tackles and one hit that remains a vivid memory—at least after he regained consciousness.

"When you look on the highlight film, Mike would be in the middle of it because he made those kind of explosive plays," fellow defensive lineman Tom Randall said. "He was just so amazing."

61 Tom Randall

As Earle Bruce sat down to watch recruiting footage on 8mm film, the tape kept cutting in and out. He evaluated the flickering images as best he could, but while he was watching one particular player, he'd had enough.

"I don't know," Bruce told assistant Randy Hart. "Let's just go see him."

So Bruce and Hart made the drive to Mason City to watch Tom Randall, who was in the middle of basketball season. Randall didn't think much of football, having only played on varsity as a high school senior. An injury on the fourth day of practice as a sophomore and playing junior varsity as a junior didn't help him develop a love for the sport.

Small college basketball was ultimately the end goal, but as he started getting more attention on the gridiron in October of his senior season, Randall ended up changing his mind and opening up to the idea of playing football after high school. During basketball season, the phone at the Randall household began to ring more often.

"Why are these people calling about *football?*" Randall's mom would ask.

At Mason City's basketball game with Bruce and Hart in attendance, Randall was more active than any player on the court. He fought for everything he got in that game, making an impression on the Iowa State coaches. Bruce and Hart walked out of the northern Iowa gym that night trying to decide what to make of what they had seen.

"I don't know," Hart said. "I don't know."

"I know!" Bruce shot back. "Take him! Take him! He's going to be a good player."

Bruce was right. Iowa State was about to get a player who would become one of the best defensive tackles in program history.

Randall had two options as to where he might go: Iowa State or Iowa. The Cyclones' advantage in the end? It was as simple as Iowa finishing 0–11 during Randall's senior year and him seeing a program on the rise in Ames.

As Randall entered his sophomore season with the Cyclones, Bruce paid him a visit in his dorm room. He had a proposition for his defensive lineman that was immediately met with resistance: Bruce wanted Randall to switch sides of the ball and play on the offensive line.

"No, I'm going to play defense," the headstrong sophomore replied. "I can play defense."

"You're not an All–Big 8 defensive player," Bruce said.

"I'll show you," Randall retorted. "I'm going to be an All–Big 8 defensive player."

"You can do that on offense," Bruce said.

Randall got his wish and stayed on defense. That stubborn nature he showed with his head coach served him well as he started developing into a capable Big 8 defensive player. Randall certainly had natural ability and athleticism, but teammates noticed a work ethic that you couldn't help but admire.

Alongside fellow defensive tackle Mike Stensrud, Randall became a starter as a junior and senior and was at the front of two of the best defenses in Iowa State history. The Cyclones posted three eight-win seasons from 1976 to 1978, with Randall being one of the cogs in the first two.

The staunchness of the defensive front of Iowa State was all about the mind-set. Nobody was going to outwork them in the weight room, on the practice field, or in games. Backing down was not an option. That way of doing things trickled down from Bruce, who was as tough as they come. It made his players—largely Iowa-born guys—appreciate even more what hard work could get them.

"We didn't out-talent many teams, but all of us, he just made us rock hard and extremely tough," Randall said. "We had a bunch of guys that liked to hit and a bunch of guys that wouldn't back down from a fight."

That sense of confidence led to arguably one of the best stretches of football in Iowa State history, and an opportunity for Randall beyond the Cyclones. He was a seventh-round pick by the Dallas Cowboys in 1978—where he played in the Super Bowl—and spent a year with the Houston Oilers in 1979.

When Randall got to Dallas as a rookie in '78, the Cowboys—ironically—switched him to play on their offensive line. Decades later, Randall and Bruce met again and reminisced about that argument they had in a college dorm room those many years earlier.

"Well, Coach," Randall said. "I guess both of us were right."

62 Larry Eustachy

There may be no better way to describe the relationship between Larry Eustachy and his players than that of love and hate.

Eustachy could just as well have been a drill sergeant as he was a basketball coach. There is no plausible way to sum up through words, apparently, just what a Larry Eustachy practice was. There were the three-hour practices, the entire time spent rebounding. There was the five-man weave drill that often took one hour because each time a player messed up, they'd restart. That drill oftentimes ended with suicide sprints. The list goes on.

"Coach told us we had to cut the fat and get down to the lean meat," forward Martin Rancik once told *Sports Illustrated*. "He's like a drill sergeant who tries to break you down, and you keep going only by telling yourself, 'There's no way I'm going to let this guy win.'"

Eustachy's coaching style was a combination of bits and pieces he picked up along the way, beginning as a prep standout and captain at Arcadia High School in California. Eustachy eventually played at Citrus College and then Division II Chico State before being cut. His coaching career began at age 22 when he was hired on as an assistant at Citrus. He went from Citrus to Mississippi State to Idaho to Utah and finally Ball State as an assistant. Then came his head coaching break.

In 1990 Eustachy was hired as the coach at Idaho, which he led to three consecutive winning seasons before moving on to Utah State. There he posted five more winning seasons. So when Tim Floyd left Iowa State for the NBA in 1998, he recommended his good friend Eustachy, who had coached under him while at Idaho. Larry got the job.

Eustachy coined his coaching style "Larry," meaning "All my players have to buy into Larry," he told *Sports Illustrated*. Not everyone bought in immediately. The initial season at Iowa State was a bit rocky as four players quit, forcing the Cyclones to practice with eight scholarship players. Eustachy had never posted a losing record as a head coach before, and didn't in that 1998–99 season as the Cyclones finished .500. But the adjustment took time.

One day shortly after Eustachy's arrival, Iowa State broadcaster Eric Heft saw forward Paul Shirley at a football game. Shirley had felt Floyd's practices were somewhat difficult.

"So how's that break from Floyd going?" Heft asked.

"This is *way* fucking worse," Shirley responded.

People didn't quite understand until they saw it for themselves. Shirley told his family about the arduous practices, and they shrugged it off. "Oh, yeah, I'm sure it's hard," they said. Floyd's practices had been difficult in the sense of length. Eustachy's were no match. When the Cyclones finished one of those one-hour five-man weave drills, with Shirley's brother in attendance, there was shock. "I didn't know that you meant it was, like…*fact*," his brother said.

"The drills they used to do were just killer drills," Heft said. "The ball goes into the stands, you're diving into the seats at Hilton to get the ball to get that possession so you can get your ass off the floor. It was brutal. He was tough."

McDonald's All-American Marcus Fizer was already in town when Eustachy arrived, and by his second season, Eustachy had convinced Jamaal Tinsley to come run the team. After some early troubles during the famed early season boot camp—Tinsley had packed his bags at one point—the team began to buy in. Eustachy's practices sucked, sure, but the team appeared to be going places.

The players began to play *for* Larry.

He had this rule in games: If you fell or hit the ground and weren't up in two seconds, you were coming out. If there was one

The notoriously fiery Larry Eustachy, left, disputes a call to referee Sam Croft on February 9, 2000, during the first half of the Cyclones' matchup against Missouri in Columbia. (Photo courtesy of AP Images/L.G. Patterson)

certainty, it was that Iowa State became one of the toughest teams around.

"You had guys that didn't want to disappoint him and definitely didn't want to come out of the game," Fizer said. "He demanded greatness, and the last thing I wanted to do, or anyone on the team ever wanted to do, was to let him down."

In only his second season, Eustachy was named National Coach of the Year after the Cyclones won a school-record 32 games, both the regular and postseason Big 12 titles, and advanced to the Elite Eight. The next season, Iowa State repeated as Big 12 champions.

Controversy eventually ended and marred Eustachy's tenure when alcoholism gave way. "We've all had our mistakes, we've all had our ups and downs," Fizer said, "but there's no questioning his leadership and his coaching ability." In five seasons at Iowa State, Eustachy won 101 games and produced one of the top stretches in program history.

"Watching practice was tough, *tough* on me to see those guys dying out there," Heft said. "Larry is one of those people that you play for and survive. You respect that, because you know what you had to sacrifice to make that happen."

63 Let's Dance

There are banners at Hilton Coliseum that list, sequentially, the years in which Iowa State has advanced to the NCAA tournament. Each of those appearances is honored with its own individual banner hanging from a concrete wall inside the team's practice facility across town. The banners certainly signify the accomplishment of reaching March Madness, but they cannot possibly put each moment in perspective. Nor can these words.

"The tournament is where you want to be," guard DeAndre Kane said in 2014 at his first-ever NCAA tournament. "[It's] where stars are born—stars are made—and it's a fun time."

When David Barrett wrote the lyrics to "One Shining Moment" after watching Larry Bird play on television from a bar in East Lansing, Michigan, in 1986, he was on to something. The NCAA tournament is not simply about banners. The Big Dance is about the journey of the season. It is about the players and their dreams. It is about those shining moments.

Moment No. 1 must be Selection Sunday, because without it, well, there are no moments. "That thing is way too much suspense," Dustin Hogue said. "It's kind of scary." Yet following a long, suspenseful season, there is no greater reward than reaching the NCAA tournament. When Iowa State pops onto your television screen and into the bracket, it's time. Let's dance.

With game after game showcasing the best college basketball has to offer, it would be difficult to argue against a better span in the sporting world than the Thursday through Sunday that concludes the first weekend of March Madness. Sure, you can hide the browser window at work and peep for updates or set up shop with multiple televisions, but nothing beats the experience of going dancing yourself. The NCAA tournament has an aura about it that can't be described. There is a feeling of new life. There is a feeling of hope and excitement. From the open shootarounds to the jam-packed arenas, there is nothing like catching a college basketball game played on hardwood with the NCAA blue outlining the court.

And who could forget the moments?

"One Shining Moment," the marquee song that concludes March Madness each season, didn't assume its role until the 1987 national championship, but had it been used one season earlier, there is little doubt the Cyclones would have made the debut montage. When Iowa State faced Miami of Ohio in the 1986 NCAA tournament, Jeff Hornacek hit a 26-foot jumper at the buzzer in overtime to give the Cyclones their first NCAA tournament win in the modern era. Hornacek's inbounds pass and Elmer Robinson's ensuing dunk in the next round helped down Michigan and send Iowa State to its first Sweet 16.

Through the years, there have been many other shining moments. In 1992 Fred Hoiberg caught a full-court pass and slammed home an eventual two-point victory against UNC Charlotte with a dunk. In 1997 Klay Edwards knocked off No. 10 Cincinnati when he drained a game-winning bucket with 32.4 seconds to play. In 2014 Kane hit a layup with 1.6 seconds remaining to send Iowa State to the Sweet 16 and the World's Most Famous Arena.

If you're going to see the good moments, there's a chance you'll see the gut-wrenching ones too. After Iowa State knocked off Cincinnati in '97, it suffered a heartbreaking 74–73 overtime loss to UCLA in the next round. In the 2000 Elite Eight, the Cyclones were five minutes from the Final Four before Michigan State surged to a win. In 2013 Ohio State's Aaron Craft provided a gut punch with a game-winning three-pointer.

Through the wins and losses are the banners. Within each individual year that marks them, there is much more to be gleaned and much more to be experienced if you just go dancing.

"It's a childhood dream," Naz Long said in 2014 following the Sweet 16. "You've got to cherish these moments, man. These moments are unforgettable."

64 Jim Doran

Consider first that Jim Doran was all of 175 pounds, and your eyebrows most likely raise when that name and the words *All-American* are thrust together in the same sentence. The odds were certainly stacked against him. Then consider this pertinent piece of information: Doran never played one snap of high school football. You could say the lightweight from Beaver, Iowa, faced a proverbial fourth-and-long.

It wasn't necessarily that Doran didn't *want* to play football, but he didn't have much choice. Growing up in Beaver during the '40s (population 126 in 1940), Doran had 11 boys in his entire school and just four in his class. So he settled for playing basketball and baseball. Some people said Doran was too slow to play college football, but when he arrived at Buena Vista College in 1947, after a stint in the navy during World War II, he gave it a shot anyway. Despite being scrawny, Doran was turned into a tackle and played on the B team. The next season, he transferred to Iowa State.

"The hard part was getting the coaches to look at you," Doran once told Buck Turnbull of the *Des Moines Register.* "I had good speed and won the wind sprints, or they might not ever have taken a look at me."

Doran saw limited action in his initial season in Ames, but by the time the 1949 season rolled around, he was ready to burst onto the scene at receiver. In a game against No. 3 Oklahoma, Doran caught eight passes for 203 yards, including an 87-yard reception, setting a then-collegiate record for receiving yards in a game. The record stood in Iowa State history for 34 years (it's now tied at No. 3). With the help of Doran, Iowa State finished 5–3–1 that season. During his senior season, the production from Doran continued.

He strung together three consecutive 100-yard games (still tied for No. 2) and reeled in three touchdown catches in a game against Missouri (now tied at No. 2).

By the time his Iowa State career came to an end, Doran's name sat atop nearly every receiving category in both Big 7 and program history. He caught 79 passes for 1,410 yards and 10 touchdowns during his three seasons at Iowa State, earning All–Big 7 honors twice and being named an All-American in 1950.

"Jim had great speed," former lineman Lowell Titus once said. "He also had great hands."

After the Detroit Lions selected Doran in the fifth round of the 1951 NFL Draft, they slotted him into their lineup not on offense, but on defense. Doran became a defensive lineman, and in 1952 he was named team MVP. During an 11-year career, Doran won NFL championships three times with the Lions (1952, 1953, and 1957) and later made the Pro Bowl with the Cowboys (1960).

The defining moment of Doran's career came in 1953. The Lions had reached the NFL championship for the second consecutive season, and while Doran wasn't supposed to play offense, he switched sides early in the first quarter after tight end Leon Hart injured his knee.

Entering that game Doran had caught only six passes during the 1953 season under similar circumstances. After switching sides, he kept telling quarterback Bobby Layne he could get behind his defender. Suddenly, Detroit trailed Cleveland 16–10, from their own 20-yard line as time wound down. Layne began looking Doran's way. Doran caught a pass for a 17-yard gain and then another for 18 yards. The Lions were then 33 yards out.

"Can you still beat that feller?" Layne asked.

"Just throw it," Doran said. "I'll beat him."

Doran lined up, got behind the defender, and the ball came his way. "Jimmy Doran don't tell lies," Layne said afterward. "If he says he can get deep, you better get him the ball." The kid from small-town Iowa, who hadn't even played high school football, watched as the pass wobbled toward him. He caught it and took it in for the championship-clinching touchdown.

65 Back-to-Back Big 12 Titles

Iowa State had already shocked the collective basketball world when it burst onto the scene by winning the Big 12 crown in 2000, but surely that luck was about to run thin one season removed from those triumphant times.

All-American Marcus Fizer had declared early for the NBA Draft. Gone, too, from the previous season's Big 12 championship team were cogs Michael Nurse and Stevie Johnson. The Cyclones still had valuable pieces, to be sure, but certainly not enough to win a second consecutive conference title in 2001, right? That's what most figured as Iowa State was slotted fifth in the preseason Big 12 poll.

The start of conference play didn't help quell those beliefs. Iowa State began Big 12 action 1–2 in 2001, but the record was not indicative of the play. Both losses came in hard-fought overtime games, including a Big 12–record quadruple overtime loss to Missouri.

Apparently that loss helped stoke a fire in the Iowa State team. The Cyclones won 10 consecutive conference games from that point on, including five road games, both school records for conference winning streaks. Iowa State was a different team from the one that had preceded it but was nonetheless a veteran group with four of its five starters being seniors. Of course, there was also Jamaal Tinsley.

Twice is Nice

Three times, Iowa State faced double-digit deficits. Three times, Fred Hoiberg's squad was on the ropes with the possibility of being bounced from the Big 12 tournament dangerously close.

Iowa State collected its first Big 12 Championship under Fred Hoiberg in 2014, and the road to defending the title for the second-seeded Cyclones proved to be as curvy as ever in 2015. Double-digit comebacks against Texas, Oklahoma, and Kansas eventually gave Iowa State its second straight Big 12 title and punched a fourth straight ticket to the NCAA tournament.

"You tell me, have we changed the culture or what?" Georges Niang wondered as confetti rained down on the Sprint Center floor in Kansas City. "I like to think so, too. These fans have come out and done a good job of supporting us and I can't thank them enough."

For three consecutive days, Cardinal and Gold apparel filled the Power & Light District and covered the stands in "Hilton South," perhaps making its biggest presence in Iowa State's win against Texas. A buzzer-beating jumper by Monte Morris sealed the first-round win, sending the dominant ISU crowd into a frenzy.

Once again down double digits against Oklahoma in the semifinals, a missed OU layup at point blank range in the waning seconds sent Iowa State to the championship. And trailing by 17 points to regular season champ Kansas in the second half there, another patented comeback gave the Cyclones back-to-back Big 12 postseason crowns for the first time ever.

"To do something like we did in this tournament just shows the world and everything about life that nothing is over until it's over," said guard Naz Long. "We just showed grit."

Iowa State's Big 12 title in 2015 was the first back-to-back championship run since the Cyclones won the conference regular season titles in 2000–01. Three wins against NCAA tournament teams in three days told Hoiberg all he needed to know.

"That's the sign of true team, and a good team, is you can handle that type of adversity," Hoiberg said. "It starts with your players."

Without Tinsley (and Martin Rancik), that 10-game winning streak may not have advanced far at all. The Cyclones' streak was sitting at just one as they trailed by one point in Lincoln, Nebraska, with 0.7 seconds remaining. Tinsley threw a perfect inbounds pass to Rancik for a layup and a 60–59 victory. Iowa State twice trumped Kansas (No. 5 and No. 6) during the streak before it eventually came to an end in the third-to-last regular-season game.

Entering the 2000–01 season, Iowa State had once—in 1943–44 and 1944–45—won back-to-back conference titles, but never outright, as it shared the former with Oklahoma. On March 3, 2001, with three conference losses, Iowa State hosted Nebraska at Hilton Coliseum with a chance to make history. Nebraska led midway through the second half before Tinsley took over. He scored 23 of his career-high 29 points in the second period, including 10 in the final three minutes. "Jamaal Tinsley putting on a clinic!" Voice of the Cyclones Pete Taylor called out in the waning minutes.

For the first time in program history, Iowa State had won outright conference titles in consecutive seasons.

"When you think about it, it's absolutely amazing what's happened on this court the last two years. It's staggering," coach Larry Eustachy said after the win. "Just look at the teams below us in our conference. You're talking about a major, major powerhouse conference. And we've been on top of this league twice now for the last two years."

During that 2001 season, the Cyclones finished runner-up in program history only to the 2000 team in both conference wins (13) and overall wins (25). Tinsley helped Iowa State take the Big 12 Player of the Year honors for the second consecutive season as he became the first player in program history to lead the team in scoring, assists, steals, and blocks. Eustachy was named the Big 12 Coach of the Year for the second straight year.

"Marcus Fizer, probably the greatest player in Iowa State history, left, and we were still able to win the Big 12 championship," Paul Shirley said after the Cyclones clinched the title. "I think that's a credit to Coach and how he has gotten us ready to play."

When all was said and done, the Cyclones lost their final two games of that 2001 season, including a first-round NCAA tournament exit following a loss to Hampton. Yet that team was one of the best ever, and capped arguably the best stretch in program history.

"This is a damn good team, one of the best that ever stepped foot in Iowa," Eustachy said when the season ended. "It didn't go right at the end, and it's too bad, but they've got the heart of a lion and they need to be thought of that way as it goes down in history. I'll remember them as league champions."

That's back-to-back league champions.

"There was never any doubt," Tinsley said. "We knew we could do it."

66 Earle Bruce

Nothing was going right. The offense was screwing up in spring practice, and Iowa State coach Earle Bruce was sick of it. He had seen all he wanted to that day. Bruce's emotions took over, and he started punching himself with both hands. Back and forth his fists collided with his cheeks, before he finally took off in a sprint. He dove into a cluster of bushes on the west side of the Cyclones' practice field, not wanting to come back out. "Get back to practice!" Bruce hollered, out of view of his players.

Nobody on the team knew exactly what was going on, but they *did* know the personality of their coach. "He was *so* passionate about football that sometimes it got away from him," Mike Stensrud recalled.

It was that passion, and overall toughness, that made Bruce the kind of coach he was. His toughness was his trademark, which was something he honed at Ohio State as a player and assistant under legendary coach Woody Hayes in the early 1950s. He returned to Ohio State as a full-fledged assistant from 1966 to 1971. In 1972 he became the head coach at the University of Tampa, taking the Spartans to a 10–2 record and a berth in the Tangerine Bowl.

That stint at Tampa was short-lived. Johnny Majors was on his way out at Iowa State, ready to take the job at Pittsburgh, leaving ISU athletics director Lou McCullough looking for a replacement while the Cyclones played in the Liberty Bowl in Memphis. McCullough and Bruce were very close, going back to their days when both were assistant coaches under Hayes at Ohio State, so McCullough called his friend for an interview. Bruce initially wanted to pass. *I'll be in the hunt for Michigan State or in the Big Ten*, he thought.

"You're coming to Iowa State, buddy," McCullough said over the phone. "You're coming to Iowa State."

"Oh, I am?" Bruce questioned.

Well, he really *was* coming, it just wasn't given to the public right away. *Bruce Quits as Tampa's Coach*, read the headline of the *Des Moines Register Peach*. A press conference was called for 10:00 AM on January 3, 1973, as McCullough was ready to introduce a new coach. But it was only a strong *assumption* that man would be Bruce. Tampa had acknowledged that Bruce resigned his post at the school and assumed he was going to Iowa State, but McCullough was dead silent on the subject.

"It's just like recruiting a football player," McCullough told the *Register*. "Until you know you have him, it's best not to say anything."

Bruce was ultimately introduced to the public that day as the Cyclones' coach, conveying the importance he placed on recruiting and winning, "with discipline, hard work, and a lot of respect for each other."

In that first season in 1973, Iowa State finished 4–7, losing four games by a combined 13 points. Two more 4–7 seasons followed, and had some questioning if Bruce was the guy to lead the Cyclones to greener pastures. During the 1975 season finale loss to Oklahoma State, fans put up signs around Cyclone Stadium. *Goodbye, Earle*, some read. *Get the hell out of here*, said others.

"I thought, *Holy hell, maybe [I'm not] supported*," Bruce remembered later. "*I ought to get a couple more [supporters]*."

Bruce *was* supported, however, by the university president and McCullough. And in 1976, he led the charge for one of Iowa State's most successful stretches in program history. The Cyclones finished 8–3 in 1976, '77, and '78, and Bruce was named Big 8 Coach of the Year in '76 and took Iowa State to bowl games in the subsequent two seasons.

After Hayes was fired by Ohio State in 1978, Bruce's name was an obvious one to come up as his replacement. By that time, though, Bruce wasn't so sure he was ready to move on from Ames. "I liked the town, I liked the people, I thought we could really build something here," Bruce said. It was because McCullough never made a strong push to retain Bruce at Iowa State that he decided to follow the tough act in Columbus and coach the Buckeyes. "You're going to Ohio State," McCullough repeatedly told him.

Bruce left Ames with a 36–32 record with the Cyclones and remains the only coach to move on with a winning record at Iowa State. Now well into retirement from coaching, Bruce hasn't lost that same fire and passion that drove him in his youth.

"If I was in a dark alley I wouldn't mind having Coach Bruce with me, because we'd figure out some way to get out of there," former player Tom Randall said. "He was a fighter."

67 Bill Bergan

Bill Bergan stood before a crowd at the podium bearing the I-State logo, completely humbled. Just behind him to his left stood a towering bronze statue in his likeness hoisting a Big 8 Conference championship trophy.

It was November 2012, at the dedication of the Bill and Karen Bergan Track, the newest Iowa State facility, that Bergan spoke about the turns his career had taken to reach that moment. Bringing the ISU track and field and cross country programs out of the depths certainly wasn't an easy task.

"I hope that all the athletes that I coached over the years, when they see this, they see what they did and what they accomplished," Bergan said that day.

And what Bergan accomplished as the head coach of the Cyclones men's track and field and cross country programs was quite a bit. During his 23-year coaching career at Iowa State, Bergan led his teams to 25 Big 8 Conference team championships and two national titles. The success under Bergan was unprecedented, as Iowa State lacked much tradition prior to his arrival.

Bergan grew up in Cedar Falls, Iowa, and went on to attend the University of Northern Iowa, where he lettered in track and cross country. After college he coached six seasons at Waterloo Columbus High School before arriving in Ames.

Bergan started as Iowa State's head cross country coach and assistant track and field coach in 1971, without much history to the program he was taking over. Iowa State had finished last or next-to-last the previous 21 years in men's track and field and hadn't won a conference title in cross country in 40 years. But Bergan was determined to make a swift change.

Three years after Bergan got to Ames, he ended the long championship drought by leading the men's cross country team to the 1974 Big 8 title. After becoming head men's track and field coach in 1976, he again took the cross country team to a league title, winning the 1981 conference championship. A winning culture had to be established, and the runners readily bought into it.

"You're always shooting for championships, always trying to do better," Bergan once said. "The most rewarding part of coaching is helping young people fulfill their dreams. That gives you a real feeling of accomplishment."

Under Bergan's tutelage, the Cyclones won the Big 8 cross country championship in 10 of 14 seasons. But his legacy was solidified in 1989 and 1994 when he led the Iowa State men's cross country team to national championships, and he took them to runner-up finishes in 1990 and '91.

It was Bergan who was one of the first coaches in the NCAA to begin foreign recruiting for his runners. When Iowa State won the men's cross country national championship in 1989, four runners were from England, two were from Kenya, and one each were from Ireland and Belgium. The success of the decade leading to that championship allowed Bergan to make an impression internationally.

"At this level of competition you can't just limit your recruiting to Iowa and the surrounding states," Bergan said. "We're just fortunate we've been able to establish a name for ourselves."

While Bergan's direction left a legacy in the Iowa State record book, the physical representation of his work can also still be found in Ames. He was instrumental in building the ISU Cross Country Course, which hosted its first NCAA Division I Cross Country Championship in 1995.

Bergan's runners achieved All-American status 110 times and won 163 individual Big 8 titles. He retired from coaching in 1996 and was inducted into the ISU Hall of Fame in 2001.

68 Ed Bock

Ed Bock stood at the line of scrimmage with open arms, awaiting the hit from Nebraska's Sam Francis. It was Bock's sophomore season in 1936, and he had already established himself as one of the toughest, most tenacious players on the Iowa State roster. This instance proved it.

As Bock prepared to make the tackle, Francis lowered his shoulder and...*boom!* The blow was so strong that it knocked three of Bock's front teeth right out of his mouth. It's the kind of hit that would stop most in their tracks. But not Ed.

"The college decided to replace my teeth at the end of the year, so I chewed up some wax and I molded some fake teeth," Bock said later. "When I smiled or talked, people really didn't know they were fake."

Ed even wore the fake teeth he fashioned during games and played with a special face mask, seeing it as an opportunity for Iowa State's benefit. In a later game against Kansas State, Bock was again hit by a running back for a sizable gain. As he lay on the turf, Ed spit his wax teeth onto the ground, pleading with the referee, who tossed his yellow flag into the air. A 15-yard penalty for unnecessary roughness was called, all because Bock had spit his teeth, much to the amusement of teammates.

"Ed played so hard he lost his teeth on several occasions," Everett Kischer once said. "We always teased him that he spent more time looking for his teeth than he did in the huddle."

Bock's contributions to Iowa State athletics were more than just gimmicks, though. He developed a reputation as an exemplary guard and a hard-hitting tackler. Growing up and playing in Fort

Dodge, Iowa, and then one year at Fort Dodge Junior College, Bock made the trek to play in Ames in 1936.

Platoon football had not yet become the standard. Conditioning and endurance were the practice of teams in the 1930s, and Iowa State was no exception. Bock's physical nature and tenacity to play hard led him to play on both offense and defense, garnering him All–Big 6 honors with Kischer as a junior in 1937.

The follow-up to his all-conference season was even better. Iowa State was on a 10-game streak without a loss heading into the season finale against Oklahoma in 1938, hoping to capture a league championship. It was a defensive struggle, and the Sooners ultimately won the game and crown 10–0. But Bock was certainly a cog in getting the team to that point. He played all but about 50 minutes that season, en route to being named Iowa State's first consensus All-American.

Bock impressed in the 1939 College All-Star Game and was drafted by the Chicago Bears that same year. He was offered $300 per month to play for the Bears, but his decision was to forgo a professional football career.

"I wanted to go to graduate school to get my [master's degree] in mechanical engineering," Bock said. "[Iowa State] offered me $200 a month to become the line coach."

After earning his degree, Bock went on to become the CEO of one of the largest chemical companies in the country, and to this day he remains the only player in Iowa State history to be inducted into the College Football Hall of Fame.

69 Catch a Bowl Game

It's the ultimate reward at the end of a season full of highs and lows. Seeing your team play past the regular season is always the hope, and nothing feels quite as satisfying as you make your way by car or plane to watch Iowa State play in a bowl game.

While it's a spectacle to attend the bowl game itself, the events of the days leading up to the game are something to behold too. Parades with Cyclones players and coaches, pep rallies where team captains and coaches speak, tailgating and the pregame spirit walk are all an essential part of the bowl experience.

Like clockwork, when Iowa State is selected to participate in a bowl game, Cyclones fans show up in force. At the 2012 Liberty Bowl, an announced crowd of 53,687 packed into the stadium in Memphis, Tennessee, which was predominantly a sea of Cardinal and Gold. In more than 10 bowl game appearances, Iowa State has always had a reputation for bringing enthusiastic fans to the host city, dating back to the Cyclones' first bowl game in 1971.

As the postseason eluded Iowa State for many years, the team finally had a chance in 1971 when the Sun Bowl committee arrived at Jack Trice Stadium to watch the Cyclones take on Oklahoma State. ISU coach Johnny Majors was told before the game by the Sun Bowl rep that if the Cyclones won, they would get the invite. Majors knew his team was ready, and it showed.

The Cyclones beat Oklahoma State 54–0 that day and were selected to play in the 1971 Sun Bowl against No. 11 LSU on December 18, 1971. A sellout crowd witnessed Iowa State come within four points of the highly rated Tigers in the fourth quarter, but the Cyclones ultimately fell 33–15. The loss, while disappointing, didn't completely taint the experience, however.

"Anytime you do something—a first—no one can match it," said George Amundson. "So it's pretty cool being part of the first bowl game in school history, to be able to say that."

Finally, though, Iowa State had had a taste of the postseason, and the 1970s brought plenty more trips.

After a five-win season and a memorable tie against No. 3 Nebraska, Iowa State earned a bowl bid to the 1972 Liberty Bowl against Georgia Tech. Amundson hit Ike Harris on a five-yard touchdown pass with 1:36 remaining to bring the Cyclones within one point, but a failed two-point conversion left the team disappointed again with a 31–30 loss.

Iowa State went to two more bowl games in the '70s, earning berths in the 1977 Peach Bowl and 1978 Hall of Fame Bowl, but both times, the Cyclones came up short. A 22-year postseason hiatus was underway. Then, Iowa State finally broke through.

In the 2000 Insight.com Bowl against Pittsburgh, Iowa State fans and the team took Phoenix, Arizona, by storm. After a tightly contested game, it was a 72-yard punt-return touchdown by JaMaine Billups that locked up Iowa State's first bowl win, 37–29.

"I think the neatest aspect was there were so many Iowa State fans that I think it was probably 2- or 4-to-1 Iowa State–to–Pittsburgh fans," quarterback Sage Rosenfels remembered. "It felt like a home game to us."

Iowa State went to two more bowl games in 2001 and 2002 (losing 14–13 to Alabama on a controversial ruling on a field goal in '01). Bowl championships thrilled Iowa State fans again in 2004 against Miami of Ohio and in the 2009 Insight Bowl against Minnesota.

70 One and Done

He thought the layup was good at first. Jamaal Tinsley had gotten the inbounds pass with 6.9 seconds remaining, his team down a point, and drove the length of the floor. He split two defenders in the lane for a scoop shot that would have been a game-winning bucket. It was a shot he made 99 times out of 100. But that brief moment, where he thought the shot fell through, dissipated in a hurry.

"I heard their crowd, so I knew something was wrong," Tinsley said afterward.

The ball hung on the front of the rim for a brief moment before falling off. Final: No. 15 seed Hampton 58, No. 2 seed Iowa State 57. It's a moment in Iowa State history fans want to forget, but knowing how one of the most successful stretches in program history came to an abrupt halt is important.

Iowa State was without All-American Marcus Fizer in 2000–01 but returned with enough cogs to make a run at the Final Four a realistic goal. The demanding pace of coach Larry Eustachy paid off for the Cyclones as the team ran to a 13–3 Big 12 record and its second straight regular-season conference title. Iowa State, however, had an ugly 16-point loss at Texas as tournament time neared, and the wind started to get taken out of their sails.

Against Baylor in the first round of the Big 12 tournament, the regular-season champs were handed a stunning 62–49 loss. Not much fuel was left in the tank. Maybe they had peaked too early. "I think we have the potential [for the Final Four]," Paul Shirley said leading into the tournament, "but I don't think anybody is going to make the prediction that we will."

The intensity in practices was wearing on the team, so Eustachy had to act fast. Players expected to return to Ames following the Baylor loss and get run into the ground. Instead, Eustachy had a pizza party in the conference room in an attempt to salvage a season that had started with lofty goals.

Iowa State received a two-seed in the NCAA tournament shortly after and learned it would play No. 15–seeded Hampton, the MEAC champion, which was making its first-ever trip to the Big Dance. The Cyclones were 17-point favorites as they headed to Boise, Idaho.

Eustachy said ahead of the game, "There isn't a team in our league that plays a better brand of basketball than the Hampton team." Maybe he was just giving public respect to his opponent; maybe he meant it. Either way, Hampton was ready.

Iowa State was shell-shocked as it went to the locker room down 31–27 at halftime, hearing "Overrated!" chants near the end of the period. But an 11–1 run to start the second half had the Cyclones rolling. A No. 2 seed had only lost to a No. 15 seed three times in NCAA history, and it looked like Iowa State would avoid becoming part of that statistic.

With seven minutes remaining and Iowa State leading 57–48, it was as though someone had built a plastic lid and fit it neatly over the Cyclones' rim. Nothing was falling, and the Pirates rallied to take their lead as the seconds ticked away. Iowa State thought it was running out of gas against Baylor, but allowing a 10–0 stretch over the final seven minutes of a tournament game had the Cyclones stalled on the court in Boise with their tank empty.

"I think our team has been spent for a long time," Eustachy said afterward. "We had no business winning the Big 12. We really exposed ourselves tonight overall. We were massive overachievers."

Hampton had pulled just the fourth upset of a 15-seed over a 2-seed in tournament history, and its band, cheerleaders, players, and coaches flooded the court in elation. On the other side of the celebration, Cyclones players were hunched over on the floor. "I can't remember a more disappointing time in basketball," freshman Jake Sullivan said.

Sure, Tinsley's shot should have gone down, or Iowa State should have been up by double digits as the heavy favorite, but the enthusiasm of the team was long gone before that trip to Boise. Tinsley's shot just symbolized the struggle to the finish line.

"It rolls off the rim," ISU broadcaster Eric Heft said, "and that's it."

71 The XC Championships

Corey Ihmels could've gone anywhere. The North Dakota high school cross country phenom was being recruited by just about everybody after winning a National High School Cross Country championship, including longtime Iowa State coach Bill Bergan. Ihmels' college decision came down to Iowa State and Oregon—a powerhouse in the running world—but it was three in-home visits and a promise that led Ihmels to Ames.

Bergan confidently proclaimed Iowa State would win a cross country national championship as he looked Ihmels in the eye. Three years later, that promise turned into something tangible.

Already proven on the national stage after leading Iowa State to a cross country national championship in 1989, Bergan and the Cyclones were back on top in 1994. Iowa State's women's cross country program had experienced substantial success on the national scene too, and that's perhaps the best place for this story to begin.

In the days before the Iowa State women's program was a part of the NCAA, the Cyclones competed in the Association for Intercollegiate Athletics for Women. Iowa State raced in its first AIAW championship in 1975 and kicked off a historic run, winning five team national championships in seven seasons. Led by coach Chris Murray, the Cyclones claimed national championships from 1975 to 1978 and lost just one meet in that span.

Peg Neppel-Darrah was as good as they come, capturing the individual national championship in 1975. It was the first-ever individual national title for an ISU female student-athlete. Neppel-Darrah paved the way for the 1975–77 titles, while the team went undefeated in those seasons. A fifth national title came to the program in 1981 under a different coach, Ron Renko, and a new individual national champion in Dorthe Rasmussen.

As the Iowa State women kicked off the near-beginning of the 1980s with a championship, it was the Cyclones men who ended the decade on top. Iowa State had finished sixth at the NCAA meet three times and was fifth in 1958, but that's as close as it came until a breakthrough in 1989.

The one-two punch of John Nuttall and Jonah Koech was tops in the country as the duo finished first and second, respectively, at the NCAA championships. Iowa State beat second-place Oregon by 18 points behind the leadership of two of the most decorated runners in program history, but Bergan felt it was the added collection of Darrell Smith, Andrew Hollens, Roland Pauwels, Sean Mulheron, and John Burris that allowed the success that season.

"This team is blessed with outstanding depth and a great attitude," Bergan said prior to the '89 national meet. "They push each other very hard to improve."

The same could be said for Bergan's squad five years later. Ihmels had come in with the goal of winning a national championship, and the Cyclones were on the brink. But when race day came on November 21, 1994, adversity hit like a ton of bricks.

The conditions on the course in Prairie Grove, Arkansas, were extremely sloppy, and a couple Cyclones harriers had a tough road individually. Ian Robinson pulled his thigh muscle just 50 meters into the race—almost leading him to drop out—and John Kihonge fell at the 1.5-mile mark.

"If you had told me before the race that Ian would run hurt and John would fall, I would have said there was no way we could win," Bergan said afterward. Luckily, the adversity didn't last long. Robinson pushed on, nabbing a ninth-place finish, and Kihonge rallied for a 22nd-place finish. Dmitry Drozdov (12th), Ihmels (13th), and Steve Brooks (17th) rounded out the scoring runners and took home Iowa State's second team national championship.

Fast-forward to 2012 when Ihmels was well into his tenure as the Iowa State cross country and track and field coach. He couldn't help but think back to that promise Bergan had made, and how it still meant a lot for it to have come true.

"He kept his promise," Ihmels said. "That was pretty cool."

72 ISUCF'V'MB

"Ladies and Gentlemen! Now entering the field, the Priiiide of Iowa State! The Iowa State University Cyclone Football *Varsityyyyy Marching Band*!"

It's the introduction all Iowa State fans are familiar with. The voice of the PA announcer rings as loud and clear as the horns he is ushering onto the field. The Iowa State marching band (or ISUCF'V'MB as it was coined in 1978) is as much a staple on game days as the action on the field itself, and it is the source from which Cyclones fans can draw energy before the game.

From the "Go State!" to start the march to the floating ISU during pregame and the halftime tunes, it's all part of a rich tradition ISUCF'V'MB has at Iowa State, and the history only adds to the appreciation of what the 345-member marching band does on game day.

It was 1886 when a marching band was born in Ames, but it wasn't until 1952 that the Iowa State marching band we are familiar with today started taking shape. It was under director Frank Piersol that that marching band began to perfect the floating formations—playing at all home games—that are now a staple of ISUCF'V'MB's routine today.

When Meredith Willson—composer of the musical *The Music Man*—paid a visit to the college in 1953, he introduced the song "For I, for S" to the performers, giving them a pep song that would be played at every game.

In addition to open, grassy fields around campus to practice on, band members were able to learn formations through photographs from performances at Clyde Williams Field. Inside Exhibit Hall—which was located roughly where Hoover Hall now stands on campus—pictures of past performances were pinned to a bulletin board and scribbled with lines to show band members how to correct the formations.

The Iowa State marching band performed in Iowa State's first bowl game at the 1971 Sun Bowl in El Paso, Texas, and first allowed women to join the ensemble the following season. The group also has a place in pop culture, as it was the first marching band to perform Ray Charles' Pepsi jingle in 1991. Four years later the Iowa State marching band won the Coach Contest and was tabbed to record the theme song for the television series *Coach*.

Although ISUCF'V'MB has found a way to change with the times, the core of what has made the band an important part at Iowa State for more than 100 years still remains. And next time you hear the PA announcer at Jack Trice Stadium bring the band onto the field, the sights and sounds might be just a little brighter and a bit louder.

73 Megan Taylor

Megan Taylor sat hunched over on the bench with her head down. It was her senior season, and while Iowa State was leading Nebraska big at Hilton Coliseum, she had just been pulled from the game after throwing a poor pass that had sailed over her teammate's head and out of bounds. Out of the corner of her eye, she saw coach Bill Fennelly coming her way.

Come on, Taylor thought, *he can't yell at me.*

As Fennelly bent down, Taylor's head was still hanging. All she could see was a dangling tie. She yanked it. "It was just an instinct thing," Taylor said. As the crowd looked on, Taylor kept fiddling with the tie. "Everybody in the place started laughing, knowing she was probably the only person who could ever get away with that," Fennelly said.

Taylor had arrived in Ames four years prior from the small town of Roseau, Minnesota, just south of the Canadian border. She was so far north, hardly anyone knew about her. There was one person. The coach at the University of South Dakota had seen Taylor play, and knowing she wasn't likely going to play Division II, he passed a tip along to Fennelly. Soon after, Fennelly sent assistant Brenda Frese on a trip north.

On that winter day, Frese picked up a rental car and drove to the Podunk town of Badger to watch Taylor play against Badger/Greenbush–Middle River. She had encountered a snowstorm, and schools in Minnesota rarely canceled. So Frese pressed on. Unable to see much ahead, Frese followed the taillights of the truck in front of her until she finally arrived. After watching Taylor play inside the small gym, Frese had seen enough.

"Call her and offer her now," Frese told Fennelly over the phone.

"Well," Fennelly said, "I need to see her."

So Fennelly made the trip. "If you miss the exit," Taylor's high school coach told him, "you'll be in Canada."

It was cold and snowing when Fennelly arrived. "I watched her play, and I thought she was exactly what we needed," Fennelly said.

Megan Taylor, left, maintains possession of the ball despite pressure from Baylor's Chanelle Fox during the second half of a January 24, 2001 matchup in Waco. (Photo courtesy of AP Images/Waco Tribune Herald, Rod Aydelotte)

Iowa State offered, but Taylor was shy and initially wasn't all that interested in being recruited. After playing AAU as a junior, other schools began calling, and Taylor became overwhelmed. Since Iowa State had been interested from the start, Taylor made her decision. She committed on Fennelly's son Steven's birthday. "Steven, you don't understand," Bill told him. "You got a great birthday present." By the end of her senior season at Roseau, Taylor had scored 3,300 points, becoming Minnesota's all-time leading scorer for both boys and girls.

The season before Taylor arrived in Ames for the 1997–98 season, Iowa State had advanced to its first NCAA tournament in program history. With Taylor aboard, Iowa State women's basketball was about to become a perennial postseason team.

Over the course of the next four seasons, Taylor started all 132 games of her career. During her sophomore season, Taylor hit a three-pointer with one second remaining to defeat Texas. Against No. 1–seeded UConn in the Sweet 16 later that season, she hit one of five consecutive threes to help Iowa State advance to its first Elite Eight. Then, as a senior, Taylor hit a 10-foot jumper as time expired to beat Oklahoma.

"She was just a kid that refused to lose and did whatever she had to do when she had to do it to win games," Fennelly said. "And she did it for us for four years."

By the time her career came to a close, Taylor had helped Iowa State to its first-ever conference title (2000), consecutive Big 12 tournament titles (2000 and 2001), and four consecutive NCAA tournament appearances, including two Sweet 16s and the Elite Eight.

Taylor graduated as Iowa State's all-time leading scorer with 1,866 points and all-time leading rebounder with 966 boards (she's now No. 3 in both). She is tied for first all-time with 287 career three-pointers. Taylor was a four-time all-conference selection and became the third Iowa State player selected in the WNBA Draft. Her No. 51 was retired in 2004.

"You never really think about that type of stuff when you're playing; you just play for the love of the game," Taylor said. "To get those kinds of honors after really makes you look back with even fonder memories of the time you had and the friendship[s] you made."

"I think if you did a poll of favorite women's basketball players of all time, even today," Fennelly said, "Megan Taylor would be near the top of that list because of how hard she played, her competitiveness, her love for college and everything about it."

The Forgotten Championships

Underneath the bleachers at Clyde Williams Field in a small, poorly ventilated room with a low, slanted ceiling began a program. In 1961 there was no budget, and the equipment for the newly commissioned Iowa State men's gymnastics team was outdated. The only option to snag the first recruits was to pull them from the existing pool of 10,000 Iowa State students.

But 25-year-old head coach Ed Gagnier accepted each challenge as it was laid in front of him. And 10 years later, he turned the fledgling program that he built from the ground up into national champions.

Iowa Staters everywhere are well aware of the history of success by the Cyclones as national champions in wrestling, but in the early 1970s, men's gymnastics at Iowa State was a national power. The Cyclones won national titles in 1971, 1973, and 1974 and won 10 Big 8 championships. Today, however, the titles, All-Americans, and performances are just a memory, as the team was dissolved in 1994.

This story, though, must begin back in the underbelly of the Clyde Williams Field bleachers. Gagnier was a successful collegiate gymnast at Michigan and later became a teacher and high school coach in Wisconsin before he was offered a physical education job at Iowa State in 1961. He also received the opportunity to build his own gymnastics program from scratch. "You're guaranteed a spot in the lineup," was Gagnier's early recruiting pitch. In that small, cramped room with his first team, the athletes couldn't even perform a high-bar dismount routine. Still, Gagnier saw the potential.

"When you're young and you have all the confidence in the world," Gagnier said later, "all you have [are] high expectations that add self-confidence."

In 1963 the program was officially recognized as a competitive NCAA sport and member of the Big 8. Iowa State began practicing in Beyer Hall in 1964 and the following year collected its first conference title. The Cyclones were starting to draw some attention, and recruiting for Gagnier got a bit easier as he started targeting Illinois high schools where gymnastics programs were abundant.

Gagnier always hoped to return to his alma mater in Michigan for a dual meet but was denied by the Wolverines coaches for many years, until 1970, when they met at the NCAA championship in Philadelphia. Iowa State finished runner-up at the national meet to Michigan by one-tenth of a point, but the shortcomings set in motion the Cyclones' run of prominence.

In Ann Arbor, Michigan, for the 1971 NCAA championship, Iowa State trailed by 2.5 points to the leader heading into the second-to-last day but surged ahead and led the pack by a half point on the final day before holding on to win its first-ever national championship as a program. Where Gagnier took the program in only 10 years was nothing short of remarkable.

"You become a secondary factor," Gagnier said afterward. "The feeling of representing an entire university takes precedent and gives you a feeling of great satisfaction."

Little did anyone know at the time, the program was in the midst of the golden age of Iowa State gymnastics. The Cyclones won the Big 8 championship 10 times from 1965 to 1975 (finishing second in 1968) and followed their 1971 NCAA championship with more national success. Iowa State was runner-up in 1972 but won back-to-back NCAA team titles in 1973 and 1974. "They believe they are champions and want every man to share in that belief," Gagnier said following the '74 title.

"Hi, Ed!"

Ed Gagnier established his legacy in Ames as the Iowa State men's gymnastics coach for 22 years, but he had a successful athletic career himself.

Growing up in Windsor, Ontario, Gagnier got involved in his high school gymnastics team, eventually becoming Canada's top junior-level gymnast. An offer to compete at Michigan awaited him, and scholarship assistance from the Wolverines program got him his college degree. While still in school in 1956, Gagnier was Canada's only male competitor for gymnastics at the Olympics.

After college, Gagnier went on to teach and coach in Wisconsin, where his high school program won the state championship. He broke through in college coaching in 1961, when he started the gymnastics program at Iowa State. After winning three national titles with the Cyclones and retiring in 1983, Gagnier eventually became the director of the National Cyclone Club.

What Cyclones fans might remember about Gagnier is when he would host the Shoot Five-for-Five contest at halftime of Cyclones men's basketball games. He would start off by saying, "Hi, everybody!" to the crowd, which would prompt the response of "Hi, Ed!" A banner honoring Gagnier's accomplishments was hung in Hilton Coliseum in February 2015.

"He started out with nothing, but with his drive and his optimism, he knew he could have a good team and win the nationals," Gagnier's wife, Carolyn, once said. "That was his goal."

Some individual success trickled over into the 1980s as well. Iowa State finished runner-up at the NCAAs in 1981, due in large part to Ron Galimore, a 1980 US Olympic team qualifier. The senior recorded the first-*ever* perfect 10.000 in NCAA history when his vault routine brought him the national title.

After Gagnier's retirement in 1983 (with a 180–30–1 combined record), Dave Mickelson served as head coach until 1994, when the men's gymnastics team received the unforgettable news: the 1993–94 season would be the final year of competition for the Cyclones due to budget constraints and the Title IX requirement for gender equality. "We take these steps with mixed emotions," athletics director Gene Smith said.

Still, the legacy of the national power that was the ISU men's gymnastics team lives on through banners hung in the rafters of Hilton Coliseum, reminding those who look upon them of the program that was formed underneath the bleachers at Clyde Williams Field all those years ago.

75 The Monster Man

Matt Blair got in position behind his linemen on fourth down, ready to do what he did better than almost anybody else. The ball was snapped. As it left the foot of the kicker, the linebacker for the Minnesota Vikings took a running start, then jumped with as much force as he could. The kick rocketed back toward the turf, and Blair knew he had done his job. *Twenty times* in his career, Blair thwarted his opponent's chance to score. It would be pretty simple to think that countless hours of work on the gridiron would have given him that ability. But it isn't quite that easy.

Blair graduated from high school in Dayton, Ohio, looking for any chance he could to get an education. Sports were a tool he knew he could use to reach that goal, starting out at Northeastern Oklahoma Junior College. He joined the football team in 1969, earning his way onto the traveling squad (and into a scholarship) as a part of that Junior College Championship team. To earn the other part of a scholarship, Blair went out for the school's basketball team and, upon arriving, he and his teammates learned something pretty quickly: he couldn't dunk the basketball.

"The guys on the team showed me how to do it and if you tell me to work on something, I will work at it," Blair once said. "By the time I was done playing for them, I was slam-dunking with one hand, two hands, off the board, everything."

One of his coaches, when he finally landed with the Vikings, familiar with his success in basketball, explained he could apply his dunking skill to blocking kicks in the NFL. "Matt, why don't you do your basketball stuff and jump up there and slam-dunk the football?" the coach asked him.

"That's how I started," Blair said.

And once the 6'5", 232-pound Blair started, it was hard to get him to stop. He was a triple threat of speed, agility, and toughness. Blair could run alongside his fastest opponents, or stick his nose in the trenches against anybody on the other side. He was known as a monster man. But the 1971 Sun Bowl MVP, All-American, six-time Pro Bowler, and Super Bowl participant didn't just fall into his reputation. Matt Blair earned it at every level.

Blair first had to make the cut at Northeastern Oklahoma, going through tryouts with 170 participants competing for 30 roster spots. He then fought to be noticed in the recruiting process, catching the eye of Iowa State and coach Johnny Majors. Majors and members of his staff went to Oklahoma to see Blair and were as honest as they could be, telling him he could probably be on the fourth team in Ames but would have a chance to move his way to the top. "I took Johnny Majors' pushing tip," Blair said. "And I said, 'I'm going to go to Iowa State and work hard and try to make the first team.'"

In Blair's first season for the Cyclones, his impact was immediate. He was crucial in leading Iowa State to its first-ever bowl berth at the 1971 Sun Bowl against LSU. Iowa State lost 33–15, but Blair was named the defensive MVP. He was ready to take it to another level in 1972 as a cocaptain with George Amundson, but an injury in the preseason left everybody wondering what could have been.

"He got a cheap shot by a player I ended up dismissing from the squad," Majors later told the *Des Moines Register.* "He hit Matt with a blow below the knee, and he was out for the season. It was very costly to our football team."

Earning a medical redshirt that season, Blair would be eligible to compete in football the following season but had a decision to make. He was offered a spot on the ISU basketball roster by coach Maury John and was planning to play football and basketball in 1972. But accepting the offer would mean his football eligibility the next season would not exist. "He would have played with no strings attached," John told the *Ames Daily Tribune* in 1973.

Blair ultimately decided to return to football and play for new coach Earle Bruce. It was that season when he laid a hit so powerful on revered Arkansas running back Dickey Morton that the collective groan of the crowd in Fayetteville could be heard loud and clear. "Knocked him out. He let him have it," Bruce recalled. "He was a…good player and a really great young man."

As a second-round selection in the 1974 NFL Draft by the Vikings, Blair played all 12 of his professional seasons in Minneapolis. He is second in Vikings history in tackles (1,452) and has the most sacks (23) and interceptions (16) by a linebacker in team history. Blair was inducted into the Vikings Ring of Honor in 2012 and is still remembered for all those kicks he knocked down.

"To go from junior college to Iowa State and then make it to the NFL and play for 12 years," Blair said, "that is something that was just unbelievable for me to do, and I did it."

76 Hilton South

There's no place like home, and there's certainly no place like Hilton Coliseum, but there is one place that comes as close as any other to producing magic away from Ames, Iowa. That place is some 228 miles south of the Iowa State hardwood down Interstate 35.

"We know if there's something down in Kansas City—Hilton South—it's going to be an incredible atmosphere," former forward Melvin Ejim said. "It's the closest thing you're going to get to Hilton Magic."

Ah, that's it. Hilton South.

Hilton South is not a place so much as it is a mind-set. Baseline to baseline the court is 94 feet just like the rest. The hoop is 10 feet from the ground. If the arena were filled with royal blue it could just as well be referred to as Allen East and if it were filled with burnt orange it could be called Erwin North. Neither has the same ring to it. So Hilton South it is.

But what exactly is Hilton South? Well, quite frankly, it's you. It is thousands of fans decked in Cardinal and Gold chanting in the Power & Light District before the game and many more fans filling the arena to take in the action. It is Kansas City being overrun by Iowa State faithful. It is, so to speak, Hilton Coliseum on wheels.

"It's obviously a place that has been very friendly to the Cyclones," Fred Hoiberg said, "going all the way back since the Big 8 tournament has been played at Kemper Arena."

In reality, the idea of Hilton South could go back even further. It was 1946 when the Big 6 began holding an early season Holiday Tournament at Municipal Auditorium in Kansas City. Nearly 10,000 fans would pack into the arena for tournament games, and undoubtedly many were representing Iowa State. They would see Gary Thompson help the Cyclones win the 1955 Big 7 Holiday Tournament, the school's first conference tournament title. Iowa State would later win the 1959 Big 8 Holiday Tournament.

Then came the move to Kemper Arena. By 1977 the Big 8 started a postseason conference tournament, and after 1978 the Holiday Tournament was disbanded. From 1977 to 1996, the Big 8 held its postseason tournament inside the spacious Kemper Arena. Iowa State fans filled the place to watch the Cyclones finish runner-up in 1985, 1986, and 1995 before they claimed their first title in the building under Tim Floyd in 1996.

When the Big 8 became the Big 12 in 1997, the postseason tournament remained at Kemper Arena, although Hilton South became more Southern and not quite the same when the conference tried out Dallas and Oklahoma City for the tournament's site in five of seven years between 2003 and 2009. In 2000 Hilton South watched as Marcus Fizer and Co. followed up their regular-season title with a postseason crown.

Today the home of Hilton South is just across the street from the Power & Light District at the Sprint Center. The Sprint Center made its debut in 2008, and after a one-year hiatus, it has been home to the tournament since 2010. In 2014 Iowa State created Hilton South like Kansas City had never seen before.

When the Cyclones marched to the Big 12 title game on March 15, 2014, thousands of fans filled the Power & Light District. They drank and cheered and chanted. Inside the Sprint Center, there was hardly a speckle of Baylor green. Iowa State fans scrounged up the tickets, filling the majority of the 19,108-seat arena with Cardinal and Gold. "When you've got a fan base like that," Hoiberg said, "that helps you."

Then the fans cheered as the confetti fell for the Cyclones' first tournament title since 2000.

"It truly was Hilton South today," Hoiberg said afterward.

Fans willed Iowa State to three straight double-digit comebacks at Hilton South in 2015 as the Cyclones won a second consecutive Big 12 postseason title for the first time in program history.

Yet Hilton South cannot be Hilton South without the fans. So make the trip to Kansas City. Stop and get your barbeque fix at the famous Joe's Kansas City Bar-B-Que, grab drinks at the Iowa State–friendly McFadden's, and pick up a slice of pizza at the Pizza Bar in the Power & Light District. Then watch from the big screen or cram into the Sprint Center to watch the game.

Now that is Hilton South.

"I think it's an important part of Iowa State, and it's great to know that even when you're not at home and you're playing in a big venue away from home, especially during the Big 12 tournament, that there's going to be a huge amount of support," Ejim said. "It's a great part of Iowa State tradition."

77 Golden Memories

Through the years, there have been many wrestlers who have walked across the soil of the Iowa State campus to reach a wrestling room. They walked with a purpose and meaning, but in time, only six have walked and ultimately wrestled to the top of an Olympic podium.

It was 1948 when the first Iowa State wrestler won Olympic gold. That year in London, after he had pinned his opponent in the finals, Glen Brand stood atop the podium as an Olympic champion at 24 years old. He had become the first athlete in Iowa State history to win Olympic gold and the first wrestler in the state of Iowa to claim an Olympic title.

The legacy was only just beginning.

It was 24 years before another Iowa State wrestler claimed Olympic gold, but at the 1972 Olympics in Munich, the Cyclones had a showing like never before. After Dan Gable lost his only collegiate match at the 1970 NCAA championship, he trained harder than ever in the two years leading up to the Olympics. On that US team, Gable was joined by Iowa Staters and 1972 NCAA champions Ben Peterson and Chris Taylor.

"The effect that I had on the Olympic team and that USA squad, especially within the town of Ames, Iowa, to me was like, 'Wow,'" Gable said. "I loved every moment of that team aspect."

There was no way Gable was losing, not after what he had been through. The Soviets said they would find a wrestler who could beat him. Gable proved otherwise. Wrestling on an injured knee, Gable did the improbable, winning six matches and Olympic gold without surrendering a single point. Peterson pinned two opponents, won two decisions, and wrestled to a draw to claim Olympic gold while Taylor took bronze. "We encouraged each other and prodded each other along with an awful lot of Cyclone pride," Peterson said.

In 1992 Bobby Douglas took the reins of the Iowa State wrestling program, but not until he first coached the US Olympic wrestling team. When he traveled to Barcelona, along with him was former Iowa State wrestler Kevin Jackson, who had finished runner-up in 1987 at the NCAA championship. In an early match at the Games, Jackson had gotten into a fight with a Spaniard, and then he heard boos following a controversial call. When he stood atop the podium later, he heard the national anthem as Iowa State's fourth gold medalist.

"Those were some of the most thrilling and exciting moments and times of all of our lives," Jackson said. "It's something that lives with me forever. I can always find a smile or happiness or enjoyment out of just reminiscing about that moment."

No Iowa State wrestler has likely faced more pressure to win Olympic gold than Cael Sanderson. After he finished his college career a perfect 159–0 with four national titles, the world expected Sanderson to dominate internationally.

"There was no other option other than winning the gold medal," Sanderson said. "You win a gold medal for your country, that feels pretty darn good." After trailing in the quarterfinals, Sanderson battled to overtime before earning a win. In the finals, he tripped his opponent with a single-leg takedown in the final minutes to win Olympic gold.

Somewhere Jake Varner watched Sanderson win that gold medal and dreamed of doing the same. After he wrestled for Sanderson for three years at Iowa State and then for Jackson as a senior, Varner became Iowa State's sixth wrestler to claim Olympic gold in 2012, with Sanderson—whom he drilled with—in attendance. "When I won, it was kind of a feeling of, 'You did it,'" Varner said. "It was just one of the greatest feelings I've ever had."

Those memories of Olympic gold will carry on forever.

"There is great honor in carrying the flag for your country," Sanderson said, "but even carrying the flag for your institution and carrying on that legacy is a great thing."

78 Tim Floyd

Within 24 hours of his introductory press conference, Tim Floyd was already nervous. The new Iowa State men's basketball coach and his wife, Beverly, were out to eat at Wallaby's in Ames with athletics director Gene Smith and his wife. The Cyclones-themed restaurant is always sure to be filled with Iowa State fans, so when Floyd was approached at dinner, he made time for those who wanted to meet him.

Up to Floyd's table walked a kid, not quite six feet tall, who looked like he might be 14 years old. Floyd's first thought was that he must be coming up to get an autograph. It shocked him to his core when this "kid" introduced himself as his new point guard. That was the first time Tim Floyd met Jacy Holloway.

"I broke out in a cold sweat," Floyd remembered later.

When Floyd arrived on the job at Iowa State, he tried as hard as he could to find any high-caliber player to replace Holloway. It's not hard to understand his reservations. Iowa State was coming off a second-to-last-place finish in the Big 8, and Floyd would have to replace the legendary coach and personality who was Johnny Orr.

Floyd was coming off a six-season run at the University of New Orleans, where he had taken the school to five postseason tournaments. When he was approached by Iowa State president Martin Jischke, Smith, and former Iowa State standout Gary Thompson about the job, he made the trip to Ames to experience the facilities and city because he was so unfamiliar with the area. He returned home to think over his options, but two days later, he announced he would stay in New Orleans.

It was the thoughts swirling in Floyd's head that made him hesitate. He had heard veteran coaches like Charlie Spoonhour and

Rick Majerus had turned down offers to coach the Cyclones, and here he was in his late thirties at a crossroads. He knew what his decision would mean for his coaching future. "I was trying to make it to the finish line at age 60, and it seemed like a daunting task," Floyd said. But it was the persistence by Iowa State and a particular phone call from Thompson that swayed him.

Thompson left a message on the Floyds' answering machine, so Beverly took the recording to her husband's office in New Orleans for him to listen to. Once he heard Gary's words, he began reflecting on all of the positives he had heard on his trip to Ames. He decided this was a move he needed to make, and one that finally felt right.

After Tim Floyd took over for legendary ISU coach Johnny Orr in 1994, he led the Cyclones to three straight NCAA tournaments for the first time in school history. (Photo courtesy of Getty Images/Allsport, Stephen Dunn)

"Wise guys change their mind," Thompson had told him. "Fools stay with it."

It was apparent in Floyd's first season that the move would be beneficial for Iowa State and its new coach. Floyd was inheriting some talent, headlined by Loren Meyer and Fred Hoiberg, and his first team won 23 games en route to an NCAA tournament berth.

Picked in many preseason polls to finish last in the Big 8 in 1995–96, Iowa State blew away expectations, winning a then–school record 24 games while claiming the last Big 8 tournament title (earning Floyd Big 8 Coach of the Year honors) and advancing to another NCAA tournament.

High expectations were placed on Iowa State in Floyd's third season, and the Cyclones responded by going to the program's first Sweet 16 in 11 years, before bowing out to UCLA. Keeping up with the high expectations meant putting in hard work. Floyd was demanding of his players to do the hard stuff in practice.

"My first weekend of practice at Iowa State we practiced for three hours on a Saturday morning, three hours on a Saturday night. Three hours on Sunday morning, three hours on Sunday night," Paul Shirley remembered. "I thought, *Wow, this is a little different than high school.*"

Following his fourth season at Iowa State, Floyd made a big move when he took over as head coach of the Chicago Bulls, immediately following the Michael Jordan era. The move was made purely for the financial security of his family, and because of the uncertainty that surrounded college coaching at the time. "Now, given what coaches are making at the college level, I might have revisited it a little differently," Floyd said.

During his four-year run at Iowa State, Floyd owned an 81–47 record with three straight NCAA tournament appearances. To the pleasure of Iowa State fans, it was a blessing that Floyd had a change of heart about leaving New Orleans.

"I'm glad we went, and it was the best thing I ever did," Floyd said. "It was a great, great move and great for me professionally, and it was a great time in my career."

79 Marv's Miracle

It was unlike anything Marv Seiler had ever seen. He turned the corner off the right side of his offensive line with the ball clutched in his hand, and saw nothing but green grass in front of him. Seiler pumped his legs as hard as he could to the roar of the Cyclone Stadium crowd.

The fifth-year senior had never had a breakaway run in his life, but there we was, smack dab in the middle of the biggest run of the season. To the 40...30...20...15...Seiler just kept going. "I kept waiting for someone to catch me," Seiler said later. Somebody finally did, but not until Seiler had cranked off a 78-yard run to set up Iowa State at the 2-yard line for the win against No. 7 Nebraska, one of its biggest victories in school history.

Nebraska was coming to Iowa State on November 14, 1992, Senior Day, as a 29-point favorite. The Huskers hadn't lost to the Cyclones since 1977. Nebraska athletics director Bob Devaney, former NU coach, said it was the best team he had seen at Nebraska in 31 years. Tom Osborne, in his 20 seasons as coach, had never lost to a team with a losing record. And to make matters worse for Iowa State, the quarterback situation was far from perfect.

Jim Walden wasn't left with many options. After Bob Utter was injured in the seventh game of that 1992 season, Donnie Smith had started the two games leading into Nebraska and Seiler played sparingly. Smith hadn't shown enough to secure the job, and Walden decided to go with the fifth-year senior who had never made a start in Ames. "I'm really not sure why I was picked," Seiler said later.

Why he was picked didn't matter. Seiler was getting the start against the No. 1 rushing defense in the Big 8. Iowa State and Nebraska traded field goals early before Nebraska quarterback Tommie Frazier threw a touchdown pass. That was followed by two field goals from Iowa State kicker Ty Stewart to give the Cyclones a 12–10 halftime lead.

Iowa State was in the game. Frazier had sustained a left knee bruise near the end of the first half, and the Huskers were already without their top two targets at tight end. Plus the Cyclones' option offense was working. Iowa State managed to fumble the ball four

Other Notable Nebraska–Iowa State Games

1976: Iowa State 37, No. 9 Nebraska 28
It had been 16 years since Iowa State had last beaten Nebraska, and things got off to a good start with the Cyclones getting on the board first. With the Huskers drawing the score to 10–7 in the first quarter, ISU returner Luther Blue took a kick 95 yards through traffic for a touchdown to push Iowa State to a convincing win.

2002: No. 19 Iowa State 36, No. 20 Nebraska 14
Iowa State was off to a 4–1 start to the season and had not beaten a ranked team since 1993, and responded with its largest margin of victory against Nebraska since a 34–0 win in 1899. The Cyclones scored 17 points off Huskers turnovers and never looked back en route to the blowout win, with a sea of Cardinal and Gold storming the field.

2009: Iowa State 9, Nebraska 7
Winless at Nebraska since 1977, Iowa State strolled into Lincoln without its starting quarterback and running back, and responded with one of the most shocking wins of its season. The combined 16 points were scored in the first half, but the Cyclones forced eight Huskers turnovers to hold on for the first big win of Paul Rhoads' tenure.

times against Nebraska without losing *any* of the miscues. The ball was bouncing the right direction and Seiler was leading the charge.

It had been two years since Seiler had made the highlight reel, completing a 23-yard pass on a fake punt to help push Iowa State to a 33–31 win at Oklahoma, but he was about to trump that in a big way. The Cyclones held on to their 12–10 lead as the fourth quarter began but had yet to hit pay dirt in the end zone. But on one option read, Seiler held on to the ball, turning up the field for that 78-yard gain. He stayed up even when the initial tackler tried to knock the ball loose at the 15-yard line, running all the way to the 2-yard line.

Fullback Chris Ulrich made the Huskers pay on the next play, plowing his way into the end zone for a 19–10 lead. There was still 10:50 remaining, and this was *still* Nebraska, but Seiler felt a bit of magic in the air after that score. "That's when I felt we had our best chance," Seiler said afterward. "After that, I believed in my heart that we could win."

His feelings turned into a reality. The clock read 0:00. The score: Iowa State 19, Nebraska 10.

It was the biggest upset in school history, and the 42,008 in the stadium treated it as such. Fans poured onto the field. Goal posts came down. And the unlikely hero, the backup's backup who only had one Division I offer coming out of high school, was the player of the game. Seiler carried the ball 24 times for 144 yards and permanently etched his name into Iowa State history. "I can't really put into words how good I feel right now," Seiler said afterward. "I'll probably remember it the rest of my life."

On the losing end of five of its previous six games, Iowa State racked up 399 yards to Nebraska's 246, with Seiler making the most of his sudden opportunity. "I'll be an answer to a trivia question," Seiler said. "I definitely don't feel like a legend, but it's enjoyable to leave your mark behind."

80 Jayme Olson

What Jayme Olson experienced when she made a return trip to Hilton Coliseum gave her the warmest feeling. It had been many years since she starred at Iowa State as a four-time all-conference selection and All-American, but out of the blue, she decided she wanted to check out her old team. She walked up to the window at Hilton Coliseum to purchase a ticket. As she began to scan the piece of paper to see where she would be sitting, the numbers led her straight to the upper level.

"Everyone was like, 'You can't get better tickets?'" Olson remembered hearing. "But I thought it's great this is where people have to sit, because when I started, we couldn't give tickets away. We begged people to come and did everything we could."

What a change it was from when Olson showed up on campus in 1994. The Bettendorf, Iowa, kid liked what she saw academically from Iowa State—having her sister already at the school was a bonus—but the athletic task ahead intrigued her too. "I liked the idea of being a part of a building program," Olson said. "I liked the idea of being able to come in and challenge myself to see if I could help to build [up] a struggling program."

The challenge under then–ISU coach Theresa Becker proved to be daunting. Iowa State struggled to an 8–19 record, and despite being selected to the All–Big 8 team and earning Big 8 Freshman of the Year honors, it was a tough year for Olson, particularly after a loss at Colorado. "I remember calling home to my parents and them telling me they must have gotten the score on the ticker across the bottom of the screen wrong," Olson recalled. Only the score *wasn't* wrong. Final: Colorado 83, Iowa State 38. The turnaround was nowhere near where Olson was hoping it would be.

Following that season, Becker left Ames, and Iowa State ushered in Toledo coach Bill Fennelly. Fortunately for Olson, she already had a rapport with her new coach, as he had tried to recruit her to Toledo. Plus they had a connection in that both were from the Quad Cities. But it was the first meeting when Fennelly got to Ames that they both knew it would be a good fit.

"New coach, I didn't recruit you here, what do you think?" Fennelly asked Olson.

"'Coach, I want to win," Olson replied.

The winning started without haste. "He brought a whole new attitude to the program," Olson said. Iowa State won 17 games in Olson's sophomore season, but it was her junior year in 1997 when the Cyclones had their biggest breakthrough. For the first time in history, Iowa State qualified for the NCAA tournament while Olson earned All–Big 12 first-team accolades and was named to the GTE All-American team.

Through all of the successes, the instances where Fennelly and Olson *didn't* see eye to eye on things stand out to both. "We both wanted success, we both wanted to improve, we both wanted to see the program grow," Olson said. Never did it hinder the team on or off the court, it only showed the will of a player and coach to be successful. "Just sometimes we had a different view of how to get to the same place," Fennelly explained.

While Olson was maybe the first headstrong player Fennelly had at Iowa State, she wasn't the last. But you *could* consider her to be one of the best. As a senior and honorable-mention All-American, she led the Cyclones to a second consecutive NCAA tournament and Iowa State's first-ever win in the Big Dance. She held 13 season and 15 career school records at the time of her graduation, including scoring (1,799 points). Olson's No. 53 jersey was given the ultimate honor by Iowa State and retired in 2004.

"Sometimes when I look back I think I was just doing what I was recruited to do, and that was play basketball, which was something I loved," Olson said. "To be recognized by other people, who felt that I had contributed that much to make that big of a difference, is great."

As Jayme Olson sat in the upper level of Hilton Coliseum that day to watch her alma mater and former coach carry on the tradition that started in 1995, she couldn't help but find herself in disbelief about how the program had come full circle. Fennelly knows just how much Olson meant to where the program is today, now more than 15 years since her last game.

"She was on the first team that got this thing going," Fennelly said. "I don't think there's any question her legacy is a pretty good one."

81 Dexter "Money" Green

The cartilage in his right knee was severely injured and he hadn't practiced all week after missing the previous week's game against Utah, so Dexter Green sat in the visitor's locker room uncertain if he would play against No. 7 Missouri in 1976.

Coach Earle Bruce stopped over to see if Green had made a decision. He hadn't, so the team left him in the locker room to decide if he wanted to play. That's when injured teammate Mike Williams stopped by. "Homie, what you gonna do?" Williams asked. "If I could throw away these crutches and help the team any kind of way I could, I would."

So Dexter decided he would play.

What followed, on an injured knee and all, was the greatest game of Dexter's career. He rushed for a 65-yard touchdown in the first quarter, eventually carrying the ball 37 times for a career-best

214 rushing yards and two touchdowns in a 21–17 road upset. If there was one game that could sum up the rest, it was this one. In the biggest moments—and against the best of the best—Dexter Green rose to the occasion.

"They called him by his nickname, Money, and in big games he got even bigger," teammate Tom Randall said. "He just had a way. That was Dexter."

Dexter had other obstacles to overcome before he could earn such a nickname. Growing up in Woodbridge, Virginia, Green was a tiny running back from Gar-Field High School. Iowa State stumbled upon him somewhat by accident. It was nearing the end of Green's senior season and the two crosstown rivals—Gar-Field and Woodbridge—were both 9–0 and playing each other to go to the state playoffs. The stadium was packed with an estimated 15,000 fans. Iowa State's scouting staff was in attendance. The Cyclones were there to see Woodbridge's Russell Davis, a back who would eventually go to Michigan and then to the NFL. Instead, Iowa State left Virginia wanting Dexter.

Even once Green arrived at Iowa State, the little running back faced doubters.

"Dexter was small, and everybody said he couldn't play in the Big 8," Randall said. "A lot of us guys…he was a year or two younger, and some of us questioned, 'Is he going to be durable enough?'"

By Green's sophomore season, those worries were quelled. "He was amazing," Randall said. He might be 5'9" and sitting at 170 pounds, but Dexter had an elusiveness about him—which one teammate compared to Hall of Famer Walter Payton—that few others did. The key wasn't bringing Green down, but rather catching him.

As Green took off as a sophomore, surpassing 1,000 yards on the ground, so did Iowa State. The Cyclones surged from 4–7 in 1975 to 8–3 in 1976 and then went to bowl games in both 1977 and 1978 with the help of Green in the backfield. By the time his career came to an end, he was an All-American and a two-time All–Big 8 selection who had become Iowa State's all-time leading rusher with 3,437 yards (now No. 3) and a school-record 34 rushing touchdowns (now No. 2).

Dexter was at his best when Iowa State needed him most.

Missouri went to Ames in 1977 seeking revenge on Iowa State after the Cyclones had used Green's performance the previous season to spoil the Tigers' homecoming. This time, Green bounced outside for a 28-yard touchdown run in the fourth quarter to lift Iowa State to a 7–0 victory. Green's performances on the ground helped Iowa State upset Nebraska in 1976 and 1977, both times when the Cornhuskers were ranked ninth. He rushed for 172 yards in the 1977 Peach Bowl, an Iowa State bowl record.

"He could break the game open, and he was only a little thing," Bruce said. "He wasn't a big guy, but he was quick, he liked the game, and he played hard. He just gave it a great effort every time he went out there."

Green passed away from cancer in 2003 at the age of 46 but left a lasting legacy as one of the first great running backs in Iowa State history. In the big games, against the big teams, Dexter was money.

"He was always smiling, and you knew you could count on him," Randall said. "The guys knew he was tough. He wouldn't come out of a game. He played hurt. Guys knew it, and they respected it."

82 Three Straight for Iowa State

It was the end of an era. The legendary Johnny Orr was stepping down as Iowa State's coach in 1994 after 14 years, and Tim Floyd had been tapped to replace him.

Given the title as the father of Hilton Magic, Orr was certainly at the forefront of many of the most memorable moments in Iowa State basketball history. So when Floyd was chosen as the man to take over for a larger-than-life figure, the shoes he had to fill were quite massive in the public eye. But Floyd responded in a huge way, by taking the Cyclones to three straight appearances in the NCAA tournament, from 1995 to 1997, for the first time in program history.

While Iowa State did have those key individuals in the past like Barry Stevens, Jeff Grayer, or Jeff Hornacek who produced some big moments, the *collection* of players who comprised the rosters of those three NCAA tournament teams is what made them special.

When Floyd arrived in 1994, Iowa State had missed the NCAA tournament that previous season under Orr but would return a healthy helping of talent. Hurl Beechum (a future pro overseas), Jacy Holloway, Fred Hoiberg, Julius Michalik, and Loren Meyer would all return. With Hoiberg's sharpshooting; Holloway's competitiveness as a point guard; Michalik's ability, at 6'11", to step outside the lane; and Meyer's presence down low, the pieces for success were well aligned.

That first Floyd-led team returned to the Big Dance, finishing with a 20-plus-win season while reaching the second round of the NCAA tournament before bowing out to North Carolina. The culture was beginning to be established, but there would be some big questions heading into the 1995–96 season, largely dealing with replacing Michalik, Meyer, and Hoiberg through the recruiting trail. And recruiting against other Big 8 schools proved to be quite the challenge.

"We were trying to recruit against Eddie Sutton and Norm Stewart, Roy Williams, one of the top 100 high school guys, and we couldn't get it done," Floyd remembered. "We had to find guys that could play for them that they weren't recruiting."

That started by getting transfers like Kelvin Cato from South Alabama, who Floyd had seen while he was coaching at New Orleans, and Kenny Pratt. Dedric Willoughby entered the mix after coming from New Orleans, and Shawn Bankhead joined the fold too.

Iowa State won 20 games in the regular season in 1995–96, but it was the Big 8 tournament, which was the last ever due to the formation of the Big 12 the next season, where the Cyclones made the most noise. Narrow wins against Nebraska and Missouri put Iowa State in the final against No. 5 Kansas, where the Cyclones won the final Big 8 tournament title 56–55. It was that tournament

1996 Big 8 Champions

Iowa State had reached the Big 8 Conference tournament championship game three times since the event began in 1977, each time coming up short. In the last-ever Big 8 tournament in 1996, the chance to finish on top meant leaving its mark in history.

Picked to finish last in the Big 8 in preseason polls, Iowa State notched wins against Nebraska and Missouri in the first two rounds to earn a date for the league championship against No. 5 Kansas on March 10, 1996, in Kansas City.

A tightly contested game throughout, Kansas' Raef LaFrentz put the Jayhawks up one with 7.1 seconds left, but Dedric Willoughby, the best free-throw shooter in the Big 8, was fouled with 5.5 seconds remaining, making both free shots. He finished with 20 points, and the Jayhawks' final shot clanked off the rim. Cyclones players ran onto the floor, closing the door on the Big 8 as its final champions.

environment Floyd hoped would prepare his group of transfers and new players to perform in Iowa State's second straight appearance in the NCAA tournament.

"The atmosphere at the NCAA tournament will not be any greater nor the caliber of teams any greater than we faced with Kansas and the intensity of the crowd in Kansas City," Floyd said. And that's the way Iowa State, in fact, approached that 1996 national tournament. The Cyclones slid past California by 10 in the opening round, but the magical season came to an end against Utah. One thing was certain, though—Iowa State had gained the experience and was poised for a deeper run.

In 1996–97, the regular season produced the highest national ranking ever by an Iowa State team (No. 4) and saw the Cyclones once again win 20-plus games. This finally *had* to be the year Iowa State got past the second round of the tournament.

After dispatching Illinois State in the first round, a matchup with Cincinnati—ranked in the top 10—awaited. Pratt scored 21 points in 36 minutes, and a last-second, half-court shot by the Bearcats ricocheted off the backboard, preserving a 67–66 Iowa State win and sending the Cyclones to the Sweet 16 for the first time in 11 years. After all the excitement of finally breaking down the barrier, the dream run was halted 74–73 at the hands of UCLA.

The Cyclones missed the NCAA tournament in 1998, Floyd's final season before he departed to be head coach of the Chicago Bulls, but the mark left by those players on Iowa State basketball was undeniable, and it is still one of the most significant stretches of Cyclones basketball history.

83 The Story of Cyclones Baseball

As each spring passes and the first pitch ceases to come with each one of them, the memories of America's pastime fade further and further away. Tucked away behind a row of houses sits a baseball field, the old Iowa State logo painted dead center onto the dugout walls. When spring turns to summer the field sits empty. There is no crowd to smell the freshly cut grass. No spectators to hear the crack of the bat and watch the ball fly into the distance. No fans to toss their peanut shells to the bleachers and roar for the Cyclones.

It wasn't always this way.

When what was then Iowa Agricultural College joined the Iowa Intercollegiate Baseball Association in 1892, baseball at Iowa State was alive and well. The school had joined a league with the likes of Grinnell College, State University (Iowa), Drake University, and Iowa College (UNI). By the next year, Cornell College (Mt. Vernon) joined the association. Baseball began to thrive in Ames, Iowa.

It was 1924 when Iowa State claimed its first conference title, with a Missouri Valley championship. In 1936 Iowa State added a Big 6 crown. Two seasons later the program began to take shape. It was in 1938 when Leroy "Capp" Timm took over as coach of the Cyclones, but in 1942 he departed to join the war effort. The ascension of the program really began with his return in 1947.

Timm was a steward of the game, serving on the national rules committee for 11 years. He was also keen on fundamentals and taking advantage of strategy with all of his exotic plays. With a speedy runner on second, for example, he'd bunt for a hit and the runner from second would just keep running, rounding third to home. There was another play where he'd emerge from the dugout and make a demonstrative signal to walk a hitter. Except a certain signal meant they'd pitch him a ball before piping a strike down the middle.

"It's better to die in childbirth than to get a called third strike," he'd yell to his players.

He cared so much about his players that he took money he received and split it among the team for books and lodging. One day, Iowa State was set to play Missouri and needed to get the games in. So Timm poured gas on the infield and burned it in an attempt to dry it. "And we got the games played," said Gary Thompson, who was a multisport athlete and played shortstop for Timm until 1957.

It was around that time when Timm's coaching began paying dividends. The Cyclones won the Big 7 title in 1957 and then reached the College World Series for the first time. That summer, Iowa State arrived at Municipal Stadium in Omaha and beat Notre Dame before losing to California in the second game. It was double-elimination, so the Cyclones were still alive. They beat Connecticut in the third game to set up a rematch with California. Things were going well the second time around, until California scored eight runs in the sixth inning to win. Iowa State finished third.

The Cyclones claimed Big 8 titles in 1970 and 1971, advancing to their second College World Series in 1970. Following the 1974 season, Timm retired with a 340–373–5 career mark, having coached the Cyclones to three conference titles and two World Series appearances. Baseball at Iowa State continued until 2001, when the program was dropped due to budget cuts.

After 109 years and 2,775 games, Iowa State baseball disappeared into the distance.

84 Harris from Perris

For the good part of three years, Danny Harris had been dedicated to reaching this particular moment. All the time spent at the Southwest Athletic Complex in Ames with Iowa State assistant Steve Lynn, all the strategizing, all the workouts, all the discipline, and all the sweat had been for this moment. Harris was in Madrid, staring at the distinguished Edwin Moses and his unprecedented streak.

It had been nine years, nine months, nine days and 122 races since Moses had lost in the 400-meter hurdles, and he stared blankly back at the 21-year-old from Perris, California.

The reason Harris had chosen to attend Iowa State in the first place was actually to play football. That was his first love, and while other schools coveted him, they wanted him solely for track. Boise State coach Jim Criner wanted him as a defensive back, and when Criner left to take over the Iowa State football program, Harris followed. He arrived on a football scholarship with the understanding that he'd be able to run track, and during his first year, Harris went from football to track. He made an immediate impact as a hurdler, breaking the world junior record in the 400-meter hurdles in his third race.

Only months removed from his freshman season, at 18 years old, Harris ran 48.02 in the 400-meter hurdles at the Olympic Trials, again setting a world junior record, which still stands. He had finished second to Moses and qualified for the 1984 Olympics. The next month he arrived at the Los Angeles Coliseum to run in the prestigious event. Harris looked around and saw the baby grand piano and the arches of the Coliseum. He was awestruck.

"Trying to describe what that feels like is trying to describe what it's like to walk on the moon," Harris said. "[I had] the realization that I was in something that was way bigger than anything I had ever been a part of or would ever be a part of again."

Harris finished behind Moses again in the Olympics, taking silver as a teenager. Then he was back to Ames to begin his sophomore season on the gridiron. But after sustaining a knee injury that fall, Harris decided to focus on track and ended his football career. By 1987 Harris had become a star. He won four Drake Relays titles and three national championships in the 400-meter hurdles, going 37–0 against collegiate competition. Following his third season, Harris made the difficult decision to focus on the professional circuit. He remained at Iowa State but stopped competing for the Cyclones.

Lynn and Harris remained a tandem as they prepared for Moses. There were two-a-days, and oftentimes the two were the only ones to be found on the track in Ames. "All of that was designed for me to be able to beat Edwin," Harris said. "Steve was the architect of that." In his last practice with Lynn in Ames before he readied to fly to Madrid in June 1987, Harris ran 500 meters at the Southwest Athletic Complex in 58 seconds. Then he did 300 meters in 33 seconds. And finally 200 meters in 21 seconds. He was ready.

"Hey," Lynn told Harris before he got on the plane, "you're ready to run 47.5."

Harris wasn't even sure Moses would be in Madrid. He was told by a promoter that he would be, but he had heard that several times before and Moses hadn't shown up. Harris had originally planned to race in Italy, but Moses had reportedly been dodging competition, so when he heard he might be in Spain, Harris changed his plans. When he stepped out of his car in Madrid, Moses was sitting on the steps of the hotel eating gelato.

"He had no idea I was coming," Harris later told the *Des Moines Register.* "I still remember the look on his face."

The two runners hadn't faced off since Moses took first and Harris second in the 1984 Olympics. "If I beat him," Harris had told reporters before the Olympics, "I would go down in history as the guy who finally beat Edwin Moses." Here was another chance.

On the afternoon of June 4, 1987, Moses jumped out to a lead over the first two hurdles, but Harris passed him on the fifth and never looked back. When Moses clipped the final hurdle, Harris finished him off. The longest streak in track history was over as Harris glanced up at his time: 47.56. It was just as Coach Lynn had predicted.

"I was convinced that today would be the day that I would beat him and end his run of victories," Harris said afterward. "This is a great day for me."

Harris from Perris as they called him—the kid from Iowa State—is remembered as the man who *finally* beat Edwin Moses.

85 Keith Krepfle

As Keith Krepfle trotted onto the field in Philadelphia for the first day of NFL training camp as a rookie—his blonde, medium-length haircut swaying in the breeze—he was about to get a rude awakening to life with the Eagles. The guy with a well-scrubbed, boyish face was about to meet middle linebacker Bill Bergey. *Whack!* Bergey threw his elbow right across Krepfle's face. It was his way of saying, "Welcome to Philadelphia."

Krepfle got up, shook off the hit, and walked back to the huddle. *Okay, now we'll see what this guy is made of,* Bergey thought.

On the next play, Bergey saw Krepfle coming across the middle and the ball in the air headed his way. Putting the hit of the previous play out of his mind, Krepfle soared into the air and came down with the ball in traffic, serving almost as an in-your-face response to the hit before. "I knew right then he was a football player," Bergey said later. "Keith doesn't hear footsteps. He makes the other guy hear *his* footsteps."

The rough persona on the playing field didn't necessarily match his choirboy appearance, but that was the way Krepfle always played. He earned the nickname Captain Crunch in his first year with the Philadelphia Eagles as a special teams player, but it was a mentality he carried with him since he was a four-sport athlete in Potosi, Wisconsin.

It was his hard-nosed approach, catching ability, and size that drew Iowa State to Krepfle initially as a wide receiver, but he spent his freshman season as a defensive back. Krepfle earned the last available scholarship from coach Johnny Majors in 1971, but it wasn't until tight end Bob Richardson was injured that Krepfle got his chance to catch the ball in his second year. "Moving to tight end was a big break for me," Krepfle later told Buck Turnbull of the *Des Moines Register*. He had put on 25 or 30 pounds after his freshman season, and even after the return of Richardson, Krepfle never gave up his spot.

In his sophomore season in 1971, Krepfle accounted for 40 catches and seven touchdowns, which was a sophomore school record. "One of my goals last year was just to make the traveling squad and get some experience," Krepfle said then. "In my high school, there were only 25 or 30 guys out for football, so I was pretty awed when I came here." Pretty soon, coaches and teammates alike were awed by Keith's ability.

"Dynamic from every standpoint," Majors said. "I've never had a better tight end in my whole career in 29 years. Never."

During his three-year career in Ames, where the 6'2", 220-pounder amassed 94 catches, 1,368 yards, and 15 touchdowns, Krepfle was also named All–Big 8 as a junior and senior. One of his most memorable performances came in 1972 in Iowa State's 23–23 tie against No. 3 Nebraska at Clyde Williams Field, where he caught two touchdown passes. That tie snapped the Huskers' 24-game conference win streak.

"He was 100 miles an hour, he went the whole time," quarterback George Amundson recalled. "If I could run a touchdown or throw him a pass this short, I'd throw him a pass this short. He deserved it…but there was no way anybody was going to stop him. Just like pinball, boom, boom, boom."

That grittiness on the field, with simultaneous finesse in the air as a receiver, made Krepfle an obvious candidate for the NFL, and he was drafted by the Eagles in 1974. But Krepfle made the decision not to report to Philadelphia immediately. His thought was that his skills weren't where they needed to be and he wasn't prepared to oust All-Pro tight end Charle Young. The World Football League and Jacksonville Sharks were where he went first. "I figured if the WFL would get off the ground," Krepfle told Gary Ledman of the *Evening Independent*, "I would have a better chance."

After the team folded the next year, Krepfle reported to Philadelphia and took his lumps from guys like Bergey, but never wavered in his ability. Krepfle was a rock in Philadelphia from 1975 to 1981 before spending his last season in the pros with the Atlanta Falcons in 1982. His best season came in 1979 in Philly when he caught 41 passes for 760 yards and three touchdowns. "Keith is the most intense, consistent, giving-what-he-has-to-give football player I've ever encountered," Eagles coach Dick Vermeil said.

With the Eagles, Krepfle became the first Iowa State alum to score a touchdown in a Super Bowl, grabbing an eight-yard pass from Ron Jaworski for the only Philadelphia touchdown in a 27–10 loss to Oakland in Super Bowl XV.

"Once in a while, something will pop up from the past, and it's very special," Krepfle said in 2002. "The Eagles had a Super Bowl reunion a few years ago, and that was a really nice night. But for the most part, I've put my football career in the past."

Krepfle may have put his football career in the past, but those who saw him play still think of him as maybe the best tight end in Cyclones history. He was inducted into the Iowa State Hall of Fame in 2002.

86 The Tornado Game

Some 110 years after Iowa State earned the moniker Cyclones for the football team's on-field play, and stemming from the meteorological tendencies of the university's location, the nickname became quite literal as the dark and ominous funnel clouds rolled over Jack Trice Stadium on the night of November 12, 2005.

Fans had just started streaming into the stadium and players had just taken the field for pregame warm-ups when the sirens began blaring across Ames. A tornado had moved in from Woodward and had touched down in the northwest part of town. Both Iowa State and No. 22 Colorado were called off the field and fans were told to evacuate to Hilton Coliseum. Some fans followed orders and others, well, didn't.

"I heard many of the Iowa State fans just left and went back out and tailgated a little longer in the parking lot," coach Dan McCarney said. "Taking cover was going out and having a couple more cold ones."

While the tornado touched down not far from Jack Trice Stadium, McCarney and Colorado coach Gary Barnett huddled inside with officials. The game eventually started 30 minutes late, but not without some repercussions. Already known as somewhat of a wind tunnel, the wind howled between 20 to 25 mph through the stadium on this particular night, with gusts reaching 45 mph. Iowa State kicker Tony Yelk's opening kickoff sailed 20 yards past the goal line while one of Colorado kicker Mason Crosby's PATs later landed on the Jacobson Building's roof in the north end zone. "As we all know, the wind blows in Ames, Iowa, pretty good," McCarney said. "Even more so that day, but our guys didn't flinch. Not one bit."

The crazed crowd of 49,242, many of whom had had extra time in those parking lots that McCarney referenced, created one of the rowdiest and most electric environments ever. Iowa State, meanwhile, quickly took Colorado by storm in a game that held Big 12 North championship implications.

With Iowa State leading 16–13 as the third quarter drew to a close, Colorado had just taken over at the Iowa State 34-yard line. Iowa State linebacker Tim Dobbins knocked the ball out of

The 1991 Blizzard

Apparently playing Colorado tends to bring out the worst weather, because before a tornado warning ever struck in 2005, the Buffaloes arrived at Jack Trice Stadium in 1991 in a blizzard.

While Colorado attempted to make the trip from its Des Moines hotel on November 23, 1991, it quickly encountered blizzard conditions. In one instance, the team bus was unable to stop for traffic and pushed off to the side of the road. Upon arrival, it found a desolate stadium. Estimates placed the attendance between 1,500 and 2,000 people (36,256 tickets had been distributed), and that number may even have been a bit inflated.

No tickets were taken for admittance into the game. If fans could somehow make it, they were let in. With wind chills of –15 degrees and gusts of 40 mph, the teams pressed on, and Colorado eventually won the season finale 17–14.

Colorado running back Lawrence Vickers' hands on the ensuing play, and safety Steve Paris scooped up the ball and took it 66 yards for a touchdown. When Colorado threatened again, this time trailing by one touchdown with less than two minutes remaining, CU quarterback Joel Klatt threw a screen pass right into the hands of Iowa State's 305-pound defensive tackle Brent "Big Play" Curvey, who rumbled 66 yards to seal a 30–16 victory.

"It was Cyclone weather tonight," McCarney declared afterward.

Iowa State's fourth straight win had kept it in line to tie Colorado for the Big 12 North crown, before an overtime loss to Kansas two weeks later wiped those hopes away.

Yet there has never been a time when Iowa State has been more fitting of its nickname.

"I'll always be really proud of that victory," McCarney said. "To this day, Gary Barnett blames me and says I had some kind of connection for getting that damn tornado to come in before we played that game."

87 The Gibbons Brothers

They're one of the most successful wrestling families in the state of Iowa. The Gibbons brothers won a combined 10 Iowa state titles and earned nine All-America honors as Cyclones, two individual national championships, and an NCAA team championship.

For Tim, Jim, Joe, and Jeff Gibbons, however, the titles pale in comparison to what it means to have accomplished it all together.

"Wrestling became almost a way for us to bond as a family," Jim said.

Growing up in Ames, Iowa, in the 1960s and '70s, wrestling was in its heyday within the community, and the Gibbons family couldn't get enough of it. Bill, the boys' father, was the driving force behind his kids getting into the sport, and made sure there was every opportunity available for his sons to get vast exposure. "We just pushed each other," Tim Gibbons said. "We just created a culture through our expectations."

"He taught us how to train, drill, and techniques," Jim, the second-eldest behind Tim, remembered. "We were doing things that were kind of ahead of our time."

As a 98-pounder when he was a sophomore, Jim nabbed his first Iowa state championship for Ames High, following it up with state titles at 105 pounds as a junior and 119 pounds as a senior. He rounded out his prep career with a 76–1 record but wasn't highly recruited to be a college wrestler, partly because he didn't want to be.

Just a short distance from Ames High School, the Iowa State wrestling program had won six of the last 12 national championships by 1977, and Jim knew he wanted to stay right there at home. Plus, Tim was already a student at the university, keeping the family dynamic intact.

Jim joined ISU legend Harold Nichols at Iowa State and became a three-time All-American in 1980, '81, and '82 and won two Big 8 titles at 134 pounds. But the crown jewel of his collegiate career came in 1981 with a 16–8 upset of Lehigh's Darryl Burley, giving Jim an NCAA championship as a junior. His legacy was solidified, but that win just might have been the tipping point for another Gibbons legacy to begin.

That same year, 1981, Joe, the third Gibbons brother, was a senior in high school and was highly sought after nationally by college coaches. "He had taken a couple visits, and he considered going to Iowa with [Dan] Gable," Jim remembered. "He went up to Wisconsin and was more highly recruited." As a prep, Joe owned a 105–5 record and four state titles and didn't even allow a take-down his senior season. After weighing his options, he chose family above all else and joined the Cyclones.

"[My brothers] cleared a path for me, and I made it wider," Joe said. That path led him to two Big 8 championships and a national title in his junior season, just like his brother. Joe holds the record for most wins in a single season (53) and has the distinction of being Nichols' last NCAA champion. And when Iowa State looked for Nichols' successor, it didn't have to turn its eyes very far.

Upon exhausting his eligibility, Jim became an assistant with the Cyclones, coaching for two seasons before being hired as the head coach in 1985, on his 26th birthday, to replace a living legend. Being tapped certainly thrilled Jim, but it also gave him an appreciation for the kind of people his brothers were. "I don't get the job at Iowa State at age 26 if my brothers are a bunch of yahoos," Jim said. "That doesn't happen unless those guys carry themselves in a quality manner."

Jim coached the Cyclones from 1985 to 1992, compiling a 93–32–1 mark while coaching 23 Big 8 champions and seven NCAA champions. The pinnacle of his coaching career came in 1987 when Iowa State won the NCAA team championship, ending a nine-year title run by Gable and Iowa.

In that '87 tournament, Jim coached his youngest brother, Jeff, to a third-place finish at 134 pounds, adding to the family tradition the Gibbonses established in Ames. From their success in high school, which carried on to Iowa State, the Gibbonses still relish the opportunity to do it with one another.

"Personally for me," Jim said, "winning my national championship as a family, there's no feeling like that."

88 Mike Busch

Many two-sport athletes have come through Iowa State, but it would be difficult to locate one who left a mark quite like Mike Busch, a dependable tight end on the gridiron and an imposing force in the batter's box. And to think, he nearly ended up on the other side of the state.

That's where Busch started, so it made sense. He grew up in the eastern Iowa town of Donahue and attended North Scott High School, where he earned first-team All-State honors on the football field and mashed home runs on the baseball diamond. He was a Hawkeye, and the Hawkeyes heavily recruited him, offering him a full-ride scholarship. So the box full of offers—from Wisconsin, Stanford, Michigan, Nebraska, Minnesota, and Iowa State—wasn't really needed. Busch was going to Iowa, and that was that. Until he got a call the night before Signing Day.

"Hey, listen," Iowa assistant Carl Jackson told a young Busch on the phone, "we've got five tight ends on scholarship. We'd like you to walk on the first year, and we'll have a scholarship for you the following year."

"No, full ride or I'm just going to go elsewhere," Busch—thinking of those other offers—replied.

Well, Iowa didn't offer. Busch's brother was already at Iowa State, the Cyclones were still offering a full ride, and they'd even let him play baseball. The decision was pretty simple.

During Busch's freshman year, he went from football—where he appeared in every game, mostly on third-and-long situations and special teams—to baseball. He pitched and played some in the outfield, but Busch was still banged up from football and didn't play to his full potential. With football coach Jim Criner having been fired following his freshman season in 1986, Busch wanted to make an impression on new coach Jim Walden and lock up a starting role at tight end. So he concentrated on weight lifting and football, and quit baseball.

The decision to focus on football paid off when Busch was named Iowa State's starting tight end in 1987. At 6'5" and 250 pounds, he was a big target between the numbers and he began to excel on the gridiron. During the winter, Busch kept hearing from baseball coach Bobby Randall in the weight room. He wanted Busch to come back. He couldn't pitch anymore—his shoulders couldn't handle it—but Randall told Busch he could play first base.

"About the fourth or fifth time I ran into him I go, 'You know what, I don't want to play spring ball, I'll just go out and do it,'" Busch recalled. "It worked out pretty good."

That might be an understatement. His football career took off his junior year, and then Busch hit .401 in his first season back on the baseball team that spring. By the time his Iowa State career

A Slow-Starting MLB Career

When Mike Busch arrived in the minors after being selected in the fourth round of the 1990 MLB Draft, his career started rather slowly. In fact, Busch started 0-for-21 at the plate.

"I knew I was a good player; I wouldn't have been drafted in the fourth round otherwise," Busch said. "I had every person in the Dodgers organization tell me how to hit or I should do this, that, and the other."

Finally, Dodgers hitting coordinator Reggie Smith got to Busch.

"Hey," Smith asked, "what do you remember doing last year when you were in college?"

"I just decided to be a good hitter and I was a good hitter," Busch told him.

That was the turnaround. Busch finished his first year of professional baseball hitting .327 with 13 home runs. He would later become the first replacement player called up following the 1994 MLB strike and hit seven home runs in two seasons in the majors.

ended, Busch had played in all 44 games on the football field, racking up 1,061 receiving yards while twice earning All–Big 8 honors. On the baseball diamond, he hit 17 home runs as a senior and finished with 31 career homers, both Iowa State records.

During that senior year, Busch was named the Big 8 Athlete of the Year and was an All-American in football *and* baseball.

In the midst of his senior baseball season, Busch was selected in the 10th round of the NFL Draft by the Tampa Bay Buccaneers. He was disappointed. Buccaneers coach Ray Perkins called six or more times. "You're a deep draft pick," Perkins told him, "but we've got a lot of plans for your type of ability." It was still baseball season, though, and Busch was getting some looks, so he didn't go to mini camp. Back at home that summer, a scout from the Dodgers showed up. "We're going to pick you pretty high," he said. "They're trying to figure out what order, but it's going to be the first three to four picks for us." The Dodgers selected Busch in the fourth round of the MLB Draft, and he eventually debuted five years later in 1995.

There is a professional baseball card out there somewhere that, on the back, reads: *Mike Busch—First Base*. If you look lower, there are four rows, each listing years sequentially between 1987 and 1990. To the right of each year it lists Iowa State. What the card doesn't say is that Mike Busch almost never ended up in Ames, and he nearly didn't play baseball.

89 Storm the Field

As the final seconds begin to tick away, you start inching into the nearest aisle and then slowly make your way down each concrete step. The clock hits zeros. Iowa State has won. You jump over the railing. Adrenaline hits. You run.

Some of the greatest moments in Iowa State football history are marked by memories of thousands of fans storming the field. There might be no greater instance than when 52,000 fans flooded the Jack Trice Stadium field on the night of November 18, 2011, after the Cyclones upset No. 2 Oklahoma State. (Photo courtesy of Iowa State Athletics)

There is, of course, a rhyme and reason to storming the field. You certainly don't do it by yourself (that's not really *storming*), and you don't do it for just *any* game. Maybe it comes after an emotionally charged rivalry game (See: Iowa 2011). It could be after knocking off a rival to end a long streak (See: Nebraska 2002). It certainly comes after knocking off a highly ranked opponent that was an overwhelming favorite (See: Oklahoma State 2011).

Storming the field is rooted deep in sports history, and it has a history at Iowa State. When George Amundson hit Willie Jones in the corner of the end zone at Clyde Williams Field in 1972 for a game-tying touchdown against Nebraska, some fans rushed onto the field to celebrate. "The field was covered with fans, so it took a while to get everybody off," Amundson said. The Cyclones eventually missed the extra point and settled for a tie. If there was one lesson to be learned, it is to not prematurely storm the field.

Another lesson? Storm with caution.

When Iowa State knocked off Nebraska by 22 in 2002 behind three Seneca Wallace touchdowns, it had beaten the Huskers for only the second time in its last 25 matchups and for the first time in its last 10 tries. The margin of victory was its largest against Nebraska since 1899. So fans stormed the field, and coach Dan McCarney paid the price.

"I got a fat lip from somebody out there," McCarney said with a smile afterward. "It got a little dangerous, but I'll fight my way out of danger like that any time."

That's the spirit, because storming the field comes only with the best and most memorable victories. If you're storming the field, there's a good chance it'll be a game that is etched among the finest in Iowa State history.

"That was cool, man. Everybody running on the field and ripping down goal posts," Wallace said of that 2002 instance. "All the fans, man, the energy in the stadium.… After the game, all the fans coming down there, it's so surreal."

Fans rushed onto the field in 2005 when Iowa State knocked off No. 8 Iowa. They stormed the field when Bret Culbertson's late field goal pushed the Cyclones over the Hawkeyes in 2007. They jumped over the walls in 2007 when the Cyclones stormed back from a 21-point deficit to beat Colorado. When James White turned the corner and ran into the end zone to beat Iowa in 2011, fans were already pouring out of the stands.

They have never rushed the field quite like they did on the night of November 18, 2011, when Jeff Woody broke into the end zone. "I'm not sure this field can fit all 52,000, but they're going to try!" ESPN broadcaster Joe Tessitore proclaimed to a national audience as fans rushed from every which way. That night combined an emotional overtime victory with beating the nation's No. 2 team as a 27-point underdog. So when Woody crossed the goal line, the floodgates opened and fans rushed from every section like never before.

It is that shot, with the field at Jack Trice Stadium filled with fans, that marks the signature win in program history. As you dash across the field and your adrenaline flows, you too will be part of a snapshot in Iowa State history with an undoubtedly memorable run.

90 Stacy Frese

She remembers the day when she had to tell him no all too well.

Then the head coach at Toledo, Bill Fennelly had turned his eyes on the recruiting trail back to his home state of Iowa, where Stacy Frese—a small point guard from Cedar Rapids—caught his attention. The two had an instant rapport, but when the time arrived for Frese to make a decision, she just couldn't go east.

"That was probably because I was kind of a baby and didn't want to go very far from home," Frese recalled.

Frese followed her gut and traveled the 30 minutes or so south to play for Iowa, but a coaching change after her freshman season resulted in her searching for a new home. There wasn't much contemplation over where she'd go. Luckily for Frese, Fennelly had since moved on and taken the head coaching position at Iowa State. She was ready to make the jump to play for Fennelly and leave the Hawkeyes for the Cyclones. Having her sister, Brenda, on Fennelly's new staff didn't hurt either.

"It just seemed like it was meant to be," Frese said.

Transfer rules required Frese to sit out during the 1996–97 season, but the following year as a redshirt sophomore, her career as one of the first great Iowa State players finally began. Frese's redshirt season had given her the opportunity to grow in Fennelly's system, and at just 5'8", it also gave her a chance to develop a physical stature suitable for the Big 12.

Looks can be deceiving—something Frese proved frequently. Often lighter and shorter than many of her opponents, she made up for a lack of some physical attributes with a killer instinct. Taking punishment on a nightly basis in the Big 12, Frese always got up, shook off the adversity, and said, "Okay, let's go."

With Fennelly on the sideline shouting his instructions, he had his first great floor general with Frese. She wasn't just a great leader on the court, but was also efficient offensively and a right-handed secret weapon.

"It was always funny because she did everything left-handed except shoot a basketball. She bowls, she throws, she writes left-handed," Fennelly said. "Everybody would force her to the left, but

Player Profile: Tonya Burns

She ran the floor at Hilton Coliseum a decade before Bill Fennelly awoke the once-dormant program, but during her time wearing the Cardinal and Gold, Tonya Burns wrote a big chapter in the women's basketball history book.

With second-team All–Big 8 honors as a sophomore and junior, Burns was named to the conference's first team as a senior, finishing her career holding or sharing 33 school records. Burns tallied 1,789 points and 921 rebounds and set the single-game scoring mark in 1984 with 42 points against Nebraska on 18-of-25 shooting.

Burns was the first Cyclones women's basketball player to have her jersey retired and hoisted up into the rafters, which took place at the basketball banquet following her senior year in 1985.

she was naturally left-handed, so we ran our offense backward for her. She could go to the left and be more open."

Being more open paid off. As a senior Frese averaged 14.1 points per game and shot a blistering 44.6 percent from three-point range. She scored more than 500 points in each of her last two seasons—both top 10 marks in program history—and finished with 1,494 points, which was the third-best total when her career ended.

Point guards need to be problem solvers, and Frese was certainly one of the first—and best—to do it at Iowa State. As a three-year starter and two-time Associated Press All-American, Frese developed the same kind of rapport with her teammates that she did when she first met Fennelly as a recruit. The trust and sense of togetherness was largely due to her leadership, which is something Fennelly remembered more than a decade later.

"Whatever Stacy did, whether it was practice, games, on the bus, on a plane, every single player bought into what she said," Fennelly said. "That's a rare quality in any player, but it's one I think [that] gave us that edge, that toughness."

Toughness and confidence led to memorable moments too. Frese scored 16 points in Iowa State's big win in the 1999 Sweet 16 against No. 1–seeded UConn, but it was performances against Nebraska and Drake that showed just how potent Frese could be. That same season against the Cornhuskers, Frese went 8-of-8 from three-point range and scored 29 points. Against Drake as a senior, she drained a school-record 10 three-pointers, ending the game with a career-high 34 points.

"She's this tiny little peanut of a guard and she could outwork someone, she could drive and finish a layup and get drilled," former teammate Angie Welle said. "She could make a three-pointer several feet behind the three-point line."

Now more than a decade removed from her playing days, Frese's name might not be in the rafters at Hilton Coliseum, but it is in the record books. She holds the Iowa State career record for three-point field goal percentage (45.3) and ranks fourth in career three-pointers made (274) despite playing only three seasons. That's quite a difference from where Frese was as a former Hawkeye, who as a recruit said no to joining Fennelly in Toledo.

91 Marcus Robertson

Kansas receiver Jim New had just caught the pass from Kelly Donohoe and had what looked like a clear path to the end zone. Iowa State was in town that day, October 7, 1989, and the Cyclones were in the lead. Out of nowhere came cornerback Marcus Robertson, who punched the ball loose at the 1-yard line and into the end zone for the touchback. Iowa State held on to win 24–20. "That one infamous play I'll remember forever," KU coach Glen Mason said later.

That was the kind of impact Marcus Robertson had as a lock-down cornerback for Iowa State. He was a game changer in the secondary. Robertson was a two-time All–Big 8 selection and a 12-year NFL veteran with one first-team All-Pro honor, and he is still considered to be one of the best defensive backs in ISU football history.

Robertson arrived in Ames from Altadena, California, in 1987 and hopped onto the field as a playmaker almost immediately in coach Jim Walden's first season. He made 54 tackles for the Cyclones as a freshman, but it was in 1988 when his presence started to be felt throughout the Big 8.

As a sophomore, Robertson had the ability to be drawn to the ball like a magnet, and always drew the task of covering the opponent's top receiver, which led to an upward spike in the numbers on his stat sheet. He racked up 70 tackles, three interceptions, and two fumble recoveries and was on the honorable mention All–Big 8 squad.

With the help of Robertson as a safety net for the Cyclones in 1989, Iowa State went 6–5 and 4–3 in the Big 8 (the best conference mark since 1978). Counting his game-saving play against the Jayhawks, Robertson had 11 pass breakups and 89 tackles, and was All–Big 8 while handling punt-returning duties for special teams.

A key interception, his only one of the season, as a senior in 1990 keyed Iowa State's first win against Oklahoma, 33–31, since 1961. Robertson missed the final three games that season due to a broken leg but still managed to find his way onto the All–Big 8 squad and tallied 47 tackles and six pass breakups.

Robertson's status as a trusty defender in college propelled him to be selected in the fourth round of the 1991 NFL Draft by the Houston Oilers. In just his third season with Houston, he was selected to the All-Pro team, primarily because of defensive coordinator Buddy Ryan's implementation of the "46" defense and his decision to rely on Marcus to make big plays.

"Buddy didn't put any restrictions on me and had confidence I could get the job done, and I just went out and played," Robertson said.

Robertson spent 10 years with the Oilers as they moved from Houston to Tennessee and eventually became the Tennessee Titans. He closed out his career for the Seattle Seahawks and officially retired in 2002. He played in 162 NFL games, was part of the playoffs in five of his 12 years, and grabbed 24 interceptions. He was inducted into the Iowa State Hall of Fame in 2008.

92 Enjoy Tailgating

When the game kicks off, Iowa State football fans can surely be found in their seats. From all corners of Iowa and beyond, Cyclones supporters flock to Jack Trice Stadium on game days to watch what this year's group of footballers has to offer. And while fans are screaming themselves hoarse as the action on the gridiron dictates, there is a whole other spectacle to behold on autumn Saturdays: tailgating.

The magnetism of watching the Cyclones on the field is what draws people to Ames in the fall, but it's the tailgating right outside Jack Trice Stadium that lets you share in your passion and enthusiasm for your team in other ways. Whether it's grilling burgers, brats, or chicken, eating chips and dip, or taking down a variety of desserts, all of the essential tailgating cuisine is usually spread out under a tent bearing the I-State logo. You're sure to find coolers stocked with soda, beer, and other beverages at every stop you make, as well as tailgating games like bags, ladder golf, or people simply tossing around the pigskin.

All of the sights and sounds of the tailgating experience at Iowa State are just as satisfying as the smells, food, and drinks. Nearly every spot in the parking lots between Hilton Coliseum and Jack Trice Stadium is filled with cars, buses, and RVs. Music rings throughout the maze of vehicles as you make your way to the stadium, and your fellow Cyclones fans are sure to give you a wave or stop you for a chat about the upcoming game. Tailgating lots also exist to the south and east parts of the stadium, and even spill over into the grass lots that are sure to give a rich experience for a first-time tailgater.

While the Cyclone Tents program (placed just to the north of Jack Trice Stadium) is available to rent for fans, you'll mostly see open areas in the grass or in the parking lots that are filled with friends and families, some of whom show up on Friday evenings to camp in the tailgating lots. Tailgating is permitted by the city up to six hours before kickoff, and it's those gatherings that make the game-day experience at Iowa State a special one.

"My favorite memory of tailgating as a kid was playing football with friends, hanging out, and having a barbeque with my friends and family," Cyclone Club donor Jason Loutsch told Cyclones. com in 2009. "As an adult, I love providing the same atmosphere for my kids that I was provided. It's a tailgating tradition that is a great experience for my family."

The university once estimated that there are 10 to 15 percent more tailgaters than those who attend the games, and for big games, that jumps to 40 percent. Cyclones fans not only bring their best in the stadium, they do it outside at the tailgating festivities as well. So next time you're wandering through the parking lots outside Jack Trice Stadium on game day, be sure to stop at one of the many tents with that I-State logo on top and enjoy a beer and some barbeque.

93 Lisa Koll

Believe it or not, Lisa Koll (now Lisa Uhl) wasn't much of a runner growing up. Outside of entering a couple road races with her dad in fifth and sixth grade, it wasn't something she did. It wasn't even something she was interested in. Her enjoyment came more through softball, basketball, soccer, and gymnastics. Always a competitive person, spending time on the bench in those sports as she got older was hard. She wanted the competition.

It was through chance that she even became interested in running as an eighth grader. Uhl's locker was located in the hallway right next to David Newman's classroom in Fort Dodge, Iowa, and Newman was the middle school cross country coach. He was also the father of one of Lisa's teammates in basketball and had seen her running ability on the court.

"You need to go out for cross country," Newman told Lisa one day near her locker. "You'd be great at running, you have a great stride."

Lisa Koll (now Uhl) runs in the women's 10,000-meter final during the 2010 USA Outdoor Track and Field championships at Drake Stadium in Des Moines, Iowa, on June 24, 2010. (Photo courtesy of Getty Images/Andy Lyons)

"No, no I'm going to play volleyball," Uhl said. "I really want to do that."

It was because of Newman's persistence that Lisa spurned volleyball and went out for cross country. She started as one of the slowest runners on the team, but after five or six weeks, she vaulted to the top five. That rise to the top has symbolized what Lisa's running career has entailed from high school, to setting records at Iowa State, to competing in the Olympics. It was during those early years that she fell in love with running.

Lisa blossomed into a good high school runner, finishing eighth in the 4,000 meters at the 2004 Iowa state cross-country meet, and running 10:16.71 for the 3,000 meters in track. But a state championship eluded her as a prep, and colleges weren't breaking down the door to recruit her. Lisa comes from an Iowa State family—both of her parents are alums, and her brother was enrolled at the time she was deciding where to go. She knew she wanted to study veterinary medicine (or general medicine) and wanted an athletic challenge to complement that. Enter Iowa State and former ISU coach Corey Ihmels.

After spending a year in Ames, Lisa wasn't seeing the results she was hoping for. She couldn't put her finger on what wasn't working. Finally a conversation with her future husband, Kiel Uhl, got through to her. "You're not really dedicating yourself 100 percent to this," Kiel said. It was exactly what Lisa needed to hear.

"That tough love that I got from him is what opened my eyes to, 'I'm going to dedicate myself to this a little bit more and see what I can do,'" Lisa said.

That next season as a sophomore, the girl who didn't win any state titles while at Fort Dodge exploded onto the national scene. Uhl went on to be an 11-time All-American in cross country and track, a two-time Drake Relays champion, and a four-time NCAA champion. She also became the first woman *ever* to win four Big 12 titles in the same event (10,000-meter run).

It was at the 2010 NCAA Track and Field Championships where Uhl cemented her legacy. She swept the 5,000- and 10,000-meter runs, setting an NCAA Division I record in the latter with a time of 31:18.07. That mark made her the sixth-fastest American woman in history at that distance.

"I think I had a magic day that day," Uhl said. "Someone was looking down on me that day and giving me some good vibes, because I think I was capable of doing that, but it just had to happen on the right day, and fortunately for me the weather was good, my body felt good, and it just happened."

Lisa finished fourth at the 2012 US Olympic Trials—overcoming a situation that forced her to retie her shoe—to punch her ticket to London. She finished the 10,000-meter final 13th, running a personal-best 31:12.80 at the 2012 Olympics.

And to think, she almost didn't start running competitively at all.

94 Road Trip

When attending a sporting event, the passion and enthusiasm is unparalleled in venues like Hilton Coliseum and Jack Trice Stadium. As an Iowa State fan, taking that passion and energy on the road and sharing it with a more hostile crowd can be just as enjoyable. The boos and jeers of opposing fans may come down hard on those who don the Cardinal and Gold, but cheering on the Cyclones in enemy territory is extra sweet when you're singing "ISU Fights" after a victory.

The feeling of watching your team on an opponent's turf gives you an extra sense of pride. It's an us-against-the-world mentality when you catch a game in Iowa City or Lawrence, Kansas, or anywhere else. And the best part about it? Anything can happen. The feeling as the clock strikes 0:00 after a win will make the fight song sound a little bit sweeter, and a loss will have you trying to stealthily move through the opposing crowd after staying to the bitter end. Rooting on the Cyclones in a different city gives you a new appreciation and perspective.

Iowa State has had its fair share of thrills and triumphs on the road too. Some of the biggest moments in Iowa State football history have come away from Ames, particularly 126 miles away in Iowa City. Cyclones fans have flocked to Kinnick Stadium and seen some of the biggest wins in series history.

Cyclones fans filed into Kinnick Stadium in 1998, hearing from Iowa fans about the last year's game in Ames (a 63–20 Iowa win), but fans witnessed Iowa State break a 15-year losing streak to Iowa, winning 27–9. Iowa State entered Kinnick Stadium in 2002, quickly finding itself in a 24–7 deficit. Cyclones fans had to face the ridicule at halftime, but three ISU touchdowns in the first 10 and a half minutes of the second half quickly put Iowa State in the lead, and at the end of the game Cyclones fans celebrated a 36–31 win.

The 2014 edition also provided some drama when ISU kicker Cole Netten, with the game tied, knocked through a 42-yard field goal with two seconds left to send Cyclones players sprinting over to the other side of the field to grab the Cy-Hawk trophy, celebrating the 20–17 win (much to the elation of the Cyclones placed throughout the sea of Black and Gold).

Iowa Staters have also experienced their share of horrors on the road, including a 35–7 football loss in Iowa City in 2010 to the ninth-ranked Hawkeyes. But sharing in the good times on the road also comes with taking your lumps in enemy territory. Iowa State basketball's history in Allen Fieldhouse on the campus of the University of Kansas proves that.

A 270-mile drive southwest will get you from Hilton Coliseum to "the Phog," where history hasn't been on Iowa State's side. But the wins that have come inside the field house have meant that much more to Iowa State fans sitting in the bleachers. Iowa State won its first game in Allen Fieldhouse in its previous 17 tries in 2000 and went on to win the Big 12 title that season. "This is monumental," coach Larry Eustachy said afterward. Kantrail Horton and Jamaal Tinsley led the Cyclones to a win at the Phog again in 2001, making the four-hour drive back to Iowa seem not quite so long.

Of course, there is the infamous Ben McLemore banked three-pointer and Kansas' overtime win in 2013, but Cyclones fans swallowed their pride and continued to cheer. Win or lose, Iowa State fans are there until the end, and road trips are the perfect time to test your fandom.

95 Jake Varner

There wasn't much emotion on his face, despite the magnitude of what he had just done. Jake Varner was standing tall on top of the podium at the 2012 Olympics in London. He had just captured the gold medal for the 211.5-pound freestyle wrestling weight class, but excessive celebration wasn't necessary.

Winning gold was always the plan Varner and his mentor, Cael Sanderson, had envisioned.

"[Sanderson] was going to get me to my ultimate goal, which was to be a gold medalist at the Olympics," Varner said afterward. "And that's what he did."

It was only natural that Varner started wrestling as a kid in Bakersfield, California, where his dad, Steve, and cousin Andy were both very involved in the sport. "It's in my blood," Varner said later. Andy was his high school coach and guided Jake to two state championships and a 159–10 prep record. When looking at colleges, there was one place in the Midwest where Varner set his sights. Jake watched Sanderson win Olympic gold in the 2004 Games and knew being his pupil would be key in getting him to his own dream of being an Olympic champion.

"When I took my recruiting trip to Iowa State and met [Sanderson]," Varner said, "I knew that's where I needed to be."

Varner took in every piece of Sanderson's tutelage and was runner-up at the NCAA championship as a redshirt freshman and sophomore at 184 pounds. Coming that close twice and falling short was tough. But the losses pushed Varner even harder.

"Those are things that you just kind of think of, they're in the back of your head," Varner said. "You don't dwell on them, you just learn from them."

Boy, did Varner learn a lot. After bumping up to the 197-pound weight class in 2009, Jake was right back in the NCAA finals, matched up with Nebraska's Craig Brester. Varner had just lost to Brester two weeks prior in the Big 12 championship, and a desire inside him not to allow it to happen again burned hot.

Varner led 1–0 heading into the third period but rode Brester for 1:25 and built 1:19 in riding time. Attempts at takedowns by Brester were futile as Varner scored the 2–1 win and his first national title as he raised his arms and let out a yell after a 31–2 season mark. "Coming up short, it makes you want it more," Varner said later.

As a senior in 2010, Varner would be without Sanderson, who left to coach at Penn State. Kevin Jackson was at the helm, but despite the move, Varner returned to the NCAA finals, once again against Brester. A focused third period by Varner pushed him to a 5–2 decision and his second national title. "He's the best, hands down, in the country," Jackson said afterward. Varner finished the season unbeaten at 31–0 and was a four-time All-American for the Cyclones.

After graduating from Iowa State, Varner followed Sanderson to State College, Pennsylvania, where he began feverishly training for the 2012 Olympics with the Nittany Lion Wrestling Club. Just like he had done in college, Varner was on the cusp of achieving his goal. He had made it to the Olympic finals and was matched up with Valerii Andriitsev of the Ukraine.

Thanks to an ankle pick attack, a favorite of Sanderson as a wrestler, Varner scored the win at 211.5 pounds to become the sixth former Cyclone to win Olympic gold. As Varner climbed to the top of the podium to receive his medal after, he and Sanderson shared a bear hug. The plan they both envisioned had become a reality.

96 Volleyball: The Right Fit

The undertaking was massive.

When Christy Johnson-Lynch took over as head coach of the Iowa State volleyball program on December 17, 2004, the rebuilding project was staggering. And at that point, you could essentially just call it a building project.

During the tenures of the two previous coaches, a span of seven seasons, Iowa State held a 42–164 overall record and was just 8–112 in the Big 12. One NCAA tournament appearance highlighted what was otherwise looked upon as a struggling program, but Johnson-Lynch was there to change that. And she did it quicker than most would have probably guessed.

Johnson-Lynch took the Cyclones to the NCAA tournament in nine of her first 10 years, to four second-place finishes in the Big 12, and she coached seven AVCA All-Americans in that first decade. It's the recentness of the success that has given Cyclones fans some of their greatest volleyball memories, but the history of the program is important to know too.

Iowa State started its volleyball program in 1973, but league play was still years away. Through the early seasons, the Cyclones played largely at regional tournaments and invitations. However, some single-match events were held periodically. Big 8 tournaments began in 1977, but it wasn't until 1982 that Big 8 conference play commenced.

Cyclones volleyball was in full swing by the mid-1990s, but a trip to the NCAA tournament eluded the program, which was on its seventh coach in its roughly 20-year history. Finally, in 1995, a second-place finish in the final season of the Big 8 Conference gave Iowa State the chance to go to the national tournament. That squad ended the season with a 22–12 overall record and made it to the second round of the tournament before falling to Notre Dame in South Bend, Indiana.

"We went from having the worst record when I was a freshman to making it to the tournament and having the best record," Sonya Van Helden, a key piece to that tournament team, said in 1996. "It shows what hard work can do, and we had a lot of fun too."

Despite the brief glimmer of success in 1995, a new beginning in the Big 12 Conference seemed to bring things crashing back down to Earth. From the inception of the Big 12 through the 2004 season, Iowa State won just 13 conference matches and 59 matches overall. When coach Linda Crum departed in 2004, Iowa State contacted an up-and-coming assistant at Wisconsin, who was known just as Christy Johnson in those days.

Johnson-Lynch played college volleyball at Nebraska, where she was a two-time All-American in 1994 and 1995 as a setter, leading her team to the Huskers' first-ever national championship in 1995. After spending a year teaching and coaching at her high school alma mater at Millard North High School in Omaha, she spent eight seasons as an assistant at Wisconsin, where she helped guide the Badgers to three NCAA tournament regional finals.

It's her technical knowledge and ability to find the right pieces to fit into her program that has given Iowa State the ability to reach new heights. The defensive position of libero has given Iowa State the reputation as "Libero U," with All-Americans Kristen Hahn, Ashley Mass, and Caitlin Nolan to name a few. That masterful direction has smoothly translated to success on the court.

Through 10 seasons with Iowa State, Johnson-Lynch produced a 209–101 overall record in Ames and became Iowa State's all-time wins leader on September 24, 2011.

"We just worked really hard to find the right players to fit our program," Johnson-Lynch once said of the turnaround. "It's the hardworking, down-to-earth kind of person that comes to Iowa State."

97 Follow the Tailgate Tour

The thrill of taking in an Iowa State sporting event at Jack Trice Stadium or Hilton Coliseum is unlike many others. You get to see your favorite coaches and players don the Cardinal and Gold as you lose your voice yelling "Go Cyclones!" and experience the unrivaled enthusiasm of your fellow fans. But thanks to the Cyclone Tailgate Tour, you're also given an opportunity each year to interact with those players and coaches you spend your falls and winters rooting for.

Since ISU athletics director Jamie Pollard helped kick off the Cyclone Tailgate Tour in 2007, the annual caravan around the state has become a way for fans to interact with their favorite Cyclones personalities. (Photo courtesy of Iowa State Athletics)

The Cyclone Tailgate Tour is an annual caravan of Iowa State head coaches and players who travel by bus to various destinations around Iowa in the middle of May and in the early part of June. It's a way for players and coaches to give thanks in person and further Iowa State's presence throughout Iowa. The event consists of large outdoor tents with tables and chairs and gives kids a chance to play inflatable Cyclones games, participate in a variety of sporting stations with the players, and even get their picture taken with Cy.

ISU athletics director Jamie Pollard helped spearhead the first Cyclone Tailgate Tour in 2007, when players and coaches stopped at St. Luke's Hospital and Lindale Mall—with an estimated 1,000 fans in the parking lot—in Cedar Rapids. The tailgate tour replaced the coaches' golf outing, and provided fans more accessibility to actually meet the coaches and get one-on-one time after a short, organized program.

"It's just a way for all of us to go from one spot to another and reach out to the fans who have given so much to Iowa State and say thanks," Voice of the Cyclones John Walters said. "I think that interaction creates great relationships."

In addition to the games and face-to-face time with coaches and players, food, drinks, and official Iowa State gear are available for purchase at each stop on the tour, along with door prizes that can include tickets to an Iowa State game.

"We get to do what we do because of what Cyclone fans allow us to do," Pollard said after one event. "These events continue to be great 'friendraisers' and an excellent chance to build up our next generation of Cyclones with young children."

Each leg of the tour is announced well in advance, so you can be sure to make the stop at the event closest to your area. When you're planning which game to attend next season, make sure to also plan a trip in the summer to meet your favorite coaches and players on the Tailgate Tour.

"The thing that makes it special," Walters said, "is everybody gets their chance to have that moment with the coach, whether it's a picture, an autograph, or just a one-minute conversation."

98 Melvin Ejim

Melvin Ejim stood near the top step of the ladder, cutting away his own piece of a net, smiling ear to ear. Ejim and Iowa State had just won the program's first Big 12 tournament title since 2000, and the thousands of Iowa State fans in the stands of the Sprint Center in Kansas City in 2014 stuck around to watch the celebration.

It was a moment—and season—that sticks in the consciousness of Iowa Staters everywhere, as well it should. Ejim had been named Big 12 Player of the Year, won a Big 12 championship, and helped Iowa State reach the NCAA tournament for the third straight year under fourth-year coach Fred Hoiberg.

Iowa State's Melvin Ejim dunks against the Texas Longhorns at Hilton Coliseum on February 18, 2014. (Photo courtesy of Getty Images/David Purdy)

As he stared out into the crowd of fans donning Cardinal and Gold as Kansas City buzzed with Cyclones pride, Ejim couldn't help but also think back to when the fanfare for the program—and himself—was rather quiet.

Ejim, of Nigerian descent, grew up in Toronto, as part of a very academic family. Sports came second to education, but Melvin did play soccer and run track as a kid, without a whole lot of attention paid to hoops. "Basketball was kind of the third thing I wasn't very good at," Ejim remembered. He picked up the sport in seventh grade, largely due to the persistence of his uncle, and began to thrive.

Playing for an Amateur Athletic Union team during his first year of high school in Canada, Ejim received interest from several boarding schools on the East Coast to play basketball. Melvin spent his sophomore year at St. Mary's Ryken High School in Maryland before moving to Brewster Academy in New Hampshire. It was there that he started receiving interest from college coaches. But even then, it wasn't copious amounts of attention compared to some of his teammates.

"People didn't know my name as well, but I felt like I had the ability and started going out and competing and practicing with those guys and started garnering my own individual accomplishments," Ejim said.

It was following his junior season when a high major school finally began showing interest. That was Iowa State. Assistant coach T.J. Otzelberger came first, then head coach Greg McDermott came the following year as Ejim was named the Gatorade Player of the Year in New Hampshire in 2010. Ejim had developed a rapport to commit to the Cyclones before his senior season, but the following spring, McDermott left for Creighton, and Hoiberg was hired shortly after.

One phone call, the first in fact, that Hoiberg made let Ejim know Iowa State would still be the right fit, despite the coaching change.

"Hey, Mel," Hoiberg said. "I asked my twins who's their favorite player, and they said you. They like the way you play, and mostly because of all the dunks and stuff you had."

"They were watching some of my highlight tapes in school, and that was just something he said that I thought was pretty funny," Ejim said. "He just had the right approach, and I heard a lot of great things about him."

Ejim's game wasn't flashy, but he started from day one as a freshman. Several close losses and Hoiberg's return to Ames left him relatively unnoticed. Another consistent season gave him Big 12 honorable mention accolades as a sophomore, and as a junior, he upped his game with 15 double-doubles while averaging 11.3 points per game.

In his senior year, Ejim was no longer just a face in the crowd; he was *the* face of the team. Nothing highlighted that more than his performance on February 8, 2014, when Iowa State hosted TCU. A 48-point outburst against the Horned Frogs gave Ejim the Big 12 record for points in a game. Chants of "Mel-vin Ej-im" erupted from the stands at Hilton Coliseum.

"I think it did a lot for my career and even more so gave a little more respect to me from people who maybe didn't [respect me] as much at first," Ejim said.

Ejim went on to win Big 12 Player of the Year and finished his career with 1,643 points and 1,051 rebounds, helping Iowa State reach the Sweet 16 for the first time since an Elite Eight berth in 2000. He broke the ISU record for games played (135) and games started (126) while being named an Academic All-American. Rather than one accomplishment, it's the body of work that defines him.

"That epitomizes being a four-year player," Ejim said, "waiting your turn and being productive and being involved and waiting for your final shot and making the most out of it."

99 Continue Your Cyclones Journey Online

The Internet cannot replace a fall afternoon at Jack Trice Stadium or a winter night snuggled inside the comfy confines of Hilton Coliseum. It cannot replicate the banter with friends at the local bar or the highway drive during which you listen intently to each word of the Iowa State call. No, the Internet cannot match these experiences, because it is an experience in and of itself.

The online world is a place you can go to continue living the moment of an exhilarating win, and a place where you can venture after a heartbreaking loss. You'll find intelligent analysis, stories, and memories. You'll find the bitterness and anger that comes with defeat. Yet that's what makes exploring the Iowa State online world so great.

You never know what you might find. And boy, is there a lot to explore.

Behind every nook and cranny of a Google search, there is certain to be something to learn about Iowa State both past and present. You can find old game stories that give you an inkling of being in the moment of that big basket or touchdown run. You can read feature stories to learn more about the big names in Iowa State history as well as the ones who have gone under the radar. The Internet knows no boundaries, and so the possibilities of what you might dig up—from photos to videos to stories—are endless.

On Twitter you can follow personalities to drive your Cyclones fandom. What better place is there to get GIFs of Fred Hoiberg dancing or the shot of Georges Niang basking in his Cy-Hawk moment with a cup of coffee to fuel the in-state rivalry? You can follow the players and coaches. You can follow the sportswriters who cover your team for the latest from practices and games. Never before has it been so easy to feel connected.

Then there are places on the Internet that bleed Cardinal and Gold. Communities like CycloneFanatic.com, which was started in 2006 and is now home to thousands upon thousands of fans, provide a place for you to talk Iowa State athletics. These are the places to prolong the good moments and lament the bad ones. They are the places that the Cyclones always live, even when you can't be in the stands.

100 A New Era: The Rising Cyclones

The dawn of a new era in Iowa State basketball began, oddly enough, at a dining room table in Chaska, Minnesota. In some ways, it began four years earlier with rejection, but mostly it began there, at a table, with some papers stuffed inside a briefcase. It also began with a vision.

As Iowa State searched for a new coach in March 2006, athletics director Jamie Pollard found himself driving to interview Northern Iowa coach Greg McDermott when he missed a call. Fred Hoiberg was in town and wanted to meet regarding the position. Pollard assured Hoiberg he'd pass his name along as a candidate to be an assistant coach for whomever Iowa State hired. "I'm not interested in being an assistant coach," Hoiberg told him. "I want to be the head coach." Pollard shrugged him off. *Well,* he thought, *he's like every other great basketball player who thinks he can coach.* Pollard wished Hoiberg well, and Iowa State eventually hired McDermott.

Over the course of the next four years, Hoiberg talked to McDermott's team in Ames. He and his wife, Carol, watched Iowa

State teams when they played in Minnesota. He joined the Cyclone Club. "He just did things that somebody who's trying to position themselves for a job would do," Pollard said. He also joined the front office of the NBA's Minnesota Timberwolves and saw the game from a new perspective.

On the final weekend in April 2010, after Hoiberg had finished a background check while preparing for the NBA Draft, his phone rang. McDermott had been offered a 10-year contract at Creighton and was going to take the weekend to think it over. "If Greg leaves," Pollard asked Hoiberg, "would you have interest in

Fred Hoiberg's return to Ames to coach his alma mater in 2010 kick-started a new era in Iowa State basketball. The Cyclones' return to prominence reached new heights in March 2014 when Hoiberg cut the final strands of net away in Kansas City with Iowa State as Big 12 champions. (Photo courtesy of Iowa State Athletics)

meeting with me?" Of course he was interested. Pollard had already called Iowa State president Gregory Geoffroy. If McDermott left, Pollard wanted to interview Hoiberg first and, if things felt right, offer him the job. Geoffroy granted autonomy, and soon after, McDermott accepted Creighton's offer.

Pollard called Hoiberg on Sunday and asked if they could meet the next night. "Tell me when and where you want to meet," Hoiberg said. He had one question before he hung up. "How many people are you looking at?" Hoiberg wondered.

"Well," Pollard said, "a lot of that will depend on how well tomorrow goes."

The next day, Pollard hopped in his car and drove north to Hoiberg's lakefront home in Chaska. Hoiberg was tired. He hadn't slept much the night before as he prepared. Carol had taken the kids out for ice cream, and Hoiberg and Pollard sat at the dining room table as Fred laid out his vision. He wondered if Pollard was open to transfers. "If I want to be the best, I've got to have the best," Hoiberg said. "I can't outcoach Kansas, I've got to have the same talent." He talked coaches. He talked style. He had a vision.

Hoiberg figured things were going well. He might get a second interview in Ames, he thought. After three hours or so, Pollard reached into his briefcase and pulled out a contract. "When he put that piece of paper on the table," Hoiberg said, "I knew it was real... He offered [it to] me right there."

The Mayor had returned.

Shortly before Hoiberg's introductory news conference in Ames, he wandered around his home in Chaska one night unable to sleep. Growing up he had walked the few blocks from his home on Donald Street in Ames to sit in Section 236 at Hilton Coliseum. Then he became a ball boy. Then he became the hometown hero who stayed home to play for the Cyclones. Now he was coming home. On this night Hoiberg noticed the photo hanging on the wall.

In the photo, his grandfather, Jerry Bush, who had coached Nebraska beginning in the 1950s, was walking down the street pointing and winking. "It was almost as if he was saying, 'Kid, you're going to be all right,'" Hoiberg said.

After four consecutive losing seasons and five straight years without an NCAA tournament berth, Hoiberg talked at his introductory news conference of bringing Hilton Magic back. "I want to get this program back in the right direction," Hoiberg told the frenzied crowd that day. "I think I can get the arena filled again and get the magic back in this place."

In five years time, Hoiberg did just that.

Beginning with an NCAA tournament appearance in his second season, the program's first since 2005, Hoiberg led Iowa State to four consecutive NCAA tournament bids, a program first. Under his guidance, the Cyclones started the 2013–14 season 14–0, the best mark in school history. They eventually cut down the nets in Kansas City at the Big 12 Championship and marched to the school's fourth-ever Sweet 16. They made more history in 2014–15, cutting down the nets in Kansas City once more as back-to-back Big 12 champions, a school record.

Following that fifth season, with 115 wins to his credit, Hoiberg departed to coach the Chicago Bulls. The new era ushered in by Hoiberg now continues with Steve Prohm at the helm. "Iowa State as a whole is in a pretty good spot," Hoiberg said. "I do take pride in that. That's something that I'm very happy about."

Iowa State has returned to the national spotlight.

"[Iowa State took] leaps—not even steps—leaps in the right direction under Coach Fred," former forward Melvin Ejim said. "As long as they keep picking the right guys and finding the right guys who are buying in, it'll continue to be a successful program."

Just as Hoiberg had envisioned from that dining room table.

Acknowledgments

The journey to this page certainly took a lot of time and effort. From transcribing to digging through old newspapers to writing, the hours spent putting this book together are countless. I'm also certain getting to this point took a bit of luck.

When I applied to attend Iowa State University in early 2010, I did so primarily because of what I had read about the journalism program. I went in rather blindly. The summer before my freshman year, as I scoured the roommate board on AccessPlus for a freshman roommate, I stumbled upon a journalism major named Dylan Montz. That was my first instance of luck. We became roommates first, and then good friends. Because of him I met two other close friends, Tyler Glover and Shawn Bowie, and through our four years, we made countless memories. Who could have imagined what a click of the mouse could do?

That brings up the second instance of luck. The summer after *100 Things Twins Fans Should Know & Do Before They Die* was published by Triumph Books in March 2011, I talked on the phone with then–managing editor Don Gulbrandsen about doing an Iowa State book down the road. The idea may have seemed crazy, but Don was supportive of the proposal and put in great effort to push for the book. Talks continued on and off for parts of three years to reach this point. I'm lucky that Don believed in the project from the start and that both Adam Motin and Noah Amstadter kept pushing to make it happen. The moment when the book was approved is indescribable. Words can't describe the gratitude shared for the people who believed and took a chance on this project, and that's saying something after nearly 90,000 words. I'm also thankful for the work put in by Jesse Jordan to guide this project and meticulously edit the words you see.

To say my decision to attend Iowa State to pursue journalism was one of the greatest things to happen to me would be an understatement. Not only did I meet lifelong friends, I took a quantum leap forward in journalism thanks to my time at the Greenlee School of Journalism and Mass Communication. Had it not been for my three years at the *Iowa State Daily*, under the guidance of Mark Witherspoon, I'm not sure where I'd be. The *Daily* helped me hone my craft and offered incredible experiences from covering a Big 12 championship in Kansas City to a Sweet 16 in New York City. The long nights pushing for (and sometimes missing) deadlines and the experiences inside the Hamilton Hall newsroom are hard to forget.

This book would have been much more difficult without help from so many people. Thanks to the 39 former athletes, coaches, and personalities who spent valuable time sharing memories. Thanks to Joe Castaldi for searching the database to help make many of those interviews happen. Thanks to the Iowa State Athletics Department, especially Steve Malchow for input and Mike Green for your knowledge and time spent finding the wonderful photos spread across this book. There are so many people who played a part throughout this process, and your time is appreciated.

Last, but certainly not least, thanks to my family. My mom, dad, and sisters, Katelyn and Paige, have always shown great support, and I'm certain I wrote the words in this book in large part because of you. And I guess that's one last instance of luck.

—Alex Halsted

Acknowledgments

Waking up early in the morning wasn't the easiest thing for me as an eighth-grade kid, but on one fall Saturday, I couldn't have been more ready to hop out of bed. A friend asked me earlier in the week if I wanted to go to Ames to watch an Iowa State football game that Saturday. It would be the first college game I ever attended. As the two of us made the two-hour trip west, along with our dads, the excitement was building.

It was October 8, 2005, when, for the first time, I saw Iowa State play in person. And even though the Cyclones fell short that day, I was hooked. Fast-forward to a little less than five years later when I arrived at Iowa State as a freshman in August 2010. My intrigue for Cyclones athletics had not diminished. I obtained a journalism degree from Iowa State in 2014, and my experience could not have been better, but I wouldn't be where I am today without good fortune. A big part of that is because I was surrounded by a lot of people putting in *a lot* of hard work.

First and foremost, I'd like to thank Steve Malchow, Mike Green, and the entire Iowa State Athletics Department. Without all of your help with setting up interviews, collecting photos, and working with us on questions, this wouldn't have been possible.

A sincere thanks is in order for every single person who took time out of their day to do interviews with us. Sometimes the conversations drifted off topic and took longer than expected, but your willingness to answer all of our questions certainly hasn't gone unappreciated.

Coming to Iowa State with little writing experience, the *Iowa State Daily* gave me the perfect opportunity to begin my journalism career, allowing me to learn from mistakes as I went. Additionally, I would like to send my appreciation to the Greenlee School of

Journalism and Mass Communication for my journalism degree, which I will forever be proud of.

A big thanks to our editor at Triumph Books, Jesse Jordan, who has been a tremendous help in guiding us with our many questions. It's because of his hours of hard work that this product is one we can feel good about.

After arriving at Iowa State in 2010, two of my high school friends joined me, and it has been a great journey ever since. Huge thanks go to Tyler Glover and Shawn Bowie, who have been a big part in encouraging me in my development as a journalist.

Along with Tyler and Shawn, Alex Halsted, my coauthor and good friend, has been a rock through this whole process and has taught me so many things about how to be successful in journalism and how to continue getting better. Thanks for making this experience such an enjoyable one!

Last, but certainly not least, a big thanks to my family. To my mom, dad, brother Drew, and sister Carly, who have always been there for me, especially when I've needed them the most. Without your love and support, I know I would not be anywhere near where I am today. I love you guys.

—Dylan Montz

Sources

Books

Abdul-Aziz, Zaid. *Darkness to Sunlight*. Sunlight Publishing Inc., 2006.
Day, H. Summerfield. *The Iowa State University Campus and Its Buildings 1859-1979*.
Didinger, Ray and Robert S. Lyons. *The Eagles Encyclopedia*. Temple University Press, 2005.
Offenburger, Chuck. *Gary Thompson: All-American*. Milwaukee: Hexagon Grandhaven Group, 2008.
Schwieder, Dorothy. *The Annals of Iowa Volume 64 No. 4: The Life and Legacy of Jack Trice*. State Historical Society of Iowa, 2010.
Strother, Shelby. *NFL Top 40*. Viking Adult, 1988.

Films

Cyclone Classics (B&G Productions)
Cyclones.tv
The Dirty Thirty: A Tradition of Toughness
ESPN SportsCentury, Dan Gable
Olympics: A History Making Victory from Nawal El Moutawakel

Magazines

Sports Illustrated (Andy Staples, Jeremiah Tax, John Garrity, Tim Crothers, S.L. Price)

Newspapers

Ames Tribune (Travis Hines, Erik Brooks, Williams Musgrove)
Cedar Rapids Gazette (Jim Ecker, Mike Hlas)
Chicago Tribune (John Mullin)
Daily Courier (Dan Beeson)
Daily Oklahoman (Mike Baldwin)
Daily Reporter (Steve Clark)
Evening Independent (Gary Ledman)
Des Moines Register (Andrew Logue, Bert McGrane, Bob Shaw, Blair Kamin, Buck Turnbull, Jim Moackler, Marc Hansen, Maury White, Pat Harty, Randy Peterson, Rick Brown, Ron Maly, Sherry Ricchiardi, Wayne Grett)
Dubuque Telegraph Herald (Jim Leitner)
Harlan News-Advertiser (Marvin Martens)
Iowa State Daily (Alex Halsted, Chris Adams, Harrison March, Jake Calhoun, John Kauffman, Luke Plansky, Paul C. Kluding, Mark Specht)
Kansas City Star (Ernest Mehl, Mechelle Voepel)
Lawrence Journal-World (Chuck Woodling)
Los Angeles Times (Julie Cart, Diane Pucin)
New York Post (Mark Cannizzaro)

Omaha World Herald (Corey Ross, Lee Barfknecht, Robert McMorris, Rudy Smith)
Philadelphia Daily News (Rich Hofmann)
Philadelphia Inquirer (Marcia C. Smith)
USA Today (Gary Mihoces)

News Service
The Associated Press (Chuck Schoffner, Doug Alden, Ron Speer)

Other Sources
Iowa State University Athletic Media Guides
Waldo Wegner Interview (Thad Dohrn)
Iowa State Library Special Collections

Websites
Cyclones.com (Mike Green, Tom Kroeschell)
ESPN.com (John Gustafson)
FootballFoundation.org
www.iastatebandhistory.us
http://www.isualum.org/
IowaHighwayEnds.net (Jeff Morrison)
Kagavi.com (Joshua Wagner)
Scout.com (Steve Deace)

Personal Interviews

Jim Hallihan (September 21, 2014)
Dan McCarney (September 26, 2014)
Mike Busch (October 7, 2014)
Seneca Wallace (October 7, 2014)
Cael Sanderson (October 9, 2014)
Troy Davis (October 9, 2014)
Paul Beene (October 9, 2014)
Ric Wesley (October 10, 2014)
Earle Bruce (October 10, 2014)
Sage Rosenfels (October 13, 2014)
Gary Thompson (October 14, 2014)
Bill Fennelly (October 22, 2014)
Matt Blair (October 23, 2014)
Jeff Hornacek (October 23, 2014)
Marcus Fizer (October 25, 2014)
Mike Stensrud (October 29, 2014)
Lyndsey Medders (October 29, 2014)
Eric Heft (October 30, 2014)
Angie Welle (October 31, 2014)
John Cooper (October 31, 2014)

Dan Gable (October 31, 2014)
Bobby Douglas (November 3, 2014)
Tim Floyd (November 4, 2014)
Stacy Frese (November 4, 2014)
Lisa Koll (November 4, 2014)
Tom Randall (November 4, 2014)
Ben Peterson (November 7, 2014)
Lafester Rhodes (November 9, 2014)
Jeff Grayer (November 10, 2014)
George Amundson (November 22, 2014)
Johnny Majors (November 22, 2014)
Jim Gibbons (December 11, 2014)
Paul Shirley (December 11, 2014)
Fred Hoiberg (December 15, 2014)
Jayme Olson (January 15, 2015)
Megan Taylor (January 19, 2015)
Melvin Ejim (January 21, 2015)
John Walters (January 26, 2015)
Jeff Woody (February 3, 2015)